ADMIRAL SHOVELL'S
TREASURE

and

SHIPWRECK

in the

ISLES OF SCILLY

Peter McBride & Richard Larn

First published in Gt. Britain in 1999

British Library Cataloguing in Publication Data

© McBride, Peter, & Larn, Richard

Admiral Shovell's Treasure and Shipwreck in the Isles of Scilly

1st edition

1. Association (Ship)   2. Shipwrecks

Cornwall, Isles of Scilly

ISBN
Hardback 0-9523971-3-7
Softback 0-9523971-2-9

Printed and bound in Gt. Britain by R. Booth (Bookbinder) Ltd. & Troutbeck Press, Antron Hill, Mabe, Penryn, Cornwall.
Tel: (01326) 373226

ADMIRAL SHOVELL'S TREASURE

and

SHIPWRECK

in the

ISLES OF SCILLY

Events amongst the Western Rocks of the Isles of Scilly, Cornwall during the night of Thursday the 22-23rd October 1707, are almost unprecedented in the long history of the Royal Navy. During a brief twenty minute period, four men o'war were lost, and Sir Clowdisley Shovell, a famous and respected admiral, was drowned along with at least 1,400 naval personnel and royal marines. The extent of the tragedy is only exceeded by the 'Great Storm' of 1703, in which thirteen warships and 2000 seamen were lost, as the worst peacetime disaster the Royal Navy has ever suffered. Shovell was a lucky survivor of this previous episode, experiencing great danger over a prolonged period in the *Russell*, of 80 guns.

Re-discovered 260 years later, the four shipwrecks commanded world attention when their remains were found revealing a fortune in sunken treasure and artefacts. To date, these have yielded a record treasure hoard second only, in British waters, to the £5 million in gold recovered from the wreck of the auxiliary cruiser *Laurentic*, lost in Lough Swilly in 1917.

The loss of Admiral Shovell's flagship *Association* and her consorts was a disaster of national importance that should never have happened. A major interrogation into navigational practices of the period followed, and the tragedy set in motion a train of events which finally led to the most important discovery in the long history of navigation - a method for accurately determining longitude, namely Harrison's chronometer. Thus the great tragedy contributed in no small part to the welfare and safer homecoming of future generations of seafarers.

Contents

Appendices

Sir Clowdisley Shovell. 1650-1707

Acknowledgement: National Maritime Museum

Chapter One

Voyage Homeward

'An admiral deserves to be broke, who kept great ships out after the end of September, and be shot if after'

Sir Clowdisley Shovell

The elegantly decorated and well furnished great-cabin of Admiral Shovell's powerful 90 gun flagship, *Association*, at anchor off Gibraltar on 29 September 1707, resounded to lively conversation as the five admirals and two senior captains charged with the joint command of the Anglo-Dutch fleet assembled for a Council of War. This was to be the last such meeting before the greater part of the fleet with nearly 8000 men on board sailed for England, marking the final phase of the Allied Expeditionary Force's attempt to capture the great harbour of Toulon. Already victualled and laden with a proportion of the booty, military personnel and stores embarked from the land campaign, including some sick and wounded, the twenty-one men o'war destined for home were ready to weigh anchor as soon as their commanders returned on board.

Admiral Shovell, the Commander in Chief, Rear Admiral of England and Admiral of the White, had acquired considerable private means throughout a long and successful career. A conscientious officer and genial character he had gained a reputation for generous hospitality. Even on this formal occasion his fellow officers were entertained in lavish style as they went about their business.(see page 138) As the meeting ended, orders were issued for the deployment of the few ships remaining in the Mediterranean under Admiral Dilkes before the officers took their final leave and were rowed back to their respective vessels. There was a sad irony about the occasion. The assembled leaders had been debating the future of the fleet, but none could have foreseen the very real and dismal fate in store for the famous admiral at their head, together with many of the officers, seamen and marines serving under his last command.[1]

For centuries prior to 1707, navigators had been aware of the hazards associated with making a landfall in the south-western approaches to the English Channel. On the southern side lie the Channel Islands, backed by the French coastline, surrounded by a proliferation of dangerous rocks,

1

headlands, islets and a tidal current of exceptional strength. Equally threatening to the north are the inhospitable cliffs, headlands and bays of Cornwall and Devon which are fringed by hazardous reefs and rocks such as the Seven Stones, Wolf, Longships, Runnelstone, Stags, Manacles, and Eddystone. Most menacing of all are the Isles of Scilly, a scattering of some 145 rocks and islands, situated twenty-eight miles south-west of Land's End. Over the centuries their dangerous reefs, with a phenomenally low lying silhouette compared with mainland Cornwall, and extending over an area of seventy square miles, have been the cause of some 900 recorded shipwrecks.

In the days of sail, a prevailing south-westerly was a fair wind for passage up Channel, but any sudden change in its direction or increase in strength, could transform a hitherto safe passage into a nightmare. To attempt a landfall here in bad weather or at night was considered foolhardy, and to be avoided at all costs. It was also well known to sailing masters that following a period of strong westerly or south-westerly gales, a current often set obliquely across the Western Approaches to the Channel, which in certain circumstances would sweep a vessel unexpectedly northwards. This phenomenon later came to be known as the Rennell current.[2]

The northerly set of this current almost caused the wreck of Sir John Narborough and his squadron of English warships amongst the Isles of Scilly in 1673. The similarity between this incident and Admiral Shovell's disaster some thirty-four years later are quite remarkable; the more so, knowing that Clowdisley Shovell, then aged twenty-three, was a master's mate on board Narborough's flagship *Fairfax*, and hence saw at first hand, the actual rocks which later claimed his life.[3]

The men o'war in that fleet were part of the Mediterranean squadron, convoying home a number of merchantmen under Narborough's command, when they encountered hazy weather close to the Scilly's on 22 May 1673. On board the ships was a vast amount of treasure amounting to '*nearly 2,000,000 pieces of eight and some silver.*'[4] Young Shovell's involvement makes it worth while recounting the incident in some detail, and according to Narborough's private journal:

'*the ships astern of me tacked and stood off when I fired my guns. Thirteen of the fleet carried it about on the south side of the island and stood away up channel; the Bristol and Nonsuch were two of them, the rest merchantmen. After it was fair daylight, that I could see round about me, I saw we were entan-*

gled with rocks called the Bishops and Clerks. The wind-mills on St. Mary's Island I saw plain; they bore NE by E from me. I was right before Broad Sound. I saw several breaches of rocks about a quarter of a mile within me, and but one rock without me, about 2 cables' length from me SW. I saw it was clear of rocks to the N.W'ard and the sea open, and the ships that were got within the breach, as I was, stood out that way. I caused a hawser to be passed out of the gunroom port forward and bent to the cable and roused it taut and veered out the cable, to cast the ship the right way. When the ship was cast and the sails full, we cut the cable and stood out to NW into the sea, until I was got off from the rocks out of danger. I lay by to have all the fleet get together. Not one vessel received any damage in the least, but all of them got clear off from so dangerous a place of rocks. I lost an anchor and two cables, which I cut away in eight fathoms. I could not heave ahead, the sea ran so high, my men could not stand at the capstan'.

Narborough describes why he came so close to being wrecked, illustrating the great importance placed on the use of the deep-sea sounding lead at the time:

'The cause of our failing here was a great indraught of current which sets into Severn and St. Georges Channel always, and when we neared the Island, we had a tide of flood set us strongly to the northward, which put most commanders and masters in this fleet out of their reckonings; and with our often lying by and bearing up so leewardly, ships in the time of the voyage from the Rock of Lisbon no man in the fleet could keep any good account of his ship's way. We all reckoned ourselves further shot in than we were and more southerly than we find it to appear by these rocks. Our being northerly more than expectation is by the current that do constantly set northerly; the soundings also deceived men in their depth and ground, for the same depth is 5 leagues SW from Scilly as is 5 leagues W from Scilly, and the ground fine white sand in many places; also, heave the lead three times one after another as fast as you can, and you will find the ground to differ every cast; sometimes sand and stones etc. will come up in the tallow, which deceiveth man'.[5]

Such was the primitive state of navigation in the late 17th century that even under the most favourable conditions, considerable doubt existed as to a ship's position when passing through the Soundings. Compasses were crude, fragile and often defective, and as will be shown later, on return to Portsmouth Dockyard after the Isles of Scilly disaster in 1707, of a total of 112 wooden cased compasses returned from nine ships, only four were completely serviceable. (see Chapter 5) The problems of deviation and variation were only understood by the more knowledgeable of navigators, and variation was often not allowed for in traverse calculations. A method of fixing longitude accurately had still to be discovered, and the mariner's progress east or west could be gauged only by log and line, in conjunction with the unreliable hour glass, after adjustment for leeway, and reckoned from the last point of departure. This was known as dead reckoning.

Charts at that time were not graduated for longitude and hence recourse was made to privately published navigation manuals in which latitudes and longitudes were given. These manuals differed considerably, often containing errors, so that each navigator was left to his own preference, and even in the Royal Navy there was no standard reference book, a matter still complained of as late as 1737. When we consider these manuals and the tables regarding the latitude of the Isles of Scilly, we find most placed them between ten and twenty miles north of their true position. This was a situation that Samuel Pepys was well aware of when, in 1683, Captain Greenville Collins was ordered to carry out a survey of the British coast. (see page Chapter 11 note 12) His results published privately in 1693, placed the St. Agnes lighthouse, the only light at that time on the Scilly's, at 50° 02´ N. This was still nine miles in error, the modern determination being 49° 53´ N.[6] Thus even the pilots of Sir Clowdisley Shovell's fleet, using the most up-to-date manuals, would have had a false sense of security.[7]

It was this special difficulty in approaching the English Channel, the dangers of coming into the 'Soundings' as they were called, that gave rise to what the old navigators called 'the three L's'. (i.e. Lead, Latitude and Lookout) The effective use of the lead line still largely depended on the skill and experience of the individual master, and the knowledge of depth and seabed accrued over previous voyages, whilst latitude could not be fixed without weather sufficiently clear to take the necessary sightings by backstaff.[8] The many unpredictable factors inherent in dead reckoning, or 'navigation by account', when observations could not be made, greatly increased the hazard of approaching the entrance to the Channel. As a consequence it became a practice about the turn of the century, to station 'cruisers' in the 'Soundings' to assist homecoming fleets make a safe landfall. (for information about the subsequent enquiry into navigational practice and causes of the disaster see Chapter 5)

The capture of Toulon by a joint expedition had been the prime objective in the naval war, ever since Savoy joined the Grand Alliance in 1703. Such a project if successful, would have meant the ruin of French sea power in the Mediterranean. For want of a suitable base within the Straits, from which the allied fleet could operate the whole year round, the English men o'war were forced to run the gauntlet of bad weather, in going out early and returning home late each year. *'Time is precious'*, Sir George Rooke protested to Nottingham, on 1 June 1702, *'so that I must repeat my opinion no service can balance the hazard of bringing our great ships home in the winter season'.*[9]

Horace Walpole attributed Sir Clowdisley with strong opinions on the risks involved and quotes the admiral: ' *- that an admiral deserves to be broke, who kept great ships out after the end of September, and be shot if after October.'*[10] Nevertheless, Rooke left Cadiz for England in September 1702 and Gibraltar for home in August 1704; while Sir Clowdisley remained in the Mediterranean until the end of October in 1703, and again in 1705. As the returning ships assembled at Gibraltar in the autumn of 1707, a combination of factors had led, yet once again, to a delayed departure, threatening the safety of the returning fleet - the very thing the successful capture of Toulon may have avoided.

These then were the circumstances and background to Sir Clowdisley Shovell's disastrous last passage. A total of 44 log books belonging to captains, masters and lieutenants on board various ships in the fleet have survived, to give first hand information of the fateful voyage from Gibraltar to Spithead. Of these, the late naval historian, Commander W.E. May, considered that of Lt. Anthony Lochard of the *Orford*, to be the most reliable.[11] Cdr. May had plotted the progress of the *Orford* on her homeward passage, according to Lochard's observations, and this can be followed, with other accounts from various sources.

With his flag in the *Association*, and accompanied by nineteen other men o'war, Sir Clowdisley sailed from Gibraltar on 29 September 1707, the *Panther* joining the fleet from Tangier en route. In his last despatch to Sir John Norris before leaving Gibraltar, the admiral wrote:

'Sir, I design to make use of this opportunity and wind to get out of the Straits and proceed home. Our next rendez-vous is to be at Spithead. I send you, Milord, a line of battle for the ships that go home with us and am, Sir, your humble servant'.[12]

In the final event the *Shrewsbury* and *Newcastle* remained in the Mediterranean, and the sloop *Weazle* joined the homeward ships. The line-of-battle established the relative positions of each remaining ship in the fleet, at least until 22 October, when the *Lenox, Phoenix* and *Valeur* were detached.

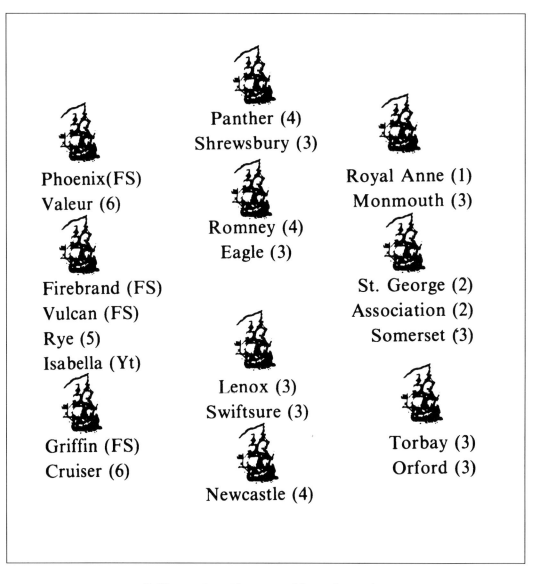

Panther (4)
Shrewsbury (3)

Royal Anne (1)
Monmouth (3)

Phoenix(FS)
Valeur (6)

Romney (4)
Eagle (3)

Firebrand (FS)
Vulcan (FS)
Rye (5)
Isabella (Yt)

St. George (2)
Association (2)
Somerset (3)

Griffin (FS)
Cruiser (6)

Lenox (3)
Swiftsure (3)

Torbay (3)
Orford (3)

Newcastle (4)

Sailing order of homeward bound squadron
(n.b. figures in brackets denote the Rate of
each ship.)

Details of the homeward bound Fleet commanded by Admiral Sir Clowdisley Shovell.[13]

There were a total of twenty-one ships in the homeward bound fleet which comprised 1 x 1st Rate; 2 x 2nd Rates; 7 x 3rd Rate; 2 x 4th Rate; 1 x 5th Rate; 2 x 6th Rate; 4 x Fireships; 1 x Sloop; 1 Yacht. Individual details are as follows:

1st Rate

Royal Anne
100 guns, 1722 tons (bm), 170 x 48ft. Built as the *St. Andrew* 96 guns at Woolwich Dkyd. 1670. Rebuilt and renamed 1703.
Flagship of Sir George Byng, Vice-Admiral of the Blue.
Captain James Moneypenny.

2nd Rate

Association
90 guns, 1549 tons (bm), 165 x 45ft. Built at Portsmouth Dkyd, 1697.
Flagship of Admiral Sir Clowdisley Shovell.
1st Captain Edward Loades; 2nd Captain Samuel Whittaker.

St. George
96 guns, 1129 tons (bm), 163 x 42.5ft. Built as the *Charles* at Deptford Dkyd, 1668. Rebuilt 1701 to 162 x 45ft, 1470 tons (bm)
Captain James Lord Dursley.

3rd Rate

Eagle
70 guns, 1053 tons (bm), 151.5 x 40.5ft. Built at Portsmouth Dkyd, 1679. Rebuilt at Chatham Dkyd, 1699, and increased to 1099 tons (bm).
Captain Robert Hancock.

Lenox
70 guns, 1013 tons (bm), 151.5 x 40ft. Built at Deptford Dkyd, 1678. Rebuilt at Deptford in 1701, and increased to 1089 tons (bm).
Captain Sir William Jumper

Monmouth
70 guns, 856 tons (bm), 148.5 x 37ft. Built at Chatham Dkyd, 1666.
Rebuilt at Woolwich Dkyd, 1700, and increased to 944 tons (bm).
Captain John Baker.

Orford
70 guns, 1051 tons (bm), 150.5 x 40.5ft. Built at Deptford Dkyd, 1698.
Captain Charles Cornwall.

Somerset
80 guns, 1263 tons (bm), 149 x 38.5ft. Built at Chatham Dkyd, 1698.
Captain John Price.

Swiftsure
70 guns, 978 tons (bm), 149 x 38.5ft. Built at Harwich 1673. Rebuilt at
Deptford Dkyd in 1696, and increased to 987 tons.
Captain Richard Griffiths.

Torbay
80 guns, 1202 tons (bm), 156 x 42ft. Built at Deptford Dkyd, 1693.
Flagship of Sir John Norris, Rear Admiral of the Blue.
Captain William Faulkner.

4th Rate

Panther
54 guns, 683 tons (bm), 131.5 x 34.5. Built at Deptford Dkyd, 1703.
Captain Henry Hobart.

Romney
48 guns, 683 tons (bm), 131 x 34.5ft. Built at Blackwall, 1694.
Captain William Coney.

Rye
32 guns, 384 tons (bm), 109.5 x 28.5ft. Built at Sheerness Dkyd, 1696.
Captain Edward Vernon.

6th Rate

Cruizer
24 guns, 280 tons (bm), dimensions not known. Build not known, ex *De*

Meric, captured from the French in 1705.
Captain John Shales.

Valeur
24 guns, 321 tons (bm), 101 x 27.5ft. Build unknown, captured from the French in 1705.
Captain Robert Johnson.

Fireships

Firebrand
8 guns, 268 tons (bm), 92.5 x 25.5ft. Built at Limehouse 1694.
Captain Francis Piercey.

Griffin
8 guns, 266 tons (bm), 95 x 25ft. Built at Rotherhithe, 1690, rebuilt at Sheerness, 1702.
Captain William Holding.

Phoenix
8 guns, 256 tons (bm), 91 x 25.5ft. Built at Rotherhithe, 1694.
Captain Michael Sansom.

Vulcan
8 guns, 273 tons (bm), 91 x 25.5ft. Built at Rotherhithe, 1691.
Captain William Ockman.

Sloop

Weazle
10 guns, 128 tons (bm), 72 x 20ft. Built at Blackwall, 1704.
Captain James Gunman.

Yacht

Isabella
8 guns, 94 tons (bm), dimensions not known. Built at Greenwich, 1683, rebuilt at Deptford Dkyd, 1703, and increased to 105 tons (bm).
Captain Finch Reddall.

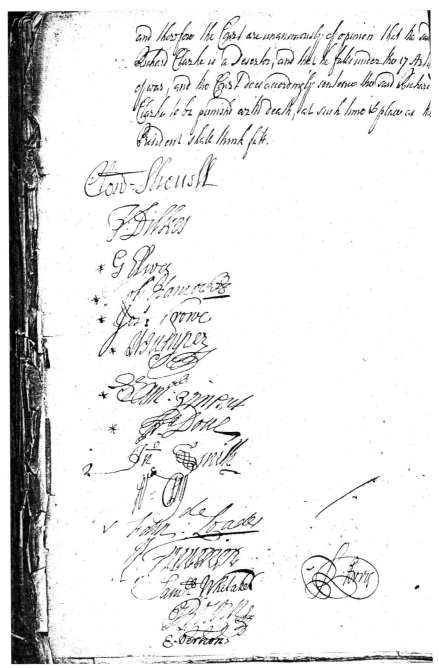

A document relating to the Court Martial of a deserter from the *Norfolk* which occured shortly before the Toulon Expedition on 22nd April 1707, and was presided over by Sir Clowdisley Shovell. The deserter was sentenced to death by hanging. It is interesting to note that no less than six of the naval officers who appended their signatures were themselves dead by the end of the year. Captains Loades, Whittaker, Hancock and Cony died in the Scillies disaster with Shovell. Admiral Thomas Dilkes, who remained in the Mediterranean with his squadron, died of an illness. (ADM1/5266)

The 3rd rate man o'war *Eagle*, 70-guns, shown at sea sometime after her rebuilding in 1699.
Acknowledgement: National Maritime Museum

The fleet took its departure from Cape Spartel, which bore *'SE about 5 leagues'*, at 8am on 30 September. The weather on passage was not good, with gales from the west between the 5-10 October, when the wind went round to ENE, dying down the following day. On the 12-13th the weather was squally, to be followed by two whole days of light airs. The wind then went round to east and blew a full gale on 16-17 October, falling away on the18th, although thick cloud covered the sky.

On the 19th there was a strong north-westerly gale, which was renewed on 21 October, following a day of north-easterly squalls. All the same, the sky did clear at noon sufficiently for some ships to obtain an observation of latitude.[14] The *Torbay* recorded 48°.57´ N, *St. George* 48°55´ N, and the *Lenox* 48°50´ N. Soundings taken that day showed between 90 and 140 fathoms, indicating that they had reached the edge of the continental shelf, but otherwise were of no assistance in establishing their position.[15]

The fleet was now seeking the *'fairway to the Channel'*. According to Greenville Collins' Coasting Pilot:

' - *the ground is finer in general; five and seven leagues to the southward of Scilly, you will have from 50 to 60 fathom of water, fine white sand with some red and black amongst it and sometimes some small shells, or pieces of shells, and at other times white sand only'*.

It continues with this advice:

'Being to the southward of Scilly about the latitude 49°30 minutes, or 49°45 minutes, and having from 60 to 55 fathom water, you may keep away east in the latitude according as you have wind and weather, and in that depth'.[16]

From now on the frequency of soundings increased. During the 21

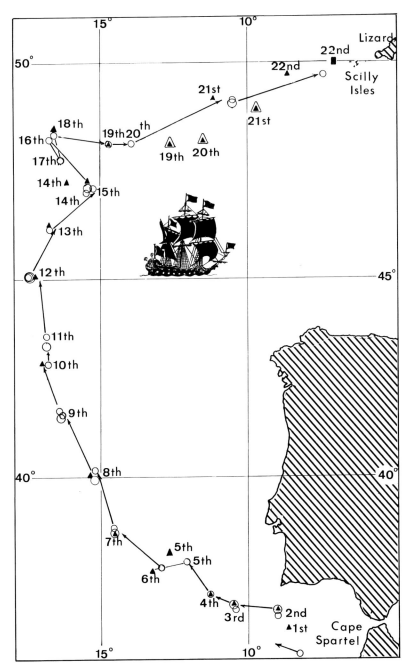

The homeward voyage as recorded in the log book of Lieutenant Anthony Lochard, of the *Orford,* as plotted by the late Commander W.E. May. It is not known which navigational manual was being used by Lochard at the time, and Commander May used 35 degrees 41′ as the latitude and the true value of 5 degrees 55′ for the longitude of Cape Spartel. The small single circles indicate dead reckoning positions at noon on respective days, the large circles the observed positions, and the triple circles the instances when both agree. The latitudes logged have been used and the differences of longitude from

Spartel measured from 5 degrees 55´W. The hard lines show the course steered and distances made noon to noon, the arrow heads the noon positions obtained. The small triangles show the noon positions obtained from the bearings and distances of Spartel. Double triangles give the noon positions relative to the Lizard, the true position of 49 degrees 58´´N and 5 degrees 12´W being used to measure them from.

Acknowledgement: Commander W.E. May. RN(Ret'd)

October the wind had backed from north-west to south-west, and then south-south-west, a sure sign that it was freshening, but nevertheless, a fair up channel wind. *'At five this evening we sounded with our boat'*, recorded the master of the *Panther,* *'having 85 fathoms, white sand with pieces of white and red shells'.* At 6pm the *Torbay* found, *'90 fathoms, fine sand'*, and the *St.George,'85 fathoms, small black sand'*. Her master noted, *'- allowed the Lizard by the depth of water to be 64 leagues distant from me, bearing ENE a quarter N'.*[17]

That same day, the frigate *Tartar* left Plymouth as a 'cruiser' with orders:
'to proceed & cruise between the lattd of 49°30´ North and the lattd of Scilly and between the meridian of the Lizard & 20 leagues West from it, to look out for Sir Clowdisley Shovell Admiral of Her Majesty's Fleet and his squadron expected from Lisbon, and to give him advice how the land bears from him, and the better to enable the captain of the said ship Tartar to give the Admiral a just account thereof you are to direct him to make the land every day if conveniently he can: to continue cruizing till he meets Sir Clo. Shovel, or hears he is passed by him'.[18]

Subsequently, on 9 October, the Admiralty forwarded a package to Captain Greenhill of the Plymouth Yard addressed to Admiral Shovell, containing orders and disposal instructions for the squadron to their various ports. This was, *'to be sent to him as soon as he appears in sight of Plymouth Sound'.*[19] Unfortunately Shovell never reached Plymouth and the *Tartar* returned to Plymouth on 24 October without once catching sight of the homecoming squadron'.[20]

Dawn on 22 October, 1707, revealed a wintry scene, with leaden sky, banks of heavy rain cloud and a persistent drizzle that filtered it's way between decks, making clothes and bedding uncomfortably damp. Although the wind was strong from the south-west, at least it was not a following sea, which made the pitch and roll of the ships in the heavy swell more comfortable than they had been for some days, but overall, conditions were pretty miserable. The fleet was now steering ENE; a risky course as experience had often shown, and in weather conditions that prevented the taking of good observations from which latitude could be calculated.

The master of the *Panther* recorded *'Strong gales and hazy'*, sounding a depth of, *'70 fathoms, white sand having things like points of needles'*. The *Somerset*'s master noted much the same, *'strong gale and great sea'*, whilst the *Monmouth* found *'70 fathoms, white and grey sand'*.[21] The depth was slowly decreasing, but the heavy layers of cloud did not allow critical observations to be made. At 11am, one hour before noon,[22] the *Association* fired a signal gun, which by prior arrangement indicated that the *Lenox*, *Valeur* and *Phoenix* were to detach themselves from the main fleet, and proceed to Falmouth. On reaching their destination they were to escort a waiting convoy of merchantmen eastwards up Channel.[23]

By noon on 22 October the master of the *Torbay* estimated his position by dead reckoning to be 49.30´ coinciding with Collins', *'fairway to the Channel'*. At 4pm the fleet brought to, and sounded yet again. *Monmouth* found *'60 fathoms, fine white sand'*; whilst the *Torbay* had *'55 fathoms, with a rocky bottom'*. The *Cruizer* recorded 53 fathoms, *'branny sand with pieces of red masked shells'*, and the *Panther*, *'47 fathoms fine white sand'*. [24]

Night was approaching. The weather was thick and it was blowing hard. The fleet was coming within the 60-fathom line unsure of their position under the worst possible conditions. A decision had to be made, and relying on their dead reckoning and apparent corroboration of soundings, Sir Clowdisley Shovell gave the fatal order to proceed. He must have believed they had the Channel open before them. Shortly after 6pm the fleet bore away.

Notes for Chapter 1

1. Minutes of Council of War, 29 Sept 1707. *Letters and Papers of Sir George Byng*, p245(NRS 1930)
2. Rennell J. *Observations on a Current*, p47-8, 55-6 (1815); *Marcus G.J. Sir Clowdisley Shovell's Last Passage*, Journal RUSI p540 (1957)
3. DNB, Vol 40 p89; ADM 33/91, Ticket 1076 (PRO)
4. Anderson R. A. Narborough's Journal, *Journals and Narratives of the Third Dutch War*, p119 (NRS 1946); CSP Dom. 1673 p297
5. Ibid, p286-7
6. Greenville Collins (Captain) *Great Britain's Coasting Pilot* (London 1693 & 1753)
7. May W. E. *A History of Marine Navigation*, p26-7 (London 1973); *The Last Voyage of Sir Clowdisley Shovell*, Journal Inst. of Navigation, Vol XIII p327
8. Laughton J. K. *Physical Geography* (London 1870)
9. Marcus G. *Sir Clowdisley Shovell's Last Passage*, Journ. RUSI, Vol C II p542 (1957); Corbett. *England in the Mediterranean*, Vol II p198 (London 1904)

10. Ibid, p542 ; Toynbee A. A. *Study of History,* Vol IV p340 (London 1951)
11. May, JIN Vol XIII p 328-9
12. Norris's Order Book, Vol I Folio 24, 29 Sept.1707. BM, Add. MSS 28314
13. The number of guns quoted for each vessel refer to her establishment which often varied depending on the circumstances of the deployment. Reference to what are believed to be the correct number of guns carried on the five ships involved in the disaster will be found in later chapters.
    (bm) indicates the tonnage as *'builder's measurement'*, a capacity measurement arrived at, from perhaps the 15th century, by calculating the number of *'tuns'* (casks) of wine that a ship could carry. Colledge J. J. *Ships of the Royal Navy*, Vol I p 9 (Newton Abbot 1969)
14. May, JIN Vol XIII p324
15. Marcus, p543 (Master's Journals, *Torbay, St .George, Lenox*)
16. Greenville Collins, *Gt. Britain's Coasting Pilot*
17. Marcus, p544 (Master's Journals, *Panther, Torbay, St. George)*
18. ADM 2/423, Adm. Sec. Fowler to Captain Edwards, *Cumberland* (for the *Tartar*) 7 Oct 1707
19. ADM 2/423, Adm. Sec. J. Fowler to Commissioner Greenhill, 9 Oct 1707
20. Marcus, p544 (Navy Board Minutes Oct 1707)
21. Ibid, (Master's Journals, *Panther, Somerset, Monmouth*)
22. By a peculiar custom of the sea, it was the practice on board English men o'war until 1805 to change the date at noon, and not midnight. Therefore at noon on board, and by admiralty reckoning on shore it was 22nd October, but in reality it was the 23rd October, a situation that led to much confusion.
23. Captain's Journal, *Lenox*
24. Master's Journals, *Torbay, Monmouth, Cruizer, Panther*

Chapter Two

Shipwreck

'One can hardly mention the Bishop and his Clerks, as they are call'd or the Rocks of Scilly, without letting fall a Tear to the Memory of Sir Cloudesly Shovel, and all the gallant Spirits that were with him at one Blow and without a moments Warning dash'd into a State of Immortality'

Daniel Defoe 1724

Unaware of the hazardous course they were sailing and the impending dangers ahead the *Monmouth* was one of the first ships approaching the Isles of Scilly to raise the alarm on sighting the St Agnes light to the eastward, and shortly thereafter, a second light on her starboard bow. The master observed, *'We wore ship and stood away to the westward, showing many lights, fired a gun etc, it being signal for the fleet of our being in danger'.* On board the *Torbay*, the master related:

'- At 8 we saw a breach on the larboard bow and rocks; then we wore and laid our head to the westward and in wearing we came near the rocks then we saw the light of Scilly bearing E by N and Sir Clowdisley's light E by S a half S, 3 miles; we saw Sir Clowdisley's light no more'.[1]

The *Association* steered E by N until 8pm or thereabouts, when the flagship and several other vessels found themselves suddenly and quite unexpectedly amongst the Western Rocks. Since there was but one survivor from the 1,315 men on board the three ships subsequently lost on, or near, the Gilstone, no comprehensive first hand account of the events survived.[2] The sole survivor was George Lawrence, a quarter-master on board the *Romney,* found clinging to a rock near the Gilstone the day following the accident and able to relate the briefest of details.[3] Herbert's account gathered a year or so later records:

'- the weather then being stormy, they could not see the light of St. Agnes, not yet knowing where they were they fired soon after which they struck on the ledge and bilged; the Romney also struck immediately and staved on the Gilstone. The Eagle was lost on the Gunner or thereabouts, by what of the wreck floated to St. Just and other places at the Lands End and up the North Channel'.[4]

Of the surviving logbook accounts, the two most graphic are those from the *Isabella* and the *Orford.* The former, kept by Captain Reddall, states:

'23rd. Wind - SSW, and WSW and WNW. Distance run - 55m lat 49°30´N, Long. 10°9´W. Cape Spartell bore dist. 280 leagues. This 24 hours hard gales of wind until 10 at night when the weather somewhat moderated. At 4 in the afternoon the admiral brought to and sounded. We likewise sounded and had between 50 and 55 fathom water, coarse sand intermixed with shells. We lay by until six o'clock at which time we heard several guns fired to the southward of us. Supposing they had discovered danger at 8 at night saw the light of Scilly bearing SE by S. distance by judgement about 4 miles. We took it to be one our admiral's lights, we steered after it until we perceived it to be a fixed light [5] and being very thick dark and rainy weather we perceived the rocks on both hands of us. We being so very near to them we immediately wore our Yacht and layed our head to the westward crowding all the sail we could to weather the rocks under our lee; we filled full and full, by god's mercy we got clear of them all, for which deliverance God's holy name be blessed and praised, which caused a great separation in the fleet, for happy was he that

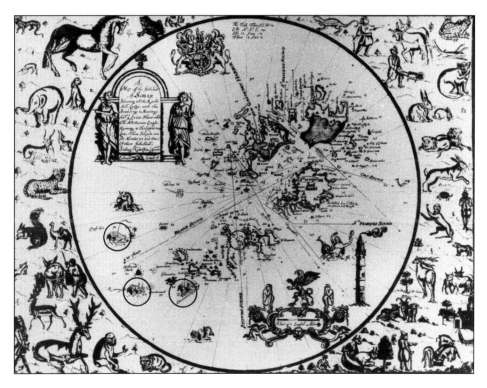

The Gostelo map or chart of the Isles of Scilly, with a completely fictitious representation of the St.Agnes light, and a strange surrounding collection of mostly wild animals. Indicated within circles are the locations of the wreck sites of the *Association, Eagle, Romney* and *Firebrand* as drawn by the artist. It is now believed that only those for the *Association* and *Firebrand* are correct.

Acknowledgement: British Library, Map Room

Ships of Sir Clowdisley Shovell's fleet amongst the
Western Rocks of the Isles of Scilly, October 1707.
Acknowledgement: National Maritime Museum

could shift himself, some steering with their heads to the southward and others to the westward and those they lay with their heads to the southward were most of them lost. In the morning we saw 5 sail beside ourselves which stood to the westward as we did. The Torbay, Sir John Norris; the St. George, one Lord Dursley; the Monmouth, Capt. Baker; The Griffin, fireship, Capt. Holding; the Weasell, Capt Gunman. My course made until I made the light of Scilly until 8 at night was by judgement E by N, a quarter N, dist 55m.'.[6]

Captain Sir William Jumper of the *Lenox*, arriving in Falmouth, was given a first hand account of the disaster:

'I am likewise to acquaint you that a small French prize laden with fish taken some days since by the Orford is arrived here. The master's mate of the Orford who commands the said prize told me this, that the 22nd instant in the evening lying about 8 o'clock he heard many guns fired as from a ship in distress, and about 9 his company cried out 'a rock' on which he set his foresail and weather it but a very little, which he says was the body of a great shipwreck and many crying out for God's sake save them which he could not, but standing on them soon cried out 'another rock' which bit he says was a wreck of a ship too but standing a little farther to the south east. About 10 o'clock they see the Bishop and Clerk two great rocks but weathered all almost attaching the bigger rocks'.[7]

The flagship of the Blue Squadron, the *Royal Anne*, 100 guns, largest warship of the fleet, with Vice-Admiral Sir George Byng on board, was rescued from great peril by the presence of mind of her officers and crew. In a desperate manoeuvre they managed to set topsails with alacrity as heavy seas were sighted breaking on hidden rocks only a ship's length away to leeward. Their prompt actions provided the extra wind power to pull her clear at the

The Outer Gilstone Rock from the air at low tide, seen from the southern side. The wreck of the *Association* lies off the reef to the bottom of this photograph.

Acknowledgement: Richard Larn

very last moment.[8] Another of the larger ships, the 2nd rate *St. George,* actually struck the same ledge as the *Association,* but the very wave which extinguished the stern lanterns of Shovell's flagship simultaneously lifted the other vessel over the reef into the safety of deep water.[9]

The fireship, *Firebrand,* fared little better, since she too struck the same reef as the *Association,* came off on a huge wave and commenced to take in water, her hull severely damaged and breached. Her captain, Francis Piercy, set the crew to the pumps, making all the sail he dared, passing along the southern side of the Western Rocks. Guided by the light from the beacon on St. Agnes he navigated her into Smith Sound where the vessel sank in ten fathoms of water not far from Menglow Rock.[10] The master of the *Salisbury* reported on the survivors: '- *the Romney with one man saved, the Firebrand fireship with capt, lieut, boatswain, carpenter, surgeon and 15 men and boys saved'.*[11]

In the meantime the *Lenox, Valeur* and *Phoenix,* previously detached for Falmouth at 11am on the 22 October, were also heading into great danger. Believing their position to be much further east than they actually were, the *Lenox* ordered a course of NE by N until 2pm, when Captain Jumper, seemingly afraid of running ashore on mainland Cornwall, altered his course to E 1/2 S, and again at dusk to ESE. The three vessels were then making about 3 knots.[12] With no observation of latitude possible all that day, the precaution of taking a south-easterly course, which should keep them clear of the land, at least until daylight, was both sensible and seamanlike. In point of fact, their northerly deviation from the fleet, followed by a long period steering south of east, brought all three ships in amongst the rocks of Scilly seven hours after the main fleet had met with disaster.

It was 3am on the 23 October when the detachment ran into danger, having unwittingly entered the North Channel, leading into Broad Sound, to run the gauntlet of the shallow water and reefs south-west of Samson, north of Annet and St. Agnes. By good fortune the *Lenox* and *Valeur* managed to get clear into the deeper water of the Sound, where they anchored until daybreak. They then sailed for Falmouth, arriving there on 25 October, seemingly unaware of the fate of the *Phoenix*.[13]

The little *Phoenix* was less fortunate than her escorts were, and Captain Sansom reported in some detail:

> '23 October, Islands of Scilly. This 24 hours hard gales and close weather with small showers of rain; about 2 last past we took one reef more in our foretopsail & handed him and also one maintopsail. At 8 we handed our maintopsail and hauled up E. at 4 Sir William Jumper handed his foresail and we reefed and handed ours and laid a try under our mizzen as the Commander did. Laid up SSE the wind at S & S by W. About 5 the Commander set his foresail and so did I and hauled up ESE; about 12 last night lost sight of his light but still steered ESE and at half past one set our mainsail. About half past 2 set our foretopsail with 2 reefs; about 4 it clearing up we saw Sir William Jumper's light again. They bore SSW about fi mile distant & and finding we ran ahead of them hauled up my mainsail & handed the foretopsail & then saw the light of Scilly, it bearing SSW about five mile.
>
> We were shot so far in that we could not weather the Smith Rock but was forced to ware ship and brought too with our head to the northward and set our mainsail and we laid up NW the wind at WSW. We wore loosing our maintopsail but the wind veered to the WNW so could not weather the NW Rocks: we put our ship to stays but would not so that we put our helm a weather and endeavouring to ware her she struck the leeward part of the rock & received a sea which almost filled her, but hove her off into 9 fathoms astern, we fired several guns: a boat came from the shore, advising with the pilot finding my ship very leaky & that we could not free her with 2 pumps & having also 8ft of water in the hold: We brought all our stream cable for a spring to cast her & cut our best bower cable away, and run in between Samson and Bryer Islands, and laid her ashore upon the sand, it being then about half flood, it was a quarter flood when we struck first upon the rock. We unbent all our sails and unrigged our topmasts and got them ashore'.[14]

According to the lieutenant, the master of the *Phoenix* initially thought the Smith Rock was a ship:

> 'the master whose opinion this was ran forward and called out there's a ship

ahead we will go under her stern and know who they are; but we soon found the mistake it being a rock'. He emphasises the danger they were in: *'in wareing a second time struck fast on a sunken rock and continued there for some minutes but a great sea that almost filled us hove us off in 9 fathom'.*[15]

In point of fact there was insufficient depth of water for her to get into New Grimsby, the deep-water channel between Bryher and Tresco, until Saturday 25 October. On board the *Phoenix*, the Captain noted in his log:

'this 24 hours fresh gale, with small showers of rain. This morning hove some of our ballast out to lighten the ship; at almost high water we run her into New Grimsby & hove her ashore upon the sand & carried the sheet anchor with the best bower cable ashore. At low water we found some part of our fore ground beat away & about 10ft of her false keel. Also five strakes from the keel about 8ft long, with several timbers, beaten in on starboard side and about 5 foot of her main keel, so that when the water flood we could not keep her free & she filled full'.[16]

The following day was Sunday. The Lieutenant of the *Phoenix* made a simple but poignant entry in his Journal:

'26th Oct This day fair and little wind. This day the Captain, I, and all our people went to church to give God thanks for the mercies bestowed on us in so miraculous deliverance'[17].

An early lithograph showing the 4th rate, 48-gun *Romney* wrecked and going to pieces, her crew attempting to clamber aboard floating wreckage.

Acknowledgement: Historical Narratives. 1812

It was perhaps fortunate that the Welsh fleet was in Scilly at the time. The *Southampton* (4th rate), *Arundel* (5th) and *Lizard* (6th) had been there for several days, having left Milford on 16 October.

Destined to join them the *Salisbury*, *Antelope* (4th rates), *Hampshire* and *Charles Galley* (5th) entered St. Mary's Roads at 4pm, only a matter of hours before the homecoming ships blundered into the Western Rocks.[18] On the morning of the 23rd boats from these men o'war and from the islands were out early, aware that there had been one or two wrecks the previous night, but ignorant of the extent of the disaster.

The master of the *Salisbury* gave a graphic account of the scene:

'Standing in the starboard gangway looking towards the SW I see several flashes of guns & told them to the number of 30 and about half an hour or more I see one more & heard the report. This morning before day being little wind, drove by us vast quantities of ship wreck as beams, carriages, drumheads of capstans, points of masts and yards and a cross piece of the bitts and as soon as daylight came on we sent our boats to see if they could save any of the men which might be washed upon the rocks. They seeing the Phoenix fireship went aboard of her. She comes almost full of water in her hold by striking against one of the rocks but got safe into Grimsby. Three being lost as we are informed; her Majesty's ship Association and Eagle and all their men, the Romney with one man saved, the Firebrand fireship with capt, lieut, boatswain, carpenter, surgeon and 15 men and boys saved'.[19]

It was the crew of a pinnace from the *Southampton* that found the first real evidence that the flagship *Association* had been lost, since they picked up a floating document addressed to a seaman on board:

'- Boats were early out the next morning in quest of the flotsam goods, very much whereof were taken up; they mattered not the wines brandy's etc. at the first, but let them swim by their boats, and pursued what they had hopes were richer, so that most of the casks staved and the liquors were lost in the ocean'.[20]

Naturally a great number of bodies were found scattered amongst the Western Rocks, mostly unidentifiable except for the occasional corpse; all traces of rank, status and identity largely obliterated by the ravages of the sea. Many floated ashore on the beaches of St. Agnes in particular. Native Scillonians will point out to this day, that part of the island, not far from the old lifeboat house, where tradition has it that many of the dead were buried in mass graves. Those men employed in searching for survivors were told to keep a sharp eye out in particular for any sign of Sir Clowdisley Shovell, who apart from being a high ranking naval officer, was a popular and respected figure of national importance.

The admiral's body was, in fact, one of the first to be cast ashore by the sea early next morning. A letter written by Joseph Addison, then Under Secretary of State, reported the discovery:

'Yesterday we had news that the body of Sir C.S. was found on the coast of Cornwall. The fishermen who were searching the rocks, took a tin box out of the pocket of one of the carcasses that was floating and found in it a commission of an admiral; upon which, examining the body more closely, they found it was poor Sir Cloudesley. You may guess the unhappy condition of his unhappy wife, who lost in the same ship with her husband, her two only sons by Sir John Narborough. We begin to despair of the two other men o'war, having yet received no news of them'.[21]

Admiral Shovell's corpse was found on St Mary's Island in a sandy cove called Porth Hellick. Not far away the bodies of his two stepsons, twenty-three year old Sir John Narborough and twent-one year old James, also came ashore. Both had been serving under his command in the *Association*. In the vicinity were the bodies of Captain Loades, Sir Clowdisley's flag-captain, and a small greyhound with a collar bearing the dog's name.[22] Part of a boat, said to be the stern of Sir Clowdisley's barge, was washed up into Porth Hellick, which gave some grounds for believing that the admiral, and some of his officers and close associates had managed to get clear of the wreck'.[23]

Among the gentlemen missing was young Henry Trelawney, the son of Sir Jonathen Trelawney, Bishop of Winchester, a Cornishman of considerable

The interior of Knowlton church, near Deal, Kent, showing the position of the magnificent memorial to the two Narborough brothers, lost with Sir Clowdisley Shovell in 1707.
Acknowledgement: Brian Turner

Enlargement of the portion of the Gostelo chart showing the site of the wreck of the *Association*. Acknowledgement: British Library, Map Room

note with a family seat at T r e l a w n e y Manor, near Looe. The subject of a famous Cornish song, he was one of the Bishops originally imprisoned in the Tower of London by King James II for refusing to endorse the Catholic King's Act of Indulgence towards the Roman Church. It is perhaps a tragic irony that in another role as the Vice-Admiral for the South Coast of Cornwall he had experienced a long and close association with the sea and the numerous shipwrecks which almost daily occurred on the rocky coast of South Cornwall.[24]

The results of a search for his son's body were communicated to the Bishop in a letter, which illustrates the scene:

'My Lord, Your Lordship's commands having been signified to my brother at Scilly, he immediately made the strictest enquiry that was possible of all the bodies that had been thrown ashore and buried and being told of one buried at St. Agnes about Mr Trelawney's age, was resolved to have him taken up in order to view him, whether is was he or not. He had seen the young gentleman at Torbay but willing to depend on his own judgement desired the captain of the Phoenix fireship that was stranded there who knew Mr Trelawney intimately well all the voyage to go with him. As soon as they had the body up they found it actually to be the same, though somewhat altered having been buried 11 days, and in the water 4. However the captain presently knew him and my brother took care to have the body brought over to St. Mary's and interred in the chancel of the church there the 8th instant with all marks of respect and honour the Island could show on such an occasion. Some captain's and the best of the inhabitants are present at the funeral. My brother

took of his hair being cut and that so very close that the left lock was not left to send over, and there is no room to doubt that it was the body of poor Mr Henry Trelawney.[25] It has not been his good luck as yet to meet with anything belonging to him but whatever of that nature happens to come to hand or knowledge your Lordship will be sure to have a faithful account of it.

They can say nothing in particular touching Sir Cloudesley's loss, only the man saved out of the Romney tells that Sir Cloudesley was to the windward of all the ships and fired three guns when she struck, and immediately went down as the Romney a little after did. Upon hearing the guns, the rest of the fleet that were directly bearing on the same rocks changed there course and stood more to the southward, or else in all probability they had run the same fate, as never enough to be admired. How it was possible men of so much experience could be mistaken in there reckoning, after they had the advantage of a great deal of fair weather before hand and no bad weather when they were lost.

The position in which the Gostelo chart suggests the *Eagle* was lost, now accepted as being incorrect, since the wreck site on the Crim is far too small, neither does it hold the number or size of cannon she carried.

Acknowledgement: British Library, Map Room

There is a great quantity of timber all round the islands and abundance of sails and rigging just about the place where the ship sunk, and a mast, one end a little above water which makes them conclude an entire ship to be foundered there because all the force they can procure is not able to move the mast. The Eagle is most certainly lost too and I wish no other of the squadron may be wanting, besides those, though I'm heartily sorry for the loss poor England has sustained of so many men and in most particular manner for the share your Lordship has in it. Your Lordship's most faithful and obedient servant, John Ben'.[26]

On 1 November, Josiah Burchett, Secretary to the Admiralty, wrote to Captain Sansom requesting an account of the damage to the *Phoenix,* Fireship, directing him to use his endeavours in saving her. He continued:

> *'My Lady Shovell being very desirous to saving the bodies of her two sons namely Sir John Narborough and Mr. Narborough who were lost with Sir Cl. Shovell I am thereupon commanded by his Royal Highness to signify his plea- sure to you to do your utmost care and endeavour to find them out and put them into coffins and that you do send an account of what you do therein'.*[27]

The remains of Captain Edward Loades and James Narborough were later interred with Henry Trelawney, in the chancel of Old Town Church, and whilst he received no special mention, it is possible that Sir John Narborough, James's brother, was also buried there.[28].

News of the accident reached Portsmouth via the *Royal Anne* at Spithead. She put in there with others of the fleet on the 25th, whilst the *Somerset* and *Monmouth*, plus two of the fireships, which must have been the *Vulcan* and *Griffin*, anchored off Deal in the Downs, on the 27th. It was not until 30 October that confirmation was received in Plymouth and then London, that the *Phoenix* was in fact still ashore, *'on the rocks, and it was hoped to be got off'*. This advice, coupled with evidence from Captain Sansom's journal, prove that the report in the London Gazette of 25 October, that the *Phoenix* had arrived in Falmouth, was incorrect.[29] The captain navigated the *Phoenix* safely into New Grimsby Harbour and beached her there on 25 October. Badly damaged and incapacitated an urgent survey was made and communicated to the Navy

Details from Gostelo's chart showing the *Romney* supposedly wrecked on Tearing Ledge, which is now generally accepted as being that of the *Eagle*. This is now a Designated Wreck Site, under the Protection of Wrecks Act, 1973.

Acknowledgement: British Library, Map Room

Board. On the 30 October her lieutenant reported:

'*This day fair. Great wrecks come ashore and many people, among them Sir Cloudsly Shovell is known and carried aboard the Salisbury,*' and on 1 November: '*Went among the wrecks and found timber to repair our ship*'.[30]

The *Phoenix* and her crew were now forced to remain in the Islands for 106 days while the necessary stores were obtained and her carpenter and crew carried out extensive repairs:

'26 Oct.   *24hrs. Fresh gale this day got most of our lumber ashore to clear the ship.*

27 Oct.   *24 hrs. Fresh gale, this day our carpenter clamped some elm beams over the leak so that the next tide we kept her with 2 pumps and we hove her further in but could not free her.*

28 Oct.   *24 hrs. Fresh gale, this day at low water we began to pump again & kept her until full seas, the tide running we hove her close to the bank but she filled every tide.*

29/30   *Fresh gales.*

31 Oct.   *24 hrs. Fresh gales. This day got our spare sails out and hauled the ballast to leeward to clear the timbers that beaten in, and began to strip the sheathing off.*

17 Nov.   *Fresh gales. This day our carpenter finished the starboard side.*

18 Nov.   *Fresh gales. This morning laid the ship on the starboard side to see what damage we had received on our larboard side, but found none.*

27 Nov.   *The carpenters of the men o'war came in (i.e. Southampton, Arundel, and Lizard) to finish the work and to endeavour to get the ship off, but durst not they finding more damage.*

29 Nov.   *Fresh gales. This morning the carpenters gave their report of the ship again, they finding four futtock riders broke, and stripping of her sheathing on her larboard side bilges, they found her very open and one of her planks sprung.*

1 Dec.   *Fresh gales. This morning began to heave the ballast out and clear the hold and clamp the riders that were sprung. (By now the fleet had sailed, and left their carpenters behind to complete the work alone).*

15 Jan.   *Hove in about 30 tonnes of ballast more.*

16 Jan.   *Hove our ship off the shore and moored her afloat with our best bower to seaward and our stream anchor fast to a rock upon Tresco Island & our small bower to westward & our spare cable fast to a rock on Hangman's Island. We lay in 10ft water at low water and 5 fm at full sea.*

30 Jan.	*This day fetched on board all our cables and spliced them.*
2 Feb.	*This day brought on board all our guns and sails, this afternoon the Southampton, Lizard & several merchantmen anchored.*
3 Feb.	*Fresh gales. All our sails and part of our water came aboard.*
8 Feb.	*Fresh gales. About our last part we unmoored. About 2 it being full sea we weighed & run off Tresco flats into St. M. arrived about 3; we anchored in 5 fm water, Nutt rock bearing N a half E, about a quarter mile distant; Gt Minolto W by N and St. Mary's castle SE by E., the lighthouse SSW.*
11 Feb.	*At 11 at noon, a signal to anchor in 11 fathoms in Falmouth Harbour.*
20 Feb.	*Reached Plymouth and anchored in the Sound.*

Signed: Mich' Sansom'.[31]

Surprisingly, the surviving vessels of the fleet did not remain in the vicinity of the Isles of Scilly for long, and whilst the majority were aware of one or more losses, they were seemingly ignorant of the magnitude of the disaster. The *Lenox* and the *Valeur* arrived in Falmouth on 25 October. The *Salisbury,* bringing the body of Sir Clowdisley, as well as the survivors from the *Firebrand* and George Lawrence from the *Romney*, reached Plymouth on the 28th, along with five prize vessels.

Lawrence was transferred to the Royal Naval hospital where he made a speedy recovery. On the 8 November Burchett wrote to the Commissioner for the Sick and Wounded at Plymouth:

'*George Lawrence now in the hospital at Plymouth being the only man that was preserved when the unhappy accident befell her Majesty's late ship the Romney and having made application to be discharged I am therefore commanded by his Royal Highness to signify his directions to you, that you do give orders, to your officers at Plymouth forthwith to release him, and give him such a certificate as will enable him to come to Town without being molested'.*[32]
Presumably the certificate requested was required to protect him from the danger of being 'pressed' into service in another ship.

Lawrence, no doubt being feted for his miraculous escape, now made his way to London to give his personal account. (see Chapter 4) Following his visit to the admiralty he had even more reason to celebrate as he was promoted and sent to a new ship in place of another. On 19 December Burchett replied to Captain Evans of the *Burford:*

'*As to John Marshall your boatswain's mate whom you recommend for boatswain of the Terrible, fireship, I am to acquaint you that George Lawrence, the only man that was saved out of her Majesty's late ship the Romney, was 3 or 4 days since made boatswain of the said fireship, otherwise your mate had been appointed for her'.³³*

It is easy to surmise that the fame of being 'sole survivor' followed George Lawrence throughout his career and wherever he went, for the rest of his natural life!

Notes for Chapter 2

1. Master's Journals, *Monmouth, Torquay*
2. The total number of men carried on board the wrecked ships will never be known since it is reasonably certain that they all carried sick and wounded from the Mediterrannean campaign. However, a further in depth study of the Treasury Neat Books of the Admiralty for each vessel has produced a more reliable figure than previously record ed, which were; *Association* - 702, *Eagle* - 377, *Romney* - 236, *Firebrand* - 48 (which includes small detachments of Royal Marines on the first 3 vessels, see Appendix II), a grand total of 1363 officers and men, of whom it is likely only 23 were saved. ADM33/249, ADM33/257, ADM33/258.
3. Master's Journal, *Salisbury* (Thomas Styles) ADM52/282.PRO. Lawrence was entered in the books of the *Salisbury* along with 20 survivors from the *Firebrand* on Sunday 26 Oct and arrived back in Plymouth on the 28th. In Herbert's report he is described as being a quarter master and butcher, but his rate was, in fact, able seaman. (see Chapter 6)
4. Cooke J.H. *The Shipwreck of Sir Clowdisley Shovell,* (Gloucester 1883)(see Herbert's account Chapter 6)
5. This was the light on St. Agnes (lat 49°54N) erected in 1680.
6. Captain's Journal, *Isabella* Yacht
7. Captain Sir William Jumper to the Admiralty, 24 Oct 1707
8. *London Gazette,* No 4380 3 Nov 1707
9. Boyer. *History of the Reign of Queen Anne,* Vol VI p241
10. *London Gazette,* 1 Nov 1707
11. Accounts differ about the number of survivors from the Firebrand. The master of the *Arundel* recorded that *'her captain and 17 men were saved in a boat, and 5 more got ashore on pieces of the wreck,'* whereas the captain of the *Salisbury* refers to *'the cap tain, lieutenant and about 20 of ye Firebrand's men who were cast away'.* The London Gazette repeats the same figures as the master of the *Arundel.* (Captain's and Master's Journals *Arundel, Salisbury*) The Admiralty Neat Book lists 22 survivors out of 48 on board
12. Marcus, p546, Captain's Journal, *Lenox*
13. Ibid, p547, Captain's Journals, *Lenox* and *Valeur*
14. Captain's Journal, *Phoenix,* ADM 51/4290
15. Lieutenant's Journal *Phoenix,* ADM 51/4290
16. Captain's Journal *Phoenix,* ADM 51/4290
17. Lieutenant's Journal *Phoenix,* ADM 51/4290
18. Captain's and Masters Journals, *Arundel, Salisbury, Southampton*
19. ADM 52/28 Master's Journal, *Salisbury* (Thomas Styles)

20. Cooke J. H. (see Herbert's account Chapter 6)
21. Pattison. JRIC, Vol I p61-5 1864/5; Addison to Cole 31 Oct 1707
22. Ibid, Pattison describes the dog by tradition as a *'faithful Newfoundland dog,'* whilst Cooke calls it an *'Italian greyhound';* Styles suggests that the dog's name was Mumper, but this cannot be confirmed. Styles S. *Admiral of England*; Cooke, J.H. *The Shipwreck of Sir Clowdsley Shovell.*
23. The supposed sternboard may, in fact, have been the main coat of arms of the *Association* which now hangs on the wall of the Petty Sessional Court at Penzance. It is also surely no coincidence that the bodies of these four men of importance and close personal association, plus Shovell's pet dog, should all have come ashore together? The distance from the Gilstone is a little over six nautical miles, which is a considerable distance for four corpses to drift, yet still remain in close proximity.
24. JRIC Vol VII p215-22 (1882). The famous Cornish ballad often sung with gusto in the ale houses of Cornwall and the Isles of Scilly concludes with the chorus:
    > Trelawney he's in keep and hold,
    > Trelawney he may die
    > But here's twenty thousand Cornish bold
    > Will know the reason why
25. This account confirms an error in Herbert's account, which says that Trelawney's body came ashore with the others on St Mary's Island. (see page 60)
26. Quiller-Couch. JRIC, Vol II p19 1866-7. (Ben. J to the Bishop of Winchester)
27. ADM 2/423, Adm Sec. J. Burchett to Captain Sansom, 1 Nov 1707.
28. According to Black's Guide, some memorials related to Captain Loades and others who perished with Shovell were removed from the Old Church to the New Church at the eastern extremity of the High Street around 1835. The reference continues: *'There are also the tombs of Henry Trelawney and Admiral Sir John Narborough, Bart., sufferers in the same sad disaster. This neat little fane was erected 1835-8, mainly at the cost of Mr. Augustus Smith'. Black's Guide to the Duchy of Cornwall*, p110 (Edinburgh 1885)
29. There were no lives lost on the *Phoenix,* and the vessel survived to be rebuilt in Plymouth in 1709, serving until 1744.
30. Lieutenant's Journal, *Phoenix,* ADM 51/4290
31. Captain's Journal, *Phoenix*. ADM 51/4290; The Phoenix is recorded by Phineas Pett as one of the ships experimentally sheathed in lead in 1678. ADM106/282.
32. ADM 2/423, Adm. Sec. J. Burchett to Commissioner for Sick and Wounded, 8 Nov 1707
33. ADM 2/423, Adm. Sec. J. Burchett to Captain Evans 19 Dec 1708

Chapter Three

Nation in Mourning

'The shrieks and doleful Cries forbear to name, and on the Rocks the Association Tost, Where Shovell and Eight Hundred Souls were lost'.

Anon[1]

Fragmented reports of the loss sustained by Shovell's squadron slowly filtered in from various quarters until, at last reaching London, the news was officially confirmed by the Admiralty revealing the full magnitude of the calamity. Broadsheets and newspapers now proclaimed the woeful news, provoking enormous concern and profound feelings of loss amongst the population. From Queen Anne and the nobility down to the common *'tar'* the great Admiral became the focus point for the grief of a seafaring nation. He had been a truly professional naval officer whose qualities of leadership, character, seamanship and bravery, had over a long and distinguished career, carried him to his ultimate command as Rear Admiral of England and Commander in Chief.

'They tell me Shovell is the best officer of his age', Queen Mary had said of him in a letter to the King when he was a young Rear Admiral of the Blue in 1691.[2] The brilliant Lord Peterborough, commander of the land forces that successfully captured Montjuich Castle in a joint operation at Barcelona in 1705 gives some idea of Shovell's character:

'he is brave, if I may say it, to a fault; and in matters he does not understand thinks that whatever is directed first must be begun, and when begun must be carried on, what accidents so or whatsoever improbabilities come in the way. He sticks close to what he calls orders and will conceive no latitude in such instructions that I think were calculated for the greatest. He is a man under that rough cast of the greatest good nature, and easily disposed on that way'.

Yet Peterborough allowed that: *'those things in which we have differed I cannot reproach Shovell for. He has had grounds for his opinions'.*[3]

Piecing together different accounts, it is possible to obtain a good overall picture of the later train of events concerning the body of the famous admiral, although there are some contradictions. In dismal circumstances the corpse, which initially had been buried in the beach at Port Hellick, was dug up again and reburied higher up in the same cove. Sometime later it was retrieved again on a third occasion, when:

An early lithographic illustration of Sir Clowdisley Shovell's tomb in Westminster Abbey, showing the elaborate carvings and overall size and layout.

Acknowledgement: Illustrated London News

' *- they carried him to Mrs. Bant's in the island, & had on shore several doctors of the ships of the fleet, but none could embalm him or embowel him.
Neither did any of the fleet take much notice of him . . . Captain (Hosier)
Commander of the Salisbury ordered him on board his ship, wherefore they put
him on board the Salisbury on a bare table, the table was Mrs Bant's and a
sheet only to cover him. The table they kept but the sheet they sent on shore* .*[4]*

The captain of the *Salisbury* recorded:

'*26 October. In St. Mary's Sound. At nine (am) the corpse of Sir Clousley
was brought on board which was taken up by the inhabitants of the island. We
made a coffin for him and the doctor embalmed him*'.*[5]*

Despite being charged with the body of the second most senior officer in the
navy, and ordered to carry it safely to Plymouth, the *Salisbury* gave chase
to two small vessels whilst on passage, and took both as prizes of war. She
arrived in Plymouth Sound on 29 October, where, '*- at 8 this evening we sent
the corpse of Sir Clusly on Shore. We hoisted our colours half-mast up and fired
24 guns all ships doing the like*'.*[6]*

Although the captain of the *Salisbury* reported his surgeon had embalmed
Shovell, it is more likely that he had only disembowelled him, since James
Yonge, the surgeon in charge of the first Royal Naval hospital at Plymouth
recorded: '*Sir Cloudisley Shovell was brought into the Citadel. He had been
unfortunately drowned 9 days, and I embalmed him and had £50 for it*'.*[7]*

The Admiral's body was now placed in a casket and conducted in a long
mournful cortege to London, the route attended by thousands of town and
country folk anxious to pay their last respects to a legendary figure, as
famous in his time, as Lord Nelson, a century later:

'*The corpse of Sir Clowdisley Shovell, after having lain in state in our
citadel, to the viewed abundance of spectators for about a week was yesterday
carried to London in a plain hearse without escutcheons and Co. and drawn
by 6 horses. They were attended out of the town by the mayor, magistrates and
common council in their formalities, and also by a regiment of soldiers; and
near 70 gentlemen on horseback, rode several miles with the Corpse. At the
same time, many minute guns were fired from the Citadel and St. Nicholas
Island*'.*[8]*

By 15 November, the procession had reached Okehampton:

'*Sir C. Shovell's corpse lay all night, and next day entered the city (of Exeter)
being met four miles out of the town by several persons of good quality on
horseback. It was near night, and they drove away in view of nearly 2000 people and lodged the corpse at an alehouse at Honiton Clift, four miles out of the
town*'.*[9]*

Sir Clowdisley Shovell's tomb and monument in Westminster Abbey, carved by Grimlin Gibbens on the Lord Chamberlain's instructions direct from Queen Anne, for which he was paid the sum of £322.10s.

Acknowledgement: Westminster Chancery Office/Richard Larn

A similar reception was given to the cortege in all the major towns through which it passed

On arriving in London the body lay in state for many days at the Shovell's town house in Frith Street, Soho, at the Queen's expense. In greatest respect ten senior admirals were asked to attend the funeral:

'Letters are to be written to Admirals Churchill, Aylmer, Fairborn, Leak, Binge, Jennings, Hopsonn, Whetstone, Wishart and Murden, desiring them as flag officers to be at the house of the Lady Shovell in Soho Square on Monday night next at 5 o'clock, to accompany the corpse of Sir Clow. Shovell to Westminster Abbey.'[10].

The funeral procession left for Westminster shortly after 6 o'clock, and following a lengthy service the body was: '- *interred with all the pomp and magnificence suitable to for so mournful an occasion, and her majesty's high regard to the remains of a brave and faithful officer'.[11]*

Sir Clowdisley's body was interred in a huge vault situated in the south choir aisle of the Abbey, a little to the west of the East Cloister door. The marble monument depicts Sir Clowdisley reclining on a couch, dressed in a loose robe, more in keeping with a Roman emperor than a great admiral.[12] The carver of the memorial was Grimlin Gibbens, Royal Carver to Queen Anne, who received payment by order of the Lord Chamberlain, by warrant dated 4 September 1708, for £322.10s.0d. For other funeral services, the Treasurer of the Chamber authorised:

'William Williams, employed by the Society of Upholsterers, for the coffin, hearse etc. to receive £480.5s.6d and Robert Trevet, herald painter, for escutcheons and other heraldry paintings for the said funeral, £138.4s.7d'.

The cost of six of the Earl Marshall's men to attend on horseback was £3 exactly and the *'fees due to St. Peter's church, Westminster, for the interment'*, paid by Daniel Williams, amounted to £46.5s.8d.[13]

The inscription on Shovell's tomb reads:

'Sir Cloudesley Shovell Kt. Rear Admiral of Great Britain and Admiral and Commander-in-Chief of the Fleet. The just rewards of his long and faithfull Service, He was Deservedly beloved of his Country and Esteem'd tho' dreaded by the Enemy, who had often experienced his Conduct and Courage. Being Shipwreckt on the Rocks of Scylly in his Voyage from Thoulon 22nd October 1707 at night in the 57th year of his age. His fate was lamented by all, But Especially the Sea faring part of the Nation to whom he was a Generous Patron and worthy Example.

His body was flung on the Shoar and buried with others in the sands, but being soon after taken up Was placed under this Monument Which his Royall Mistress has caused to be erected To Commemorate His Steady Loyalty and Extraordinary Vertues'.

O' Dreadful accident, be silent Fame,
And tell us not how, nor by what chance it came,
The shrieks and doleful Cries forbear to name,
and on the Rocks the Association Tost,
Where Shovell and Eight Hundred Souls were Lost [14]

Notes for Chapter 3
1. Anon. *The Life and Glorious Actions of Sir Cloudisley Shovell*, BM No 10815 c5
2. CSP Dom. 1690, King William's Chest 7. No 83 p53
3. Owen J.H. *War at Sea Under Queen Anne 1702-08*, p8 (Cambridge 1938); CSP Dom. 1690, King William's Chest 7 No 83
4. Cooke J.H. *The Shipwreck of Sir Cloudsley Shovell*, (Gloucester 1883), (see Herbert's account Chapter 6)
5. Captain's Journal, *Salisbury*
6. Ibid
7. *Journal of James Yonge*, London, 1963 p227. Jonge was apprenticed to a surgeon on board the *Constant Warwick*, 31guns, in 1647 at the age of nine years! Granted the Freedom of the Company of Barber-Surgeons of London in 1631, he was a surgeon for over 50 years.
8. *Daily Courant*, 15 Nov 1707, BM Burney Collection
9. Ibid
10. Adm Minute, 17 Dec 1707
11. *London Gazette*, 29 Dec-1 Jan 1707
12. The monument was much criticized at the time. Joseph Addison, Under-Secretary for

State wrote *'Sir Cloudesley Shovell's monument has very often given me great offence. Instead of the brave, rough English Admiral, which was the distinguishing character of that gallant man, he is represented on his tomb by a figure of a Beau, dressed in long periwig, and reposing himself upon velvet cushions under a canopy of state. The Dutch, whom we are apt to despise for want of genius, shew an infinitely greater taste of antiq uity and politeness in their buildings and works of this nature. The Monuments of their Admirals, which have been erected at public expense, represent them like themselves; and are adorned with rostral crowns and naval ornaments, with beautiful festoons of seaweed, shells and coral'. Spectator,* No 26 March 1711.

It is amusing to note a later description as *' lying in a recumbent position in white mar ble and may be known by his dirty face, arising from the juice of tobacco thrown at his face by British tars out of revenge. He having been the first promoter of 'Burgoo' in the navy, which seamen much dislike'.* Kelly S. *An Eighteenth Century Seaman, p267* 1925; Powell, J. MM, Vol XLIV p160, 1958.

The official Westminster Abbey Guide (1977), makes mention of two other naval offi cers buried in Westminster Abbey who are recorded as having been connected with the 1707 disaster. The first is Vice-Admiral Sir John Baker (1661-1716), buried west of the doorway which leads to the medieval sacristy, said to have been second-in-com mand to Sir Clowdisley and who brought back the fleet from the Scilly's after the acci dent. This must be a mistake, as although Captain John Baker was in command of the *Monmouth,* which was part of the fleet, there were at least four other officers senior to Baker who survived on other ships and he did not assume any overall command. The other officer is Lieutenant John Twysden, son of Sir William Twysden, who was *'lost in one of the ships'.* (p24, 26 & 32)

13. CSP Treasury, 1708, Vol XXII Pt II p108
14. Anon. *The Life and Glorious Actions of Sir Cloudisley Shovell.* BM No 10815 c5

Part of Sir Clowdisley Shovell's will, a long six page document complicated by his many blood kin, and step-children acquired by marriage to Dame Elizabeth, the widow of Admiral Sir John Narborough. The will involved estates in Morston, Norfolk, the manors of Newberry and Howberry and estates in Crayford, Erith and Bexley in Kent. It reads *'In the name of God Amen. Sir Clowdisley Shovell of London, Knight, one of the Commissioners of his Majesties Navy being now of sound and disposing mind and memory do make and ordaine this my last Will and Testament in manner following. I first commend my Soul to Almighty God my Creator in hopes of Eternal Salvation by the merits of my blessed Saviour Jesus Christ. My Body I commit to the Earth from whence it came in full assurance of a joyfull Resurrection And to be buried at the discretion of my Executrix herein after Named And as to such worldly Goods which it hath pleased God to bestow on me I will and bequeath the same in manner following. First I will that all my Debts which I shall owe at the time of my death be fully paid and satisfied immediatly after my decease. I do give and devise unto my Mother Anne Flaxman for and during the Term of her Natural Life All my Lands, Tenements and Hereditaments in Morston in the County of Norfolk with all and every of their Appurtenances thereunto belonging And from and after the decease of my said Mother Anne'.*

Amongst the interesting bequests in the will appears *'I do give and devise unto my said dear wife all my Plate and Jewells, Household Goods, Coach and Horses'.* (PROB/11/499)

Chapter Four

The Aftermath

'Had not the seas been so boisterous all the treasure before this had been fished out'

Scottish Newspaper 9 July 1710

In the spring of 1708 a long succession of widows, other next of kin and executors representing the deceased, descended on the Broadstreet offices of the Navy Treasury in London, to lay claim to the unpaid wages of their loved ones drowned in the disaster. In February the Chancellor of the Exchequer ordered the sum of £10,000, *'to be applied to pay what is due to the men cast away with Sir Cloudisley Shovell'.*[1] Even so, it was some months before the majority had received their legacies. Many who attended early were paid in March but it was not until May, 1708, that the Bank of England: *'agreed for the public service to advance £20,000, the Lord Treasurer desiring that you apply for wages of the ship's companies lost with Sir Cloudisley Shovell £15,000'.*[2]

Amongst the many claimants at Broadstreet on the 9 April 1708, in stark contrast to the bereaved, appeared George Lawrence, the only survivor of the *Romney,* to collect the balance of 28 months pay accrued since 22 August, 1705. The entry against his name in the Admiralty Neat Book lists him as an Able Seaman showing that out of a total of £33.18.10d earned, he received a balance of £30.13.7d. Small deductions had been made for *'Tobacco', 'Slopsellers Cloaths', 'Chest'* and 14s 2d for *'Greenwich Hospital'* at 6d per month. The most interesting entry of all, however, gives us some idea as to the means of his lucky preservation. In a column headed *'Whether or for What Reason'* is the brief remark: *'This man was saved on a longboat oar and appeared at this office 23rd Dec 1707'.*[3]

Putting the various reports together it would appear that Lawrence, in the turmoil and darkness of the night following the wrecking, first clung to the oar of a long-boat that was swept along by wind and tide. Providence eventually brought him close to one of the isolated Western Rocks. With great difficulty in the numbing cold and surging seas, he eventually managed to struggle, injured and exhausted, onto the rock (probably the Hellweathers) from where he was eventually rescued by boat at dawn the following morning.[4]

Details of the ship's company of the lost ships can be found in Appendix 1-4, with the names and ratings of every individual, the beneficiaries, mostly widows, and the sums of money due to their men. The Neat Book for the *Association*, which details the dates men joined and left the ship, their rank or rating and daily pay, was obviously made up with some difficulty, as the introduction notes imply, and it was certainly no easier for the other vessels:

'Association - Began sea wages 1st July 1705; ended sea wages 22nd October 1707.

His Royal Highness having by his late order of the 10th November last, directed the payment of the wages due for the service of the officers and company of Her Majestys late ship the Association, to the 22nd October proceeding (the day she was unhappily lost on the rocks near the Island of Scilly). The foregoing book has in pursuance thereof been collected from the several muster books remaining in the Ticket Office so far as they have been received either from the Captain and Officers, Clerks of the Cheque and Musters, as is set down in the front thereof, with respect to the entries, names, qualities, discharges, times of death, runs, with the deductions for slops, under the several vendors heads, as also beds, divers clothes and tobacco so far as the same is charged on any or all of the said Muster Books, and this collection is made as perfect and correct as the said Muster Books will enable and admit of'.[5]

A substantial part of the wages due were paid out at Broadstreet, on 1 March 1707-8, before Sir Richard Haddock Knt., with William Hogg and Roger Webb, Clerks for the Navy, and William Wahup and Thomas Bluett, Clerks for the Treasury in attendance. However, it was not until 21 July 1712 that the book was made up and closed showing a total amount paid out of £22,339.15s.9d.

Despite the payments made in early 1708 there were still many families in need who had received little of the allocated money by December 1708. Some in authority questioned whether various payments were in fact due. William Lowndes wrote to the Navy Commissioners that month: ' - *enclosing the petition of the poor seaman's widows whose husbands were lost with Sir C. Shovell. Please certify whether anything is due to them, and whether it has been usual upon such sad accidents to bestow bounties?'* [6]

Lady Shovell fared little better, and even she had to petition for all the money due to her late husband in respect of his service. On 26 July 1710, William Lowndes reported: '- *on the enclosed petition of the widow of Sir C.*

Shovell with the account of money imprested to him or his agent for pay of one of the Marine Regiments in the late war under his command'.[7]   Sir Clowdisley Shovell's annual salary would appear to have been £1,277.10s. With additional sums of servants and table money whilst at sea.[8] Amongst the many sums of money paid to him on board the *Association* the following are recorded:

'Salary paid to Sir C. Shovell 29 Sept. 1706, per 1/4   £250. 0. 0d.
To Hon. Sir C. Shovell 25 Dec. 1706   £250. 0. 0d.
To Sir C.S. for services,   £912.10s.0d (also £770.0.0d that
*   he has to pass on).*

Other money for ship at Jan 1707,   £10,129.19s.7d.
To Sir C.S. 29 Sept. 1707, salary   £250. 0s. 0d.
*   and £98.7s.0d for his 12 servants.'*

The handle of a pewter spoon recovered from the wreck of the *Association,* showing a crest which includes a crown over the letters AA and an incomplete mark below.

Acknowledgement: Scillonian Diving Services

Whilst an earlier reference, of 31 December 1702 quotes, ' - *Sir C. Shovell his Table Money to start from January 1703 of £365.0.0d'.*[9]

In October 1711, Lady Elizabeth Shovell and others made yet another plea to the Admiralty*:*

'- On behalf of themselves and the colonels and divers captains of the late two marine regiments, and the widows of others deceased, praying that a full and exact state be made of the pay of the said regiments as well as the time they were at sea and on shore'.[10]

The financial consequences of the disaster rumbled on. As late as 1713 it was reported:

'My Lord Treasurer is importuned by persons calling themselves the widows of seamen belonging to her Majesty's ship Romney lost with Sir Cloudisley

Shovell, which was cast away, they praying for gun money alleged to be due to them for a French privateer called the Diamond which was taken by the Romney. Please report a state of this case and your opinion on these Pretences'.[11]

A final reference cites an application for money, which was not settled until 1717, ten years after the accident;

'Ensign Peter de-la-Chappelle. This ensign never was in service being a child to whom Lord Galway gave an Ensign's Commission for the support of himself, his mother and sister, in consideration of the long service of his father, who was drowned at the same time with Sir C. Shovell'.[12]

In the few days after the incident wreckage was found ashore as far away as Land's End, and up the Bristol Channel. We do not know exactly what this wreckage was, but certainly the *Association's* stern escutcheon bearing a resplendent royal coat of arms was taken up in the islands and saved. There is also to this day the carved wooden head of a lion mounted on the wall of the Hugh Town Church, which is said to have come from the wreck, and there may also be other historic artifact material surviving in private hands in Scilly or elsewhere. On display in the Isles of Scilly Museum, side by side, are two identical silver spoons, one probably salvaged from the wreck by a Scillonian in 1707, and treasured ever since; the other recovered from the site of the *Association* in the late 1960's and recently presented in perfect condition.

For those Scillonians who derived their living from the sea it is certain there would have been rich pickings from the wrecks. Defoe, choosing to ignore the fact that lives were often saved by the Islanders, observed that after a gale on the Islands:

'The sands were covered with country people running to and fro' to see if the sea had cast up anything of value. This the seamen call 'going ashoring'; and it seems they do often find good purchase: sometimes also some dead bodies are cast up here, the consequence of shipwreck among those fatal rocks and Islands; as also broken pieces of ships, casks, chests, and almost everything that will float, or roll on shore by the surges of the sea'.[13]

Although by custom most of the wreck recovered would have been quickly spirited away and hidden by the Islanders, it is interesting to speculate on the emerging situation amongst the interested parties. The Governor of the Islands at the time was Sir Sidney Godolphin, Lord Treasurer of England and 'prime minister' of England, a man of considerable power, who by the terms of his lease was entitled to *'a moiety or half part of all shipwrecks'*, occurring in Scilly.[14] Bishop Trelawney, the Vice-admiral for Shipwreck for the South Coast of Cornwall (which presumably included the Islands) could lay claim for at least 10%, on behalf of the Lord High Admiral of England. The original owners of the vessel and cargo also had *'a year and a day'* in which to lay claim to any goods recovered. A further complication was that some of the wreck would have been the private property of members of the crew. The strongest claim naturally fell to the Crown through the Admiralty and Officers of the Navy Board.

The established agents for all the interested parties would have been quickly on site. The difficulties would have been, firstly, how to persuade the finders to declare the materials recovered; and secondly, how to legally prove any unmarked wreckage was from one of the Royal Naval vessels, as opposed to a merchantman or foreign warship. The situation has changed little over the centuries. Similar circumstances have strangely pervaded all the salvage that has gone on in the Islands in recent years. (see Chapter 8)

On 1 November Josiah Burchett, Secretary for the Admiralty, responded to Captain Benedict, Deputy Governor of the Islands:

'I am commanded by his Royal Highness to signify his directions to you to do your utmost to save what you can of the wrecks of Her Majesty's ships lost on the Islands of Scilly and an order there to you to employ which persons therein as you shall think necessary and give me an account of what shall be ordered for the information of the Prince'.[15]

In the margin of this letter is a note also advising Benedict to send an account of the charge when the saving of stores is completed. Captain Benedict, was now officially required to give priority to the crown's directions and on 20 November Burchett wrote:

'I am commanded by the Prince to write to you to desire you will give me an account for the information of his Royal Highness and his Council in what depth of water the Association was sunk and whether you think there is any prospect of recovering the guns'.[16]

It is apparent that a fair amount of stores were saved in the immediate aftermath, since on 22 December, Captain Greenhill, Commissioner for the Plymouth Dockyard, was directed:

'to send a proper officer from the yard or some other fitting person to the Islands of Scilly for putting to sale the stores saved from the wrecks of her Majesty's ships lately cast away on the Island; as also the Phoenix, Fireship'.[17]

Retrieved from amongst the flotsam in strange circumstances were documents and journals belonging to Admiral Shovell:

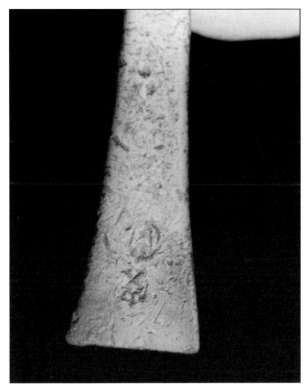

Another pewter spoon from the *Association* site,
bearing a mark of crossed swords or quills
beneath a crown.

Acknowledgement: Peter McBride

'Mr Joseph Iuath, Post Master Genl. gives account of proceedings relative to the paper thrown away by Mr Morley, the custom house officer, saying they were of no value. Sends him three books taken up by Elias Griggs, junr and Mr Paine's son. Sends also Lord Sunderland's letter as directed and a description of the said three books. Will send an explanation of Mr Morley's conduct as soon as he has seen him'.

The commission said to have been amongst the papers proves to have been left with the Governor of Scilly'.[18]

One of the enclosures is most curious, *'Nov 7, description of three books mentioned above, taken out of the River at Topsham'*, whilst the other describes the steps taken by the Earl of Sunderland (Secretary of State for the South) and two other officials to recover and transmit the papers to the Admiralty.[19] The suggestion that documents and books were recovered from the River Topsham merits deeper research. It is difficult to believe that the books could have drifted all the way from Scilly to Devon on the wind and tide. Had they been recovered by the crew of another vessel and later thrown in the river?

Very little is known about the value of the money actually carried on board the *Association* and other ships when they were wrecked, the only printed reference to the sum of money can be found in a Scottish newspaper account:

'We hear from Scilly that the gentleman concerned in the wreck of Sir Cloudisley Shovell's ship have taken several iron cannon, seven brass guns with a cable, and have found the Association in 4 fathoms of water at low tide, the hull of the ship being whole wherein there is vast treasure. The Queen's plate, several chests of money with great riches from the Grandees of Spain.

The divers go down in a copper engine and continue two hours underwater, wherein they have also met with the fireship cast away at the same time as the Association (I don't know her name). Had not the seas been so very high and boisterous all the treasure before this, had been fished out'.[20]

Apart from the obvious mistake of identifying the *Firebrand* as the *Phoenix*, this report raises a number of interesting questions regarding the early diving operations. Who were these divers and what apparatus were they using? Did the celebrated Captain Jacob Rowe, of London, employ them? The diver the Dutch East India Company hired to try and find the wreck of the *Hollandia*, which sank near St. Agnes, in 1743, was John Lethbridge, of Newton Abbot, who used a wooden diving 'engine', where-as Captain Rowe was well known for his superior copper device. Unless the 'engine' used on the *Association* in 1710 was a diving bell, or an appa-ratus belonging to a little known diver, we can reasonably assume Captain Rowe or one of his employees was the diver.

In his *'Tour of Great Britain'*, published in 1724, the celebrated journal-ist Daniel Defoe, of *'Robinson Crusoe'* fame, painted a vivid scene of the diving salvage activities going on in the Scilly's in the early 1700's. It is amazing how much the description is reminiscent of the frenzied operations on site after the rediscovery of the wreck in 1967:

'Here also is a further testimony of the immense riches to be found which have been lost several times upon this coast, we found several engineers and projectors; some with one sort of diving engine, and some with another; some claiming such a wreck, and some such and such others; where they alleged, they were assured there were great quantities of money; and strange unprece-dented ways were used by them to come at it; some, I say with one kind of engine, and some another; and though we thought several of them very strange impracticable methods, yet, I was assured by the country people, that they had done wonders with them under water, and that some of them had taken up things of great weight, and in a great depth of water; others had split open the wrecks they had found, in a manner one would have thought not possible to have done, so far under water, and had taken out things from the very holds of the ships; but we could not learn, that they had come at any pieces of eight, which was the thing they seemed most to aim at, and depend upon; at least they had not found any great quantity, as they said they expected'.[21]

With regard to the money reported as being on board the flag ship in the newspaper account, the expression *'Queen's plate'*, is used in reference to sil-ver specie or coin money. One possible source was the balance of the funds provided by the government for the Duke of Savoy's army at Toulon. At the outset of this campaign, Sir Clowdisley, as Commander-in-Chief, was given clearly defined orders as to the navy's contribution in supporting the army. In addition to providing guns *'as judged requisite by His Royal Highness',* and supplying 6-700 barrels of gunpowder, Sir Clowdisley was responsible for the carriage and security of the funds supplied to support the army:

> *'£50,000 sterling shall be furnished for the extra-ordinary expenses, and if the sum is not sufficient there shall be given such a surplus as His Royal Highness, the Duke shall think necessary and represent so, in whom there is placed an entire trust'.*

The actual document setting out these resolutions has a margin annotation, which reads *'£100,000',*[22] indicating that at some stage, the initial sum supplied had been increased.

Amongst the many reasons assigned for the failure of the expedition, was a supposed clash of personalities between the Duke, Prince Eugene and Sir Clowdisley. Of the Admirals relationship with the Duke, it was said *'Sir C.S. disgusted the Duke of Savoy, by detaining the payment of the subsidies, which were due on his passing the Var'.* This has not been substantiated, but it would seem possible in the complicated politics of the situation, which involved various allied forces, their movements, and the limited duration of the campaign. Sir Clowdisley may have felt justified in withholding a proportion of the war funds, for eventual return to the Treasury.[23] Campbell felt that the story of Sir C.S. detaining a sum of money must be without foundation since he wrote, *'before the attack, His Royal Highness must have been perfectly satisfied, otherwise he would not have undertaken it'.*[24]

Warships of today, especially those on foreign commissions, often carry very large sums of money in different currencies, necessary for payment to the crew for shore leave, the purchase of fresh provisions, and general emergencies. Even today, almost into the 21st century, a warship sent to some remote part of the world will normally carry in the ship's safe a considerable sum in gold coin. With this 'ship money', fuel oil in particular, may be purchased, should the need arise, anywhere in the world. Circumstances were very little different in 1707, and no doubt, the *Association,* and the other ships of the fleet carried similar contingency funds.

Some of the money on board the *Association* is known to have been part of the regimental funds of the Coldstream Guards, as a petition to the Lord High Treasurer from Colonel Andrew Bissett, one of the senior officers of that regiment, makes clear:

> *' - equipage, to the value of £600, to be brought to England, but Captain*

Elwes being despatched for Lisbon, put the same on board Admiral Sir Cloudesley Shovell's ship, which was unfortunately lost on the rocks of Scilly. They (J. Brydges & R. Walpole, addressees of the petition) were of opinion he ought to be relieved as to the £400, but left the consideration as to the baggage to his Lordship.[25] Despite a degree of sympathy from the Treasury, which is obvious in their letter to the Paymaster of Guards and Garrisons, recognising that: *'otherwise Colonel Bissett will be subject to the great hardship of having the loss placed to his own particular account.'*[26] The Colonel never got his money: *'- the two reports have been read to the Treasury, one the 19th February and 22nd March and the answer has been, there is no provision made by the Parliament for losses of this kind.'*[27]

Whether or not Sir Clowdisley really did have ten chests of personal money on board cannot now be substantiated, but it would seem highly unlikely, unless he had somehow accumulated that sum during the expedition. There was no obvious requirement for the Admiral to have carried such a large personal sum out of England, with the ever-present risk of it being lost by storm, accident or capture, but he may have been carrying home specie on behalf of merchant bankers. The true value of the treasure carried on board the *Association* will probably never be known.

When the wreck of the *Association* was discovered in 1967 by divers of the Naval Air Command Sub Aqua Club, the first coin brought to the surface was a gold Portuguese 4,000 reis piece in mint condition, found by Richard Voisey. This may have been part of a consignment of such coin, described in a newspaper account at the time as *'great riches of the Grandees of Spain'*. Worth some £150 in 1967, a similar coin today would fetch between £400-450.

Most probably the flagship was transporting a consignment of gold and silver 'specie' on behalf of foreign bankers or merchants, a common practice at the time. An 18th century man o'war was the equivalent of a modern security service, offering a near guaranteed delivery. In return, it was a perquisite of the admiral or captain involved to receive at least 5% of the gross sum, a lucrative additional source of income, at little or no expense to the officer involved.

Salvage work on the site of the *Association* and the wreck on Tearing Ledge, initially thought to be that of the *Romney*, but now in the light of research and investigation of the guns, almost certainly that of the *Eagle*, has produced a remarkable number of coins and artefacts. The specie is predominantly English silver, with a not inconsiderable amount of English and foreign gold, a fair proportion of Spanish/American cobs of eight, four and two reales, and some unusual coinage and tokens, including Arabian and Dutch. The oldest coins found were reales of 1598 (Phillip II), and the latest, Portuguese 4,000 reis dated 1707, the year the *Association* sank.

The English silver spans the reigns of five monarchs, from 1662 (Charles II), through James II, William and Mary, and William III to Queen Anne, the latest coin being 1705 (the year that Sea Pay commenced on the *Association*), suggesting it was money brought from England initially. Amongst the English coins are gold guineas, half-guineas, crowns, half-crowns, shillings and sixpence's, with almost no copper coinage. The latter circumstance appears unusual, since many of the seamen on board must surely have had a few pence in their ditty boxes?

Estimates as to exactly how much *'treasure'* has been recovered from the *Association* can only be speculated, but the current value must be in the order of £300,000 to £500,000. In the early days of excavation work on the wreck site, one particular diver recovered over one hundred Portuguese 4,000 reis in a day, and there have been at least two spectacular cache finds of silver and possibly more. The first of these was in September 1967, when two divers working for Roland Morris, of Penzance, found several thousand coins. The second was a substantial find of over 8,000 coins discoverd by Jim Heslin, Terry Hiron and Don Bates in July 1971. Currently, the *Association* site still yields around 200 coins a year, and seemingly will continue to do so for many year to come, although frequently many of them are in very poor condition.

There is only one documented visit to the wreck site of the *Association* from the time of the Herbert expedition in 1709, and its subsequent relocation by the Royal Navy in 1967. This occurred in August 1847, the same month that Queen Victoria and Prince Albert visited the Isles of Scilly on board the Royal Yacht *Victoria and Albert* on their way to Scotland. The account, which appeared in a West Country newspaper, reads:

> *'Scilly Islands. Interesting discovery. Sir Cloudesley Shovell's ship's guns, about 30 in number, and several round and cross-bar shot, were seen on the 17th instant near a rock called the Gilstone, to the westward of these islands, by a diver belonging to the cutter Argyle of Jersey, (Captain) Masters. He states that two of the guns could be raised with ease, but the remainder are covered over by a rock apparently of about 30 tons weight, which must have fallen upon them. He recovered two round shot of about 24lbs each, and a crossbar shot of the same weight.'*[28]

Work began on building the first Bishop Rock lighthouse in the Isles of Scilly in 1848, and was not completed until 1850. It is quite likely that divers employed in underwater construction carried out the 1847 visit to the Gilstone. They may have known the history of the 1707 disaster, or heard of it from the islanders. As far as known, this was the last occasion divers were to visit the wreck of the *Association* for 120 years.

Notes for Chapter 4

1. CSP Treasury, 13 Feb 1708, Vol XXII Pt II p6
2. Ibid, 22 May 1708, p247.
3. ADM 33/258, Neat Book of the *Romney,* 1 Jul 1705-22 Oct 1707, paid at Broadstreet 9 April 1708.
4. The notation *'saved on a longboat oar'* adds credence to Woodley's recorded account in 1833. According to Woodley, Lawrence floated on a piece of timber to the Hellweathers (2 1/2 miles from the Gilstone) and was found by a boat from St.Agnes. Woodley G. Reverend, *The Present State of the Isles of Scilly,* p44-47 (London 1833)
5. ADM 33/249, Neat Book of the *Association*
6. CSP Treasury, 8 Dec 1708, Out Letters, general, Vol XIX p20
7. CSP Treasury, 26 Jul 1711, Vol. XXV Pt 2 p388, Lowndes to Navy Commissioners
8. ADM 81/109, 17 Nov 1707.
9. ADM 18/82, D.179 p46, 31 Dec. 1702.
10. CSP Treasury, 17 Oct 1711,Vol. XXV Pt 2 p530
11. Ibid,1713, Pt 2 p237
12. Ibid,1717, Pt 3 p848-9
13. Defoe D. *A Tour through the Whole of the Island of Britain*, p245, Appendix to letter III (London 1927) First published 1724
14. The lease, previously held for 50 years by Sir Francis Godolphin, was renewed by letter patent 25th July 1698 to his successor. This was granted by King William III on *'yielding and paying to his Majesty his heirs and successors the yearly rent of £40 at the Feast of St.Michael into the hands of the Receiver of the Dutchy of Cornwall'.* JRIC, Vol 19 p292-298.
15. ADM 2/423, Adm. Sec. J. Burchett to Captain Benedict,1 Nov 1707
16. Ibid, 20 Nov 1707
17. Ibid, Adm. Sec. J. Burchett to Captain Greenhill, 22 Dec 1707
18. CSP 1707, No 48 p450; The commission is probably the one found in a tin box on a *'carcass that was floating'* (see Chapter 2)
19. Ibid, No 49 p450, 17 Nov 1707
20. London Letter, 9 Jul 1710.
21. Defoe D. *A Tour through the Whole Island of Britain*, p245
22. BM Add. Mss 28153 and 28141; Owen p158, 160.
23. Campbell, Vol. III p522.
24. Ibid, Vol. IV p258.
25. CSP Treasury, 18 Jun 1709, Vol CXIV No 55

26. Ibid, 23 Feb 1710, Vol XXV Pt 2 p183
27. Ibid, 11 Jun 1711, Vol XXV Pt 2 p300
28. *Royal Cornwall Gazette* Aug 1847.

Chapter Five

Quest for Longitude

'Nothing is so much wanted and desired at sea, as the discovery of longitude, for the safety and quickness of voyages, the preservation of ships and the lives of men'

Longitude Act - 1714

Every officer and seaman from the *Association* and the *Eagle* having been drowned, and only a quartermaster saved from the wreck of the *Romney*, there were literally no responsible senior officers left to face the usual court-martial and recount the navigational particulars of the three lost ships of the line. The surviving officers from the fireship *Firebrand,* which finally foundered inshore near St. Agnes were, however, summoned to a court martial on board the *Somerset* at Blackstakes under the presidency of Captain John Price on 21 November 1707. The findings of the court were predictable:

> *'The court having strictly enquired into the matter it appeared to the court by evidence upon oath of the surviving officers, that they were in their proper station and fell in amongst the rocks with the rest of the ships, and that both before and after she struck they used the utmost endeavours for saving the ship; the court not finding the said Fireship was lost through any neglect of duty in the officers of her. The court does acquit the said Captain Frances Piercy and the other officers as to the loss of the said Fireship the Firebrand'.[1]*

Naturally, the Board of Admiralty considered the naval consequences of the catastrophe so serious that a thorough enquiry into the circumstances and potential causes was instigated. Particular emphasis was placed on current navigational practice, in an attempt to learn new lessons for the future.

In considering the evidence little stress was put on the two other contributory causes, (ie. the delayed departure from Gibraltar, adjudged far too late in the season even by Admiral Shovell's own standards. (see page 5) and the decision to approach the Channel at night in poor weather with all the inherent hazards. (see page 2) It may be that little emphasis was laid on these factors to avoid any censure of the dead Admiral who otherwise had an unblemished record and had served his country long and well. Instead importance was placed on the navigational aspects.

'We were too much to the northward of what we expected', said the captain of

Wooden nocturnal recovered from the wreck site of the *Firebrand,* near St Agnes
Acknowledgement: Roland Morris

the *Torbay,'and likewise more to the eastward'.* Captain Sir William Jumper of the *Lenox* observed, *'I was surprised to find my ship so far to the northward and indeed can impute it to nothing but the badness of the compass which was very old and full of defects'.*[2] In a letter to George, Prince of Denmark, the Lord High Admiral, Sir William later amplified his concerns:

' *I am extremely surprised for the bad news of the Admiral....indeed I fear I should have had the same fate if I had not parted with the Admiral that day and sailed away those hours to the N to speak with two ships I took to be English Frigates to know the bearing of the land, but they proved privateers. I should have steered to the N'ward while daylight to make Scilly believing myself the length thereof; if it had not proved thick weather which made me keep my luff and steer ESE & SE by E till I met with Scilly.*

Indeed never so deceived in my life having come into the Channel above 100 times and very often when I had no observations of the sun for a fortnight or 3 weeks in the winter. Neither can I impute this extraordinary deviation from a serious consideration of my past works to anything but the age and deficiency of our compass having had a very good observation two days before, which agreed with the other ships and am pretty well satisfied this error has been in the age and deficiency of our compass, since most or all of the fleet were a head of their ships which was reckoned in navigation a very good fault giving us cautions to look out early for land or danger'.[3]

As a result of this and other reports, the Navy Board instigated a major survey of all the compasses on board the surviving ships of Shovell's fleet, including those held at naval dockyards. Captain's George St. Loe and Isaac Townsend, Naval Commissioners of the Chatham and Portsmouth dockyards, respectively, were instructed to carry out this task. Townsend had, in fact, served as captain on board the *Russell,* under Shovell in 1703, at the time of the 'Great Gale'. (see Chapter 13)

The results of this survey are enlightening. A ship of the first rate was allowed twelve wooden compasses, yet the *St. George* actually returned no less than twenty-two. The *Monmouth* carried fourteen wooden box compasses, all by different manufacturers, while an equal number in the *Lenox* were *'broke and in pieces'*. The ship's officers also said *'the remainder were useless'*. At Portsmouth of 112 wooden cased compasses returned from nine ships in Shovell's squadron (ie. approximately twelve each), only four were completely serviceable, whilst only seventy out of 370 wooden box compasses held in the dockyard store in November 1707 were found to be of any use.

One of the causes blamed for the rapid deterioration of compasses at sea was the custom of storing them in the boatswain's store. This being always damp and near the powder room, caused the nitre in the gunpowder to rust the needles prematurely, which was the main cause of malfunction.

On conclusion of the survey, it was proposed that in future brass box compasses only should be purchased. It was considered that by this means the number of compasses supplied to each ship could be reduced by a third, or even half, and a higher proportion would be found serviceable or repairable when returned to the dockyards from sea service. It was also suggested that compasses should in future be kept in a seasoned wood chest fitted with partitions, in the ship's lead lined bread-room, considered the driest part of any ship, a practice introduced from June 1708 [4]

Recent analysis of data obtained from the surviving journals of the homeward bound fleet has revealed no reference to any allowances for magnetic variation of the compass. This would have increased from four to seven degrees west as the homeward voyage progressed, and if not allowed for would have placed the ships between one and two degrees westward of their reckoning.[5]

Defective compasses apart, blame appears to have been placed on the primitive methods for estimating longitude, coupled to cloudy weather which had marred and reduced the ability of the fleet to make backstaff observations for latitude. In respect of longitude some officers in the fleet were as much as three degrees in error, the majority something less than one degree to the westward. In fact they could hardly have been expected to achieve a greater accuracy, since in 1707, estimates of longitude between Cape Spartel and the Isles of Scilly varied considerably. With a reckoning based on departure from Cape Spartel, which was usually located too far to the westward on charts anyway, it is a wonder that more ships did not place themselves in that direction.

Five incomplete pairs of brass navigational dividers recovered from the Outer Gilstone site. The steel points of these instruments have, of course, rusted away long ago.

Acknowledgement: Scillonian Diving Services

Where latitude was concerned most of Shovell's ships thought they were about thirty miles to the southward of Scilly and three in fact gave their positions correctly. Even they must have thought themselves quite safe, as most of the tables, then in use, showed the islands between fourteen and twenty miles too far north. Whilst it would seem that the 'Rennell Current' and inaccurate compasses probably contributed to the cause of the disaster, a higher proportion of blame must be placed on the inaccuracies of recorded geographical positions, and the generally low standard of accuracy of navigational practice.[6]

The search for a method of accurately determining longitude had long occupied many mathematicians, astronomers and scientists of the 17th century. The loss of the 2nd Rate *Coronation* in 1691 and the *Association*,

XSV. *Puttenham* (M.2784) alongside St. Mary's quay, Isles of Scilly, with spectators looking at the 3-ton bronze cannon slung across her stern, about to the landed.

Acknowledgement: Paul Armiger, Daily Telegraph

Eagle and *Romney* in 1707, each resulting in an exceptional number of fatalities, now served to intensify the quest. In 1713, William Whiston, a protégé of Isaac Newton's, who had succeeded him as Lucasian professor of mathematics at Cambridge and then lost his post in 1711 for holding unorthodox religious views, made public a novel, if somewhat bizarre, scheme to solve the longitude problem. The idea was conceived jointly with Humphrey Ditton, a friend and fellow mathematician from Christ's Hospital who was also co-author.[7]

Citing Admiral Shovell's recent demise in justification the scheme proposed that a number of specially commissioned vessels would be anchored in the ocean at 600-mile intervals, at points of latitude and longitude calculated from observed eclipses of the moons of Jupiter. Alternatively solar and lunar eclipses could be used. Each midnight a cannon on each stationary ship would fire a bomb at maximum elevation which, exploding at approximately 6440ft could be seen for 100 miles. By this means mariners in transit would obtain a sound and visual fix, which could be improved by reference to local time. If clouds obscured the flash, the sound would suffice.

The many impracticalities of the scheme, published for the first time in the *Guardian* July 1713, are obvious. However, it was refined and re-published in a second article in the *Englishman* on 10 December of the same year under the title *'A New Method for Discovering the Longitude both at Sea and Land'*.[8]

By dogged determination the impoverished Whiston, supported by his partner, managed to unite the maritime interests of London in a common cause. In the spring of 1714 they produced a petition signed by *'the Captains of Her Majesty's Ships, Merchants of London and Commanders of Merchantmen'*. The document demanded that the government focus attention on the longitude problem by offering rich rewards to anyone successful in finding an accurate method. The government was pressured into setting up a parliamentary committee. A committee including Sir Isaac Newton and Edmund Halley were consulted and the former produced a paper summarising the options. These included; a telescope for observations of the satellites of Jupiter, use of a magnetic needle and: *'a watch to keep time exactly, But by reason of the motion of the ship, the Variation of Heat and Cold, Wet and Dry, and the Difference of Gravity in different Latitudes, such a watch hath not yet been made'*.[9]

In July 1714, after due debate, the Longitude Act of July 1714 was issued. The opening preamble reads:

'It is well known by all that are acquainted with the Art of Navigation, That nothing is so much wanted and desired at Sea, as the Discovery of Longitude, for the Safety and Quickness of Voyages, the Preservation of Ships and the Lives of Men'.[10]

Three levels of prize were offered for the discovery of an effective solution, dependant on the degree of precision achieved. Strict criteria for judging the competition were incorporated and a Board of Longitude was established to preside. The greatest reward was £20,000 for a method achieving an accuracy of half a degree on a great circle, which translates to thirty nautical miles at the equator.

Offered solutions had been plentiful even before the act and after 1714 the

Two bronze breech loading cannon, less their breech-blocks, lignum vitae sheaves from pulley blocks, and two sounding leads. Acknowledgement: Richard Larn

number of contestants proliferated. The most successful competitor and the person credited with the eventual discovery was Edward Harrison, a carpenter turned clockmaker, who first addressed his genius to the development of a chronometer in 1725. Supported by grants from the Board he produced a succession of innovative and progressive designs over many years. It was not until 1773, after a lifetime of skilful endeavour and frequent disappointment, that he finally overcame considerable opposition to collect the last instalment of the prize money with his fifth prototype.[11]

Whiston, the main instigator, appears to have profited little from the race he was instrumental in promoting and encouraging. Nevertheless, over the years he continued to submit projects for the safety and welfare of mariners. In 1717 he petitioned the Officers of the Board of Ordnance:

'praying an allowance and other things necessary for putting into practice a method for the preservation of ships near Scilly by balls of fire and the sound of a mortar or great gun'.[12] His proposal was that a ball of fire should be thrown up from St. Mary's: *'every midnight and three times a night'* and that it should: *'afford a light above a degree of a great circle or 60 geographical miles; and the sound heard above one third of the same distance'.[13]* It is interesting to speculate on the likely reaction of the population of St.Mary's to this extreme proposal!

Between 1719 and 1722, Whiston put forward, and attempted to develop, a new method for establishing longitude by magnetic dipping needle, using a central iron magnetic core turning slowly on axis from east to west. It was thought the dip of the needle towards the core could be computed and the intersection of lines of equal dip with lines of latitude could give the longitude. The theory was put to a sea trial in 1722, when each captain of four ships were entrusted with an enormous dip-needle hung in gimbals to be placed near the ship's *'centre of motion'*. Unfortunately no consistent results were achieved.[14]

Finally, as late as 1741, he received a grant of £500 from the Board of Longitude:

'for procuring a new Sett of Astronomical Instruments for finding out the Longitude on the Coasts of this Kingdom with the Variation of the Needle and for enabling him to make Observations with them'.[15]

The exclusive use of the chronometer for finding longitude has now largely been superseded by the modern invention of satellite navigation. However, over a period of two centuries, generations of mariners were indebted to Edward Harrison, William Whiston and the unfortunate souls sacrificed with Admiral Shovell for contributing to the safer navigation of the world's oceans.

Notes for Chapter 5

1. ADM 1/5266
2. Marcus G. *Sir Clowdisley Shovell's Last Passage*, JRUSI Vol CII p547, 1957; Captain's Journals, *Lenox* and *Torbay*
3. ADM 1/1981, 29 Oct 1707
4. May W.E. *Compasses in 1707*, JIN, Vol VI No 4 p405-6, 1953; Navy Board Letters (In) ADM 106/617
5. May W.E. *Last Voyage of Sir Clowdisley Shovell*, JIN, Vol XIII p331-2
6. Ibid, and May W.E. *A History of Marine Navigation*, p28 (London 1973)
7. Taylor E.G.R. *Reward for Longitude*, MM, Vol XLV p59-65, 1959; Andrews J.H. (Editor) *The Quest for Longitude*, p142-145 (Harvard Symposium Nov 1993)
8. Ibid, Whiston W. and Ditton H. (London 1714); DNB, LXI p10-14 (London 1900)
9. Ibid, Sobell D. *Longitude*, p50-52 (London 1995)
10. Howse D. *Britain's Board of Longitude: The Finances 1714-1828*, MM, Vol 84 p400, Nov 1998
11. Ibid, p402; Sobell, *Longitude*, p50-52
12. CSP Treasury, 25 Jan 1717-18, Vol XXXII pt II p168, Treasury Warrants, Bk IX p371.
13. Woodley G. Reverend,*The Present State of the Isles of Scilly*, p320 (London 1833)
14. Taylor, *Reward for Longitude*, p64
15. Howse, *Britain's Board of Longitude*, p413

William Whiston, mathematician and protégé of Isaac Newton. Prompted by Shovell's disaster, Whiston's longitude project led to the '*Act for the Discovery of Longitude, 1714*' and Edward Harrison's prize winning '*Chronometer*'.

Chapter Six

Herbert's Expedition - Legends

'This part of Cornwall may be truly said to be inhabited by a fierce and ravenous people'.

Daniel Defoe - 1725

Two whole years after Sir Clowdisley Shovell's tragic shipwreck a venture was proposed in London to salvage the wrecked ships. Associated with this was the desire to gain, at first hand, details of the incident from the Scillonians, since it would appear that the Admiralty had little real knowledge of events. The task of salvaging, or establishing the feasibility of salvage, fell to twenty-four year old Edmund Herbert, an unemployed 'gentleman' of good background, who later obtained a clerkship in the office of the Paymaster General of the Regiment of Marine, and eventually rose to become Deputy Paymaster.[1]

Although the extent of Herbert's expedition is unknown, he arrived in the Isles of Scilly in 1709, and appears to have remained there for the best part of a year. It is not recorded whether his undertaking was considered a success, but certainly in the year following his visit, salvage by an unidentified team resulted in the recovery of material from the wreck of the *Association*.[2]

Despite the lapse of two years, and some unsubstantiated errors, Herbert's is the single most comprehensive account of events, which in 1883 formed the basis of a paper presented to the Society of Antiquaries by James Herbert Cooke, FSA, in London.[3] Cooke was probably a descendant of Edmund Herbert, and his paper records that he had access to some notes provided by R. Marsham-Townsend [4]

'Sir. C. Shovel cast away 8hr 23, being Wednesday, between 6 and 7 at night, (others say between 4 and 5, between night and day.) off Guilstone (south) by west, was found on shore (at Porthellick Cove) in St Mary's Islands, stripped of his shirt, which by confession was known, by 2 women, which shirt had his name at the gusset at his waist: (where by order of Mr Harry Pennick was buried 4 yards off the sands; which place I myself viewed & as I was by his grave came by said woman the first saw him after he was stripped). His ring was also lost from off his hand, which however left the impression on his finger, as also of a second. The Lady Shovel offered a considerable reward to any one who should recover it for her. In order thereto wrote Captain Benedick,

Deputy Governor & Commander in Charge of the Islands of Scilly, [5] (giving him a particular description thereof), who used his utmost diligence both by fair and foul means, though could not hear of it. Sir Cloud, had on a pair of thread stockings and a thread waistcoat. (Others say a flannel waistcoat and a pair of drawers.)

Mr Child. (Mr Paxton) Purser of the Arundel caused him to be taken up and knew him to be Sir Cloudesley by a certain black mold under his left ear, as also by the first joint of one of his forefingers being broken inwards formerly by playing at tables; the said first joint of his finger was also small and taper, as well as standing somewhat inwards; (he had likewise a shot in his right arm another in his left thigh.) Moreover he was well satisfied it was him, for he was as fresh when his face was washed as if only asleep. His nose likewise bled as though alive, which Mr Child (Paxton) said was because of himself, for Sir C. had preferred him to purser of the Arundel and was his particular friend.

Many that saw him said his head was the largest that ever they had seen, and not at all swelled with the waters, neither had he any bruise or scar about him, save only a small scratch above one of his eyes like that of a pin. He was a very lusty comely man, and very fat. Captain Loads, Commander of the Association, (Sir Cloudisley's Captain as Admiral, but Captain Whitacre was Captain of the ship) which Sir C. was on board of when cast away, was also taken, up on St. Marie's Island, (in the same cove near Sir C.) and buried in Old Town Church whose burial it was reported cost £90, but Mr Withe who

was manager of it says half that sum. (This Mr Withe raised a report that Mr. Pennick buried Sir C. before cold, but had said gent lived it would have cost him dear, but himself had misfortune to be cast away.

Mr James Narborough (others say Sir John Narborough) and the Lord Bishop Trelawney's son,

The supposed site of Sir Clowdisley Shovell's first burial on the foreshore at Porth Hellick Cove, St. Mary's, Isles of Scilly, in Victorian times. Today the site is marked by two large stones, one bearing a brass inscription plate.

Acknowledgement: Frank Gibson

was likewise buried in said Church very honourably. Sir C. had a naked small greyhound cast on shore in the same cove with, and not far distant, as about a bowshot, from him with a collar of his name &c. around its neck. There came on shore in or very near the same cove the stern of Sir C's barge, which gives ground to believe he had time to get in it with some of his crew, though most people are not of that mind. Captain Loads, Sir John and Mr James Narborough, also the Bishop of Trelawney's son, being all cast on shore on St. Mary's Island, give further matter of credit. [6]

The Association 2nd rate and the Romney - rate, and the Eagle - rate were all cast away on said rock, & but one soul saved from off the rock, called —— ——-, who was quartermaster of the Romney, a north country-man near Hull, a butcher by trade, a lusty fat man but much battered with the rocks. (Most of the Captains, Lieutenants, Doctors &c. of the Squadron came on shore and asked him many questions in relation to the wreck, but not one man took pity on him, either to dress or order to be dressed his bruises &c. wherefore had perished had not Mr Ekins, a gentleman of the island, charitably taken him in: and a doctor of a merchant ship then in the road under convoy of Southampton &c. searched his wounds and applied proper remedies). At the time this horrible accident happened there was in Scilly the Welsh fleet with men o'war viz. the Southampton —-, —-, —-, whose boats were early out the next morning in quest of the flotsam goods, very much whereof were by them taken up; they mattered not the wines and brandys &c. the first, but let them swim by their boats and pursued what they had hopes were richer, so that most of the casks staved and the liquors were lost in the ocean.

The Squadron consisted of 20 men of war and 2 fireships, and had with them also one prize. About one or two afternoon on the 23rd (22nd) October Sir C. called a council & examined the masters what latitude they were in; all agreed to be in that of Ushant on the coast of France, except Sir W. Jumper's master of the Lenox, who believed them to be nearer Scilly, & that in 3 hours should be up in sight thereof (which unfortunately happened) but Sir Cloud. listened not to a single person whose opinion was contrary to the whole fleet. (They then altered their opinion and thought themselves on the coast of France, but a lad on board the —— said the light they made was Scilly light, though all the ships crew swore at & gave him ill language for it. Howbeit he continued in his assertion, and that what they made to be a sail and a ship's lantern proved to be a rock and the light aforementioned, which rock the lad called the Great Smith, of the truth of which at day-break they was all convinced). Whereupon despatched the Lenox & —-, ——, ——, for Falmouth which ships were drove in between the rocks to Broad Sound where they came to an anchor about 2 in the morning of the 24th (23rd) after the wreck had happened, though to those

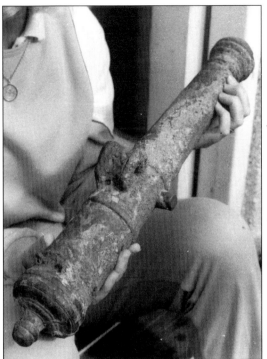

A small bronze signal gun, complete with decoration, miniature lifting dolphins, and a hinge attachment for a vent cover, recovered by Scillonian Diving Services as late as 1983. This was found beneath huge boulders on the *Association* site.

Acknowledgement: Scillonian Diving Services

ships as yet unknown. About day-break they weighed and sailed for Falmouth as ordered, with news of wreck on Scilly rocks; but knew not what sail were lost.

After the departure of the ships from the fleet, according as Sir William's master had believed, they were indeed engaged with the rocks: the weather being stormy, they could not see the light on St. Agnes; not yet knowing where they were they fired ——, soon after which they struck on the ledge ——, and bilged: the Romney also struck immediately and staved on the Gilstone. The Eagle was lost on the Gunnar or thereabouts, by what of the wreck floated to St. Just and other places at the Lands End & up the North Channel'. [7]

A number of legends have grown out of the tragic loss of Sir Clowdisley and his four vessels, two in particular concerning supposed events on board the *Association* the day she was lost. One concerns the council of sailing masters reported and propagated by Herbert that has been repeated in almost every pamphlet or book on the history of longitude over the centuries. The other is the story of the hanging of a seaman for insubordination against Sir Clowdisley.

Recent research and analysis of the information retrieved from forty-four surviving log books from the vessels that escaped being wrecked on 23 October has revealed that the first is almost certainly a fabrication. Not one officer mentions a meeting of sailing masters, or of a single sailing master being summoned to the flagship at sea. Since the *Lenox*, *Phoenix* and *Valeur* had been detached earlier that day; it would not have been possible for Sir William Jumper to be present at such a meeting to express his doubts regarding their position. [8]

All the ships in the main fleet record heaving-to at various times to take soundings. The last occasion was between 4pm and 6pm on the 23rd (which was still the 22 October by modern reckoning) when, by consensus, the *Association* and most of the fleet sounded. Deep-sea sounding normally involved the practice of launching boats, and it is possible that this task was misconstrued, giving birth to the more romantic, but false tale that a grand meeting of captains took place.

The second legend, grown since Herbert recorded the first seeds, would have us believe that on the 22nd, a seaman on board the *Association*, a native of Scilly, approached the admiral telling him he was steering too far to the northward. He advised his superior that unless the course was changed, the fleet would find itself on the rocks of Scilly. For this gross insubordination, Sir Clowdisley was said to have ordered the man to be hung from the mainyard, the only favour being granted the unfortunate sea-man in mitigation of his punishment, was permission to read aloud, before his execution, the 109th psalm, in which occur the imprecations: ' - *let his days be few, let another take his office, let his children be fatherless, and his wife a widow . . let his posterity be destroyed and in the next generation let his name be clean put out'.*[9]

The broken barrel of a standard Admiralty issue musketoon hand gun, similar to a blunderbuss, much favoured by seamen in boarding parties. This is one of several found on the Outer Gilstone, Tearing Ledge and Crim Rocks sites.

Acknowledgement: Scillonian Diving Services

None of the journals of the *Association* are known to have survived with evidence to the true circumstances. With no survivors out of the 702 or so souls on board, who could possibly have transmitted this story to the shore? An extension of this story is the tradition that as a consequence of the admiral's cruel action, no grass will ever grow on his original gravesite on the foreshore at Porth Hellick Cove.[10]

Another tale passed down is that the chaplain of the *Association* went on board another ship the morning before the disaster in order to administer the sacrament to some dying people, and by this means his life was saved'.[11] This has not been verified. The only chaplain listed in the Admiralty pay books as being on board at the time was Peter Penny (alias Pury) who joined the *Association* from the Britannia on 23 August 1706, accompanied by his servant Thomas Harrison. Penny had previously been the chaplain of the church on Lady Shovell's Knowlton estate near Deal. Unfortunately he did not survive the wrecking and his widow Mary attended the Treasury Office on 3 March following the disaster to collect his pay of £13.6.2d. In addition, under the curious system of deducting 4p per month from the pay of each member of the crew for the chaplain's services, a subsequent entry recorded:

A pewter container, about 80mm tall, once fitted with screw top, the purpose of which remains unknown, recovered from the wreck of the *Association*.

Acknowledgement: Scillonian Diving Services

'*Received this 4th June 1708 for the Fourpence due on this book to Mr. Peter Pury late Chaplain of this ship the sum of two hundred eighty one pounds seven shillings and three pence - I say rec'd by me Attorney to his widow Mary Adm[x]. Thos D'Aeth'.*[12]

There is no reference in any known logbook to a chaplain of the *Association* leaving his ship for another and the only other chaplain record-ed in the pay book was Edward Roach who was discharged in 1706 to go to another ship.[13]

A little known legend, surviving in Dorset, concerns the untimely death of a close relative in mysterious circumstances in the immediate aftermath of Shovell's death. Near Sherborne there is a pond surrounded by old trees known as Woodbridge Copse, which was once known as 'Shovell's Pit', named after a nephew of Sir Clowdisley. It is recorded that this nephew and heir, also in the navy, set out on horseback to ride from Portsmouth to

Exeter to settle his uncle's affairs carrying a sum of mony in his saddlebags. He spent the first night at Blandford and was due to spend the second at Sherborne, but never arrived. Rumour had it that he had been robbed and murdered, his body being thrown into the pond. Within living memory, when Shovell's Pit was being cleared out during a dry spell, part of a blue uniform with silver naval buttons appropriate to the period was found.[14]

The last of the legends concerning the wrecking would have us believe that the admiral was murdered for his valuable rings. It is said a Scillonian woman confessed her crime to the local clergyman, many years later, when on her death-bed. Shortly after the wrecking a report appeared in a London newspaper:

A pewter goblet and two spoons from the *Association* site.   Acknowledgement: Terry Hiron

'The country fellows belonging to the Islands of Scilly, finding Sir Cloudesly Shovel's corpse, took a fine emerald ring from off his finger, and buried him seven foot deep in the sand; but quarrelling about the said Ring and Mr Paxton, Purser of the Arundel, having some information on the matter ordered him to be dug up, and put on board the Arundel; where Captain Windall ordered it to be embalmed, and afterwards put on board the Salisbury which was then sailing to Plymouth. Last Saturday morning a hearse was sent thither, to bring Sir Cloudesly's corpse, by order of the Lady'.[15]

This account appears to bear out Defoe's following description of the islanders, most of whom at that time lived in hovels and survived mainly on a meagre sustenance provided by the sea.

'This part of Cornwall may truly be said to be inhabited by a fierce and ravenous people; for they are greedy and, and eager for the prey, that they are charged with strange bloody, and cruel dealings, even sometimes with one another; but especially with poor distressed seamen when they come on shore by force of a tempest, and seek help for their lives, and where they find the rocks not more merciless than the people who range about them for their

prey'.[16]

The details reported in the newspaper account about the finding of Shovell's corpse vary to some degree from Herbert's, but it is apparent that the rings were never actually seen. Despite a large reward offered for their return by Lady Shovell and a supposedly diligent search by the Governor of the Islands, they were not forthcoming. In neither version is there any suspicion of foul play against Sir Clowdisley, other than the theft of the rings from his corpse.

Another version of this legend has it that the woman actually cut off his fingers in order to steal the rings, but again this is totally untrue, since no mutilation of the body was recorded at any stage. The tradition rests on the basis of a draft letter only,[17] in the handwriting of Robert, second Lord Romney. As Sir Clowdisley's grandson, twenty years of age when his grandmother, Lady Shovell, died on 15 March 1732, he would certainly have known if either ring had been recovered.

Some time after 1790, Captain William Locker, compiling a naval history, was in communication with Lord Romney about Sir Clowdisley's career and background. Captain Locker, later to become Commodore and Governor of the Naval Hospital at Greenwich, and one of Admiral Nelson's early mentors[18], had reason to be interested in naval shipwrecks. In February 1760, Locker, as a young Lieutenant, had been appointed to join the 2nd rate, *Ramillies,* refitting at Plymouth and scheduled to re-join the British squadron blockading the French port of Brest. His commission from the admiralty failed to arrive in time for him to join her as she sailed from the port. Two days later she was wrecked on Bolt Tail, some twenty miles east of Plymouth, in a tremendous gale and Locker was witness to the terrible aftermath, describing the wreckage and some of the 800 or so bodies which came ashore in Bigbury Bay.[19]

Lord Romney's reply to Locker, dated 31 May 1792, eventually appeared verbatim in Charnock's '*Biographia Navalis*', and it is assumed it was supplied for the sole purpose, the latter being published in 1794. The letter commences:

> '*Lord Romney and Mr. Marsham present their compliments to Captain Locker, and inform him that on enquiry they find that the family papers relative to Sir Cloudely Shovell's public transactions have from length of time and other accidents been destroyed'.*

Briefly summarising his naval career it continues:

'There is one circumstance relating to Sir Cloudisly Shovell's death that is known to very few persons, namely; he was not drowned, having got on shore where, by the confession of an ancient woman, he was put to death. This many years after, when on her death bed, she revealed to the minister of the parish, declaring she could not die in peace 'till she had made this confession, as she was led to commit this horrid deed for the sake of plunder. She acknowledged having, among other things, an emerald ring in her possession, which she had been afraid to sell lest it should lead to a discovery. This ring, which she delivered to the minister, was by him given to James, Earl of Berkeley, at his particular request, Sir Cloudesly Shovell and himself having lived on the strictest footing of friendship'.[20] One source suggests a fine emerald ring set with diamonds, was originally a present to the admiral from James Lord Dursley, when captain of the St.George.[21]*

Compiled from information gathered by Robert Marsham-Townsend, a direct descendant of Shovell, who carried out extensive research into his ancestry in the 19th century, the letter elaborates:

'the ring itself, unfortunately altered into the form of a locket, but with the emerald surrounded by its diamonds in its original setting, and with the name of Sir Cloudesly and date of his death engraved on the back, is still in the possession of a member of the Berkeley family. I saw it in 1879, when it belonged to the late Mrs Rumley, fourth in descent from the third Earl of Berkeley, and the wife of the late General Randal Rumley. It had come down to her by descent as Sir Cloudesley's ring, but he had never heard any of the details concerned with it'.[22]

The magnificent carved wooden coat-of-arms, over 6ft (1.83m) across, which hangs in the Magistrates Court, Penzance, which once graced the stern of Sir Clowdisley Shovell's flagship, the *Association*. Recovered from the sea at the time of the wreck, it remained in the Isles of Scilly until the mid 1800's when it was given to the people of Penzance in gratitude for a boat load of potatoes sent over during a time of great hardship and famine in the islands.
Acknowledgement: Penwith County Council & Richard Larn

The present whereabouts of the locket

cannot be ascertained, nor can it be proved that part of it once comprised one of the rings stolen from the body of Sir Clowdisley. However, Marsham-Townsend's collected evidence has a certain ring of authenticity about it, and it seems highly unlikely that he and Lord Romney would have fabricated such a lie.

It is probable that the *'ancient woman'* may have made her confession and restitution between 1732 and 1736, as Lady Shovell, to whom the ring would naturally have been given, died at the beginning of that four year period. James, the third Earl of Berkeley and Clowdisley's close friend died at the end. A further interesting aspect, is the general belief in the Isles of Scilly that one of the rings remains there to this day, in the possession of descendants of the woman who stole it some 277 years ago.

Pattison records that on a visit to the Scilly Islands in 1864, he was told that the body of the admiral was washed ashore on a grating, on which was also the dead body of his faithful Newfoundland dog. A woman named Thomas, living at Sallakey farm, a short distance from Porth Hellick, found them early in the morning following the wrecking.[23] She was said to have buried the body, with help obtained from Sallakey, in the inner part of the cove.

Herbert's account mentions two unnamed women, and Thomas may have been the second of these, the first having committed the crime before summoning help. No record of a Mrs. Thomas has been traced, but in an attempt to put a name to the woman who confessed to the crime, a detailed search of the burial records of St. Mary's reveals some interesting information. The earliest surviving register commences January 1726, with the handwritten comment on the first page: *'It is said that the Registers prior to 1726 were destroyed by fire in the house of William Crudge in the Holy Vale.'*

The parson in Scilly at the time the *Association* was wrecked was the Reverend Henry Penneck. He had arrived in the Islands in 1707 following the death of the Reverend John Maurice. The latter had served this isolated community for sixteen years, being buried in the Old Town churchyard on 20 January of that year. Perhaps the strain of being involved in such a large scale disaster, with the internment of so many dead from the four shipwrecks, proved too much for Penneck. The Register simply states that '- *he went away the same year'*, and was not replaced until well into 1708.

In seeking a tentative identification of the woman, the only clues are that she possibly died between 1732 and 1736, was elderly and a widow.

Between 1732 (twenty-five years after Shovell's death) and 1744, only four widows were buried on St. Mary's, namely:

Jane Morrice	*5 Jul 1732*	*Reverend Richard Symons*
Joan Friend	*13 May 1733*	*Reverend Richard Symons*
Mary Mumford	*1 Feb 1735*	*Reverend Richard Symons*
Margaret Edger	*10 Jun 1744*	*Reverend Paul Hathaway* [24]

If there is any truth in the deathbed story of the ring, then Mary Mumford is the most likely candidate since her surname, one of the oldest in Scilly, still survives, and her death occurs in the right period. An extension of the legend surrounding the second ring, taken from Sir Clowdisley's body at Porth Hellick and hidden, is that should it ever leave the islands, they will sink.

Another tradition strong in the islands was brought back to life some twenty-two years ago. It is said that if the Scillies are ever in great danger, the 'ghost wreck' of the *Association* will be seen off St. Mary's under full sail. In 1963, the Scilly Isles suffered the worst storm for centuries, so powerful that the sea breached the isthmus between Porth Cressa and the town's harbour, putting the fresh water supply at risk. At the peak of the gale, an old lady living in the hospital, looking out to sea saw an old ship under full sail. Shortly afterwards she related her experience in detail to the ward nurse, who knowing nothing of the superstition, dismissed the idea as the ramblings of a very old lady. Several days later, the nurse mentioned the matter to an islander familiar with the story. He visited the old lady, who repeated the details of the vision, giving a very convincing account.

Notes for Chapter 6

1. Edmund Herbert was the elder son of Thomas Herbert, the Deputy Woodward and Superintendent of the Royal Forests of Alcey and Whittlebury
2. See Chapter 4 concerning the Aftermath
3. Cook J.H. *The Shipwreck of Sir Clowdisley Shovell*, 1 Feb 1883 (Gloucester)
4. See Chapter 10 concerning Clowdisley Shovell's Family Background
5. One of the traditions recorded by the Reverend Woodley in 1833 was that a soldier recovered Sir John Narborough's body for which he received a pension for life from Lady Shovell. As the Deputy Governor, Captain Benedict, an army officer, Captain of the Garrison, was involved in the retrieval of the bodies and was most probably the soldier referred to. Woodley G. *Reverend Present State of the Isles of Scilly*, p47(London 1833)
6. In actual fact Trelawney's body came ashore on St Agnes where it was initially buried and later recovered. (see page 24)
7. Assuming that Herbert would have been given access to Admiralty letters and docu-

ments before proceeding to Scilly, and that he would have made use of these in compiling his report on return, it is remarkable that he was unable to insert so many names of individuals and ships.

8. It is generally agreed that the *Lenox* and the other two ships detached from the main fleet at 11am, as logged by her captain, although his two lieutenants reported 7am and 10am. The captain of the *Phoenix* recorded 8am and of the Valeur 11am.

9. Woodley ascribes this story to the survivor George Lawrence, but in this he is incorrect as Lawrence was on the *Romney*. He appears to think that Lawrence was from the *Association*. Woodley G. Reverend, *Present State of the Isles of Scilly*, p46-7 (London 1833)

10. Pattison S.R. *Sir Cloudesley Shovell*, JRIC Vol I p61-5 (1864-5)

11. Campbell R. *The Lives of the Admirals,* Vol III p525 (London 1812)

12. ADM 33/249, Neat Book *Association.* PRO

13. Ibid; Two payments recorded in the Neat Book to Chaplain Edward Roach and his widow, in March 1708 and May 1714, originally suggested he was lost in the wreck. It has recently been discovered, however, that he left the ship to join the *Triumph* in April 1706, and the payments were for service on the *Association* prior this date.

14. Coffin L.W. *Holwell and Villages*, *Past and Present*, p172 (Bridport 1990). The story has a ring of authenticity about it. There were several relatives with naval rank or connection in Shovell's extended family, some bearing his surname. (see notes to Chapter 10) However, the only nephew mentioned in Shovell's will is William Jenkenson, the son of Shovell's uncle, Clowdsley Jenkenson, who was naval Deputy Judge Advocate in 1690.

15. *The Post Boy*, No 1945 1-4 Nov 1707

16. Defoe D. *A Tour Through The Whole Of The Island Of Britain*, p 245 (London 1927) First Published 1724

17. Said to have been in the possession of the Earl of Romney at the time

18. Nelson served as Second Lieutenant under Captain Locker in the *Lowestoft,* 32 guns, in the West Indies in 1777. Nav Chr. Vol 3 p163-4, 1800

19. Locker E.H. *Memoirs of Celebrated Naval Commanders*, p12 (London 1832)

20. Marsham-Townsend, R. Notes and Queries 6th Series, Vol X p518-519(1884)

21. Styles *S. Admiral of England*, p170 (1973)

22. At one time it was reported as being in the possession of Sir George Cranfield Berkeley. Notes and Queries 6th Series Vol 10 p519(1884)

23. Pattison, JRIC, Vol I p63

24. *Isles of Scilly Burial Registers*, CRO DDP 206/1/1

Chapter Seven

Search and Discovery

'£1M treasure may await frogmen probing 260-year-old wreck'.

Sunday Times - July 1967

By 1964, 257 years after the disaster, very little local tradition of the death of Sir Clowdisley Shovel and the tragic loss of his four warships had survived in the Isles of Scilly. The legends had almost faded into obscurity due to a decline in the number of long established local families to pass on the tradition and the large influx of outsiders from the mainland, which had occurred over the last half century. The burial place of the Admiral at Porthellick was still well marked. Various guidebooks and publications recorded differing accounts of his death, but the incident was otherwise almost forgotten.

The islands' museum on St Mary's was still very small, and there was no local history reference collection such as there is today. The only published shipwreck information relating to Scilly was Charlotte Dorrian-Smith's original shipwreck list produced in August 1950 and Juliet de Boulay's articles in the 'Mariner's Mirror'(Journal of the Society for Nautical Research December 1959 and May 1960.) These were supplemented by the Gibson family's quite remarkable collection of local shipwreck photographs.

As for the shipwrecks themselves, they remained underwater where they sank, untouched. Even the Penzance based Western Marine Salvage Company, which was very active in Cornwall and the Isles of Scilly from the late 19th century well into the 1930's, and had carried out extensive salvage amongst the Western Rocks, does not appear to have visited the Outer Gilstone area. Despite the lure of a small fortune in non-ferrous metals on some two dozen steamship wrecks, and the potential of treasure on board Sir Clowdisley's men of war and six Dutch and English East Indiamen in the area, no sport divers showed any interest in the Isles of Scilly prior to 1955.

It is impossible to establish exactly who was the first person to dive amongst the islands using self-contained compressed air apparatus, but the first Scilly's resident to dive there was Geoffrey Coldwell in 1960. He and his wife Pamela started the first underwater centre on St. Mary's, a sort of

The Receiver of Wreck on St. Mary's, Isles of Scilly, HM. Customs & Excise officer 'Bill' Saunby, in the Queen's Warehouse in Hugh Town, examining the first finds from the wreck of the *Association,* handed in by the Royal Navy team that found the site in July 1967. The large cannon, breech-loader and signal gun were all bronze, as were the four spoked pulley-sheaves which would have been part of her cathead lifting tackle for the anchors. Also shown are lead sounding weights, scupper pipe, sheathing and musket shot.

Acknowledgement: Paul Armiger, Daily Telegraph

holiday with basic instruction in snorkelling and aqualung for beginners. They named the business 'Seasport' but after two years were forced to close, insufficient divers being attracted to the Islands to make it a viable business.

One of Geoff's enthusiastic companions was the late Barrie Fairest, then the islands' dentist, who, along with Noel Jenkins, the first native Scillonian to dive there, read every book on diving they could find, and literally taught themselves! In the same year 1963, they started 'Divework', a small business selling compressed air, taking out groups of divers and performing local underwater work. Towards the end of the 1960's, 'Divework' was sold out to two newcomers, Terry Hiron and Jim Heslin, London divers, who had arrived in the wake of publicity announcing the discovery of the *Association.*

This perfect sphere or 'ball' some 30mm in diameter, is something of a mystery. Dark green in colour, made of a very hard polished material, but neither glass, china or stone, it was found on the Gilstone wreck site. A billiard ball comes to mind, but it remains unidentified .

Acknowledgement: Scillonian Diving Services

Amongst the first outside sport diving groups to visit from the mainland were the Guildford BS-AC and the Coventry Sub-aqua Club, who pottered around a couple of the shallow wreck sites in archaeological exploration. In the very early 1960's, Bob Rogers and the 'Blue Seas Divers', with whom Terry Hiron and Jim Heslin worked much later, were also visitors, but none of them did any serious diving, or made a search for historic wreck around the islands.

Although the Royal Navy encouraged fleet 'outward bound' recreational type facilities in warmer climates, they had no official sport diving organisation, until the formation of NAC-SAC (Naval Air Command Sub-Aqua Club) in 1961. This was later to become Special Branch No.66 of the British Sub-Aqua Club, of which Lieutenant Roy Graham was the first Chairman, with Chief Petty Officer Richard Larn the club Diving Officer. Between them they initiated several expeditions; that for 1963 using a Royal Navy motor fishing vessel tender to take a dozen divers to the islands. HMS *Seahawk,* the naval establishment at R.N.A.S. Culdrose, near Helston, supported this. A chart of potential wreck targets both certain and uncertain, was plotted in advance,

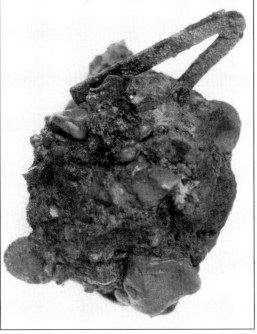

A concreted lump of silver coins, gunflints and a brass folding rule.

Acknowledgement Scillonian Diving Services

from researched sources.

As an initial project the club set out to see if anything remained of the *Indipendenza*, a wreck on the Barrel of Butter, just off the Garrison shore, sunk in 1881. It was thought possible that some of her animal horn cargo might still survive. The Navy team arrived in Scilly on 23 June, spent time looking for the first wreck, found no artefacts, then went on to St. Agnes where they located the ss. *Italia,* a steamship which a visiting German team later claimed to have found some eight weeks before. On 27 June the team found two iron cannon in deep water off the Old Town Gilstone rock, raising and presenting one to the local Museum next day. Unfortunately, there were no conservation facilities on the islands at the time and the gun gradually disinte-

An incomplete brass arm of a weighing balance, probably used to measure food.

Acknowledgement Scillonian Diving Services

grated over the years. In hindsight the gun, now believed to have come from the wreck of an 18th century transport, should never have been recovered from the seabed.

From that chance find emerged the whole saga of the discovery of the *Association* site three years later. It has been said that the Navy team commenced their search for the *Assocation* on the wrong Gilstone in error, which is not true. The early dive cited took place on Old Town Gilstone, five miles from the Western Rocks or Outer Gilstone, and was a dive location selected

Another lead container recovered from the Gilstone wreck site of the *Association,* whose function remains unknown.
Acknowledgement Scillonian Diving Services

One of the many bronze guns salvaged from the *Association* site being landed on the quay at St. Mary's by the Roland Morris diving team in 1967.
Acknowledgement: Paul Armiger, Daily Telegraph

at random with no particular target. The subsequent discovery of cannon came as a complete surprise and provoked a wider search of this old wreck site revealing little else, other than a stockless iron anchor. Only later, when the significance of the name Gilstone had sunk in, did the team begin to think that this might be the location of one of Sir Clowdisley's ships. By nightfall, having landed the cannon on St. Mary's Quay, the significance of the second Gilstone, far off shore, was realised. Although they had been diving near the wrong Gilstone, imaginations had been fired.

The idea of a naval diving team relocating a sunken man of war as historically important as the *Association* had significant attractions, and certain poignancy. The following autumn, at the next committee meeting of NAC-SAC, Richard Larn proposed that the search for the *Association* should be adopted as a long-term project of the organisation, a motion that was approved. The year 1965 therefore saw a larger, better equipped and more informed Navy team in the Isles of Scilly, on board the much larger Auxiliary Service Vessel *Puttenham*. She was an inshore minesweeper of the '*Ham*' class, crewed by members of the Penzance branch of the RNXS (Royal Naval Auxiliary Service), under the command of the late Lieut.Cdr.

A lump of concretion holding a large number of coins found on the wreck of the *Association* in 1984.
Acknowledgement: Scillonian Diving Services

Ted Barter, RN (Retd).

Ted was a first class choice as skipper for such a project, and commanded every navy diving team expedition well into the 1970's. He grew to know and love the islands so well that he was able to manoeuvre the 120-ton vessel close inshore to put the team on variety of diving sites. Often so close that local boatman at the Mermaid Inn ran a 'book' and speculated on where he would eventually run his ship ashore. However, they were to be disappointed!

Diving in 1965 commenced on 28 June, with the intention of finding the 'Big A', as the *Association* became nicknamed, and as tide and wind allowed, other days were devoted to searching new areas looking for the *Eagle* and *Romney* and any modern wreck that might turn up. During their stay in the Scilly's that year, the Navy team raised an intact stern-gun from the *ss.Italia*, on Wingletang Ledge, found the main condenser and loose bronze propeller blades on the *ss.Hathor*, the capsized hull of the *ss.Plympton*, and further afield located more modern wrecks. These included the *Mando, Delaware, Brinkburn, Sussex, Zelda* and many others.

The first of dozens of newspaper accounts relating to the wreck of the *Association* appeared in the Western Morning News in July 1965, under a banner headline of '*Underwater expedition finds uncharted rock pinnacle and wreck of Italian ship - but no sign of HMS Association*'. Unfortunately the world was now aware of the identity of the ship the Navy team sought.

During the following winter months extensive research was carried out in London; at the British Museum, Public Record Office at Kew and elsewhere, to establish more details of the 1707 incident. As a consequence the navy divers who assembled at Penzance in the summer of 1966 were far better informed and even more determined in their quest. This time the media were waiting for them at Penzance before they sailed '*Navy Search for Treasure ship of 1707'* screamed a national daily. *'Eighteen divers look for wreck'; 'Hunt for wrecks in Scilly's'*, said others.

Other parties claiming salvage now fed half-truths and lies to the press. The Western Morning News, a Plymouth based daily paper, reported: *'also in the Isles of Scilly searching for the Association is a private group, which includes Bob Rogers and David Harrison. They have an agreement with the Admiralty to share the spoils 50/50'*. This statement bore little resemblance to the truth, and published statements that the 'Blue Seas Divers' knew exactly where the *Association* lay were based on a blatant lie. Bob Rogers claimed that he had already found the wreck, and was only waiting for the Navy team to leave before recovering the treasure. In fact, neither he, nor any of his team, had been anywhere near the Outer Gilstone. The statement regarding an agreement with MOD(Navy) was true, but the percentages were fiction and again the 'Blue Seas Divers' were merely shadowing the Navy team who had already signed a similar contractual agreement.

Over the winter of 1965-6, simultaneously with the ongoing documentary research, the NAC-SAC team, through its Chairman, Lieut.Cdr. Jack Gayton, supported by Lieuts. Roy Graham and Terry Montgomery had made an application to the Contracts Division of MOD (Navy), Bath. This was for a contract to *'search for and if successful, salvage the wrecks of 1707, in the Isles of Scilly'*. The intention was to protect the position of the Navy team in law, in the event of actually finding one or more of the wrecked warships.

At this time it was thought

Newspapers from around the world reported the discoveryof the wreck of the *Association* by Royal Navy divers in1967, including the Singapore Straits and Hong Kong Times.

Acknowledgement: Richard Larn

that such a contract would allow unhindered salvage to be conducted in the best interests of the Royal Navy and the nation. In this manner heritage would be protected and the latter would benefit by ownership of artifact material. This request was probably unprecedented in the history of the Senior Service. It sent the crown solicitors and naval legal department scurrying to their law books in a spin - a team of Navy divers asking

An old and corroded iron cannon found on the Old Town Gilstone wreck site by Richard Larn, shown on St Mary's quay during the navy's first expedition to Scilly in 1964. This led to the relocation of the *Association* three years later.
Acknowledgement: Richard Larn

the Royal Navy for a commercial contract to salvage navy ships whilst the divers were still on active service! No wonder their official reply was a long time coming!

Meanwhile, after getting wind of the Navy diving team's plans, two similar applications were made by leaders of rival civilian groups on the

grounds that they were perfectly entitled to similar, and equal, treatment in law. The applicants were; Bob Rogers leader of the 'Blue Seas Divers', and an entrepreneur, the late Roland Morris, owner of the Admiral Benbow restaurant at Penzance.

Douglas Rowe(left), and Geoffrey Upton(centre) were the two divers working for the late Roland Morris(right), and made the first large coin discovery at the bottom of a miniature cave on the Gilstone site.
Acknowledgement: Paul Armiger, Daily Telegraph

The outcome was the eventual issue by the Ministry of Defence of three similar, but not identical salvage documents, the first of which went to the Naval Air

Command Sub-Aqua Club, but allowing all three groups to search for and salvage the same shipwrecks! The Navy team, and no doubt the other contract holders, presumed and certainly expected that on eventual location, the lucky finders would be granted exclusive rights, and that the licences of the unlucky teams would be revoked. This was not to be.

Pewter eating utensils which would have been the personal property of officers on board the *Association.*

Acknowledgements: Scillonian Diving Services

Diving and commercial salvage operations had become established on a more than modest scale in the Scilly's by 1966. A well known character *'Dougie'* Rowe, later employed by Roland Morris on the *Association*, lived on a converted ship's lifeboat which doubled as a diving platform, and was hard at work recovering non-ferrous metals from steamship wrecks. Explosives were being used on several of the now well known wreck sites, but many were left untouched. Elsewhere, in the deeper waters of the Crim and Bishop Rock areas, crayfish divers were making more than a good living.

More determined than ever to find the wreck of the *Association* the Navy team took the XSV. *Puttenham* straight out to the Western Rocks on arrival in July of the same year. Unfortunately they had not anticipated bad weather and over a twelve-day period, only twenty minutes of diving were possible in the target area. The Gilstone and Gilstone reef were obscured by a heaving mass of white water, and massive swell, quite unworkable using inflatable boats. The only consolation was that if the Navy

A lead container from the wreck of the *Association,* the function or purpose yet to be established.

Acknowledgement: Scillonian Diving Services

team were frustrated and unable to dive, neither could any one else. The 1966 season closed with the *Association* still eluding discovery.

Another winter passed, more research was carried out, and XSV. *Puttenham* was back in the Isles of Scilly on the 1 July 1967. This time leadership of the expedition was jointly shared between Lt.Cdr. Jack Gayton, Lieut. Roy Graham (Diving Officer), and Lieut. Terry Montgomery (Recording and Research), Chief Petty Officer Larn having been sent to join HMS *Bulwark* in Singapore shortly before the divers sailed. Other members of the eighteen-man team included Lieut. Andrew Lindsey, Lieut. Minchin and thirteen other divers. The 2/3 July saw rough seas and a huge swell on the Outer Gilstone, but one team did manage a memorable but wasted dive, describing the experience later as similar to being inside an revolving washing machine!

Combs carved from wood, bone, ivory or tortoiseshell are common in shipwrecks of this period. These have widely spaced teeth at one end, and much finer teeth at the other, in order to remove head lice.

Acknowledgement: Scillonian Diving Services

On Tuesday 4 July, the weather having moderated overnight, and the sun now shining on a flat calm sea, the third group of divers to descend in the vicinity of the Gilstone Rock that morning located a single iron cannon. Great excitement ensued as a more detailed search revealed at least twenty others, plus a large stockless anchor. Returning to the site the following day the teams found yet more ordnance. There was much jubilation when a pair of divers, Jack Gayton and Paddy Minchin, surfaced and reported discovering an ornate bronze gun with lifting dolphins, some nine feet in length capable of firing an 18 pound iron shot.

Throughout the course of the day divers were exhilarated as they found a succession of gold and silver coins. The most significant of these was the first of many Portuguese 4,000 reis coins bearing a date confirming that here, positively, was one of Admiral Shovell's fleet of 1707. There was no evidence as yet, to suggest the identity of the wreck, but as the small minesweeper made her way back to the safety of St. Mary's the Royal Navy diving team were already celebrating - their discoveries had exceeded their wildest dreams.

The members of the Navy team and the RNXS crew members were sworn to secrecy and news of the discovery was kept from all ashore except MOD(Navy). An urgent signal was dispatched to the Admiralty advising of the find, and the fact that bronze guns and treasure lay on the seabed. At the same time a request was made for the expedition to be extended for an additional seven days. This was granted immediately and the salvage and exploration continued.

The first attempt to raise a 3.5ton bronze gun on the 6th failed, simply because the team had no lifting bags on board and the number of empty forty gallon oil drums available offered insufficient buoyancy lift. The following two days were lost due to a combination of bad weather and *Puttenham*'s need to return to Penzance for a crew change, and refuelling, during which time suitable lifting bags were flown out to the Scilly's from RNAS Culdrose by helicopter.

Late in the day on 10 July the *Puttenham* finally entered St. Mary's with the magnificent bronze cannon slung across her stern. This was landed on the quay to the immense interest of a large crowd of spectators including locals and visitors. Merely an unconfirmed rumour up until now, the fact that the *Association* had been found could no longer be concealed from the media or the public.

The gun was later identified as a 16 pounder of French origin cast in Le Havre around 1652 for *'Francois de Vendome'* (The Duke of Beaufort),the Tower of London Armoury reporting it as *'a find of international importance'*. Apart from assisting a French TV crew to make a film concerning the discovery, the remaining time in the Scilly's was spent in tagging iron cannon, completing a rough survey of the site, recovering coins and artefacts and anxiously contemplating the future of the site.

On 14 July, having kept the discovery a secret for the agreed period, the Navy team departed for the mainland and service duties. Unfortunately, before the team was able to formulate a new strategy, Lieut. Andrew Lindsey, the Public Relations Officer, who had returned to duty earlier than the other divers, being unaware of the need for continuing secrecy, released detailed information to Southern Television and the media. This immediately alerted the general public to the presence of treasure and threw the

Association site (although identification had yet to be confirmed), open to anyone who could dive.

The other contract holders, who now moved on to the site and started salvaging, were equally upset when it became apparent that they were to be given no more protection or right to work on the site than any other rogue diver. They also suffered the futility of holding a legal agreement, acknowledging admiralty ownership, which was not worth the paper on which it was written.

Chapter Eight

Salvage or Archaeology

Leading to the Act for the Protection of Historic Wrecks - 1973.

The discovery of the *Association* by the divers of the Royal Navy raised many issues, which the legal representatives of MOD(Navy) had not considered when they granted the three independent contracts. There had been no precedents and as the situation unfolded MOD(Navy) found itself in difficulties. Presumably the decision not to grant a single exclusive contract to the NAC-SAC team was grounded on the vulnerability of the government to public criticism about the continued use of naval manpower and resources. A project that, initially, had been considered merely an interesting recreational naval training exercise was now becoming an embarrassment.

It is fair to say that in the early days of the search none of the parties involved had any knowledge or proof that the *Association* was a treasure ship in the real sense, nor if any part of the wreck had survived unrecorded contemporary salvage. The media were largely responsible for raising expectations and broadcasting the possibility of treasure far and wide. The members of the Naval Air Command Sub-Aqua Club were initially motivated by the possibilities of finding a historical Royal Naval wreck site of some fame from which they could raise interesting marine artefacts.

The natural dilemma with all historic 'treasure wrecks' is the conflict of interests between straight forward 'salvage' and properly controlled 'archaeological excavation' with all the inherent disciplines. Maritime archaeology was in its infancy in the United Kingdom in the 1960's. The growth in the popularity of SCUBA diving and excavation of Henry VIII's great ship *Mary Rose* at Portsmouth had yet to focus the nation's attention on the historical and archaeological potential lying unexplored around the British coastline.[1] Having issued the sought after contract to the Navy team, MOD(Navy) was unprepared for the consequences of the actual discovery, and the raising of the *Association's* profile to that of a major treasure ship, and an archaeological discovery of significance, by an escalating succession of valuable finds.

The Lords of the Admiralty initially gave the team unreserved support, supplying the opportunity and resources required. In addition, Prime

The late Prime Minister, the Hon. Harold Wilson, later Baron Wilson of Rievaulx, with a group of divers from the Roland Morris team on St. Mary's quay, discussing some finds which include a breech loading gun. Harold Wilson and his wife were frequent visitors to St. Mary's, where the family still have a holiday bungalow.

Acknowledgement: Paul Armiger, Daily Telegraph

Minister Harold Wilson, an aficionado of the islands with a holiday home on St. Mary's, used his personal influence to sustain the Navy team's period of involvement, but it was inevitable that without direct government intervention this continuing support would gradually wane. The political will required to go forward with a controversial project of this nature was not forthcoming, an understandable but regrettable situation.

Apart from a need for manpower, support vessels and equipment; the recognition that this was a potential major archaeological, as well as salvage project, would have initiated an ongoing requirement for all manner of costly expertise, together with facilities for the conservation and storage of artefacts. MOD(Navy) as a consequence, chose not to revoke any of the licences, claim any of the salvaged material, or get more embroiled in the controversy over treasure. They left the situation to be resolved under the terms of the Merchant Shipping Act, which were quite inappropriate for a wreck of this nature.

The Royal Navy team tried to keep things in perspective by simultaneously conducting a survey of the site, but successive events, now out of control, initiated a free for all, in which the wreck was scavenged for treasure by rival diving teams. The valuable maritime information which would have been forthcoming from a systematic archaeological excavation of the wreck, yielding a unique collection of priceless artefacts, was largely destroyed in the salvage process and the underwater site today resembles an abandoned battlefield, littered with broken guns.

From the perspectives of national heritage, and marine archaeology, the lost opportunity will be forever regretted and it is easy to cite the contrary example of the Swedish King Gustav's great galleon *Vasa* which foundered in the Baltic in 1628. Discovered by Anders Franzen in deep water off Stockholm in 1956, she was used as an ongoing training facility for successive waves of professional divers from the Swedish Royal Navy, who were employed in dredging and excavating the hull over several years. Recovered intact, in 1961 the *Vasa* is now housed in a great purpose built museum in Stockholm, where she remains a Mecca for marine archaeologists from all over the world.[2] On the bonus side, almost as a direct consequence of the demise of the *Association* and one or two other historic wrecks, government legislation was initiated to prevent the situation from repeating itself. In 1973 the Act for the Protection of Historic Wreck was finally introduced.

Four gold coins from the *Association* site, showing both sides of a gold guinea and a Portuguese 4,000 Reis.
Acknowledgement: Richard Larn

Just over a month after the initial discovery of the site, on 19th August, the Navy divers were back again under the same leadership, having put forward a strong case to their Lordships to continue the project. This time the principal diving platform was the naval minesweeper (XSV) *Shipham*, with her sister ship *Odiham* remaining alongside the quay at St. Mary's as an accommodation vessel for eighteen divers. In competition with other groups, every minute of available underwater time was spent surveying the Gilstone, searching the gullies and crevices for artefacts and coins. The largest item located was a stockless anchor eighteen feet in the shank, weighing some three tons, which was placed on the seabed close to Nut Rock, later salvaged and taken to the mainland.

All the artefacts recovered from the wreck were duly declared to Bill Saunby, the Customs Officer on St. Mary's who was also the Receiver of Wreck. The law required that copies of wreck declarations were posted on a public notice board on the quay for all to see, therefore the various diving

A uniform brass button found on the Association site. Probably worn by a Royal Marine, it shows King William and Queen Mary beneath a crown. Acknowledgement: Richard Larn

groups were well aware of the recoveries made by rivals. The range and quantity of salvaged material declared was a matter of conscience, bearing in mind the valuable nature of many of the artefacts, and not all the groups were honest in reporting their finds.

Gold and silver coins were offered freely for sale in the local pubs and later their were rumours of divers travelling abroad and offering illegal gold coins for sale in the gold markets of Paris and France. At the time, gold 4,000 reis coins were being sold off in the gentlemen's toilets of the Mermaid public house for around £20 each. Elsewhere and among coin dealers they were fetching £185, which later made some of the contracted civilian divers on the *Association* site somewhat disgruntled when they realised their true value. This particular naval visit came to an end on 25 August.

One final expedition for that momentous year followed when, between the 9 and 22 September, all three minesweepers, *Puttenham*, *Odiham* and *Shipham* were available. Two of these were used to support diving whilst one remained alongside as accommodation vessel, which relieved the divers of domestic chores. During this visit another ornate bronze cannon, with both lifting dolphins missing, was brought to the surface, having been dis-covered close to Rosevear Island. Since this is some distance from the Gilstone, it is conjectured this gun may well have been lost in some early salvage attempt, possibly the Herbert expedition.[3] This gun was later offered to the Isles of Scilly museum but declined, the local council appearing to view the NAC-SAC team with some hostility for finding the wreck and the media focus it had brought to the islands. The gun was therefore sold to the Tresco Estate where it was mounted on a gun carriage and remains in the

Valhalla Collection.

Some time later a successful bid, equivalent to scrap metal prices, was made by the Tower of London for the large ornate bronze gun found on the previous expedition. They paid for all transportation costs from the Scilly's to London and sent a cheque for £600 to NAC-SAC in payment. Unfortunately, the receipt of this money immediately disqualified

A pewter medical syringe, which may have been part of the surgeon's medical chest carried on board the *Association*

Acknowledgement: Scillonian Diving Services

the diving club from receiving any further support grants from the Nuffield Trust Fund. This situation continued until the funds raised from the *Association* sales were exhausted.

The Navy team also raised two bronze breech-loading guns, which went into the Receiver of Wreck's warehouse on St. Mary's; Roland Morris's team raised one similar, but badly eroded and damaged. When the Navy team later went to view their guns they found one of them had been switched, possibly in error. The badly damaged gun remained, whilst the best of the three guns had been personally collected from the warehouse by the late Roland Morris for conservation, prior to displaying it in his museum collection.

Because of the political difficulties the Navy team were forced to

A collection of silver, pewter and brass uniform and shoe buckles, found on the Gilstone and Tearing Ledge sites

Acknowledgement: Scillonian Diving Services

abandon the wreck to the civilian salvors in 1967. Of all the civilian diving teams that subsequently worked on the wreck site up into the 70's, when Terry Hiron and Jim Heslin assumed the position of 'salvors in possession', the most successful were the late Roland Morris's divers. Some hard words have been said about them and their employer, but Roland Morris was the only individual prepared to gamble his own money on the venture, paying divers and boatmen, providing equipment, and reaping a just reward. It is a matter of fact that Morris's divers recovered three bronze cannon and more gold and silver coins collectively than any other team for the period they worked the site. Even if the Royal Navy diving team had been given exclusive rights to the wreck of the *Association* and unlimited time on site, it is doubtful if they would have achieved more.

The divers who worked for the late Roland Morris included Doug Rowe, Geoff Upton, Mike Hicks, Mark Horobin, Terry Par, David Regalado, Peter Grosche and others. If any criticism of the late Roland Morris was justified, then it was his continued refusal to acknowledge that the Navy team actually found the *Association* and not he or his divers. In several books written by him or on his behalf, he claimed either to have found the wreck first, or having known all along where the wreck lay, neither of which was true. In fact, Morris, an opportunist, did not assemble a team or commence diving activities in the Isles of Scilly, let alone appear any where near the Gilstone, until August 1967, one month after the team from the Royal

Spanish American silver 8 reale cob coins, recovered from the wreck sites of the *Association & Eagle*. The letters 'P' and 'M' on the left side indicate that they were minted in Potosi and Mexico, the letters 'B' and 'F' below being the initial or mark of the mint master or ensayador. These were worth about 4 shillings 9 pence, and whilst a little below the value of an English 'crown' was considered its equivalent and certainly more acceptable world wide. Acknowledgement: Richard Larn

Navy had declared their first finds.

If there were bad feelings between the various diving teams the reasons were understandable. All three contract holders, and particularly the Navy team, felt something should be done to prevent outside groups from recklessly plundering the wreck. Instead, the Gilstone had become infested with individuals seeking only the treasure, in fierce competition, without regard for many historic artefacts they were uncovering and damaging in the process. As work progressed, however, an unspoken code of co-operation, restraint and mutual respect developed between the rival divers, all of who were working in a difficult, often dangerous location. In addition many of them were sharing mutual accommodation on board a converted barge named *Queen*, tied up alongside St. Mary's quay, which helped, in no small way, to alleviate the competitive atmosphere.

An extremely decorative example of early 17th century bronze ordnance, recovered from the wreck site of the *Association* in 1969, by the 'Blue Seas Divers', led by Bob Rogers. The inscription in Latin reads: *'Charles Earl of Devonshire and master of ordnance commissioned Thomas Pitt the maker, year 1604.'* This type of gun, known as a Falconette, was valued by Sotheby's at £20,000, and can now be seen in the Isles of Scilly Museum on St. Mary's.
Acknowledgement Frank Gibson

The late Roland Morris was a colourful character who claimed to have been a professional hard-hat salvage diver in his younger days, but never gave any indication of this ability by diving on the *Association.* It was rumoured, in fact, that he never really had been a diver. True or not, his obsession with the sea and ships resulted in conservation, restoration and research into many items from the *Association* and *Eagle* sites, which in the hands of other salvors, would probably have found their way to the antique or scrap metal market. There is no complete record of the vast array of artefacts recovered. Only the completed WRE5 Wreck declaration forms kept by HM Receiver of Wreck give any indication as to the range and value of items salvaged, and it is reasonably certain that only a small proportion of the material was declared.

Two brass barrel taps, probably used by officers on board the *Association* for pouring brandy or Madeira wine.
Acknowledgement: Scillonian Diving Services

The sales catalogues of Sotheby's and W.H. Lane & Sons, Penzance, who offered *Association* wreck material at seven auctions from 1968 onwards, are probably the best pictorial evidence remaining of artefacts recovered. It would now be necessary to travel half the world in order to view the full range of artefacts and coins recovered.

Some of the thousands of items recovered, which for the most part have now vanished into private collections include; gold finger rings, jewellery, gunner's rules, pistol and musket trigger guards, side and butt plates, lead shot, shot-moulds, inkwells, sanding pots, chamber-pots, complete or fragments of ship's bells, lead containers, buckles, parts of musical instruments, buttons, buckles, pocket watches, signal guns, forks and spoons.

Unique amongst the gold rings found were a number of 'posy' rings (from the French *'poésie'*) each poetically inscribed and dedicated in love to an unknown sailor. Simple expressions of love wound round the inside of each: *'God Above Increase our Love'*, *'Not the Value But My Love'*, *'True Love is Endless'*, *'In thy Sight is my Delight'*. One proved to be an English

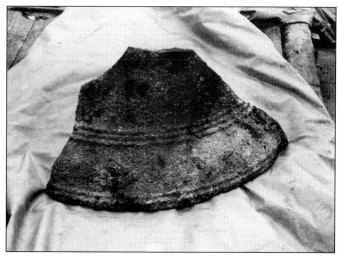

A fragment of the bronze bell from the wreck site of the *Association*.   Acknowledgment: Richard Larn

Three bronze cannon recovered from the *Association* site on the Outer Gilstone rock.
Acknowledgment: Richard Larn

version of the ring the French archaeologist Robert Stenuit had recently found on the Spanish Armada ship *Girona,* wrecked in Ireland in 1588. This time the motto read in English: *'I have Nothing More to Give Thee'.*

Material from the *Association* on public display in this country is predominantly in Cornwall; at the Isles of Scilly Museum, the Museum of Nautical Art, Penzance, and the Charlestown Shipwreck Centre, near St Austell. There is also a small collection in Rochester town hall, Kent, since Sir Clowdisley Shovell once represented that town as a Member of Parliament.

Salvaged items declared to the Receiver of Wreck in Scilly, came up for disposal from July 1968 onwards. By that time the statutory waiting period of a 'year and a day' for unclaimed wreck goods, as laid down in the Merchant Shipping Act, had expired. For the individual divers and communal groups not in possession of a MOD(Navy) contract, this presented no problems, the only question being what percentage of the value of the goods would they be allowed? For example, the reward to the salvor for an item valued at say £100, for which a salvage award of 80% might be offered,

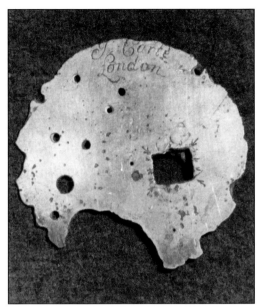

Part of a pocket or deck watch timepiece, showing the name of the maker *'J. Carte - London'*. The small square on the right, with arrows engraved around its sides are for adjustment of the mechanism.
Acknowledgment: Richard Larn

meant that in hard financial terms the salvaged goods could be retained on payment of the difference, i.e. £20. The salvor was then free to dispose of the item(s), as they felt fit.

For the contract holders the issue was unfortunately more complicated. The wording of the individual contracts stated that the contractors could retain 100% of all salvaged items that could be shown *'to have originally been government property.'* On the other hand all items deemed to have been private or personal, which including all specie, would have to be treated as unclaimed wreck and subject to the usual 'year and a day' requirements.

As a legal consequence it was essential to the contract holders that the wreck was somehow positively identified as the *Association* at an early stage, if possible before August 1968, the end of the first major declaration 'period' of a year and a day. The reasoning was simple; the government was prepared to allow all the items marked with a broad arrow, including the five valuable bronze cannon recovered, to be retained by the contract holders, provided it could be reasonably proven that this was one of the lost 1707 warships. Other items, such as coins, rings, buckles etc, which were considered personal property, had to be

A pewter chamber pot found on the wreck of the *Association,* the property of one of the gentlemen on board, possibly Sir Clowdisley himself.
Acknowledgment: Roland Morris

treated under the Merchant Shipping Act as normal unclaimed wreck, the salvor accepting what ever percentage salvage award the Department of Transport officials deemed reasonable.

The divers of the Royal Navy, together with those of Roland Morris and the 'Blue Seas' teams, had all recovered and declared a variety of valuable items.   Many of these carried the 'broad arrow' mark denoting they

Detail of the crest on the silver plate recovered by the Roland Morris diving team. This shows the crest combining the arms of both the Shovell and Hill families, the latter being the maiden name of Lady Elizabeth Shovell.

Acknowledgement: Roland Morris

were government property. The latter were quite obviously ship's fittings from a Royal Naval vessel but no artefact positively confirmed or suggested the identity of the ship. All of the valuable bronze cannon, except the smaller breech-loaders, carried French crests and gunfounders marks and were worth around £3-4,000. Some were actually inscribed *'Vigo'*, on the breech reinforce, which suggested they had been captured by Sir Clowdisley when charged with bringing home the guns of the sacked treasure fleet in 1703, and retained on board ship as trophies. However it could not be proven they were ever added to the flagship's complement of guns or actually taken on board.

In the ensuing arbitration, a Ministry official stated that it was his genuine belief that a separate French warship had subsequently sunk on top of the 1707 wrecks, which was a possible but highly unlikely, scenario. In an attempt to resolve the situation, MOD(Navy) stated that they were sending someone down to look at all the salvaged material, which now partially filled H.M.Custom's 'Queen's Warehouse' on the Scilly's.

Fortunately for the contract holders, the late Roland Morris's team came to the rescue. With literally only days to spare before the visit, Mark Horobin, who now lives near Porthhallow, Cornwall, then the youngest diver in Morris's team, is alleged to have found a silver plate that carried Shovell's personal coat of arms. The rim of the plate was engraved with a combination of his personal crest and that of the Hill family, pertaining to his wife, Elizabeth.

The following historic description of the crest was given to the late Roland Morris by W.J.G. Verco, MVO. Chester Herald of Arms, of the College of Arms, London:

'The Arms of the dexter half of the shield (ie. on the left as one looks at the shield) are blazoned: Gules a chevron ermine between two crescents in chief argent and fleur-de-lis in base or. This coat, together with its accompanying crest (not depicted in the achievement) namely, out of a mural coronet gold and demi-lion gules holding a sail argent with an anchor sable, was granted direct to him and his descendants by Letters Patent under the hands and seal of the then Garter and Clarence aux Kings of Arms, bearing the date 6th January 1691-2 and wherein it is simply stated that the grant was made in consideration of the many eminent services performed at sea by the said Sir Clowdisley Shovell, Rear Admiral of the Blue Squadron of Their Majesties' Fleet, as for his good affections to Their Majesties'.

Auctioned by the late Roland Morris at Penzance in 1973 and purchased for a sum in excess of £1,000, by the town council of Rochester, the borough which Sir Clowdisley represented in Parliament, the plate is the only known piece of silver from the wreck site bearing the Shovell personal crest, a strange circumstance considering his reputation for lavish entertainment. (see page 138) One other piece of silver, a dessert spoon bearing the crest of his Flag Captain, Loades, was found later by the Navy team. Shortly before leaving Gibraltar and sailing for home Sir Clowdisley is reported to have held a dinner party on board the *Association*, at which some forty-eight officers and gentlemen were guests.

The lack of cutlery bearing the Admiral's crest and the absence of any gold tableware known to have been on board are a mystery. No substantial quantity of stern window glass, shoe buckles, side arms and navigational instruments have been revealed. Coupled to the scarcity of silver and pewter utensils; plates, porringers, dishes and tankards in the quantity one would expect of a large warship, these facts suggest the stern section of the *Association* has yet to be located. To date, only one bronze gudgeon and pintle, of which there would have been at least eighteen supporting her giant rudder, has been found. All these circumstances support an unverified account credited to a man named Quimley, that *'the stern section of the flagship broke off and floated away for fourteen minutes before sinking'*. It is understood that the current 'salvors in possession' intend to mount a search for the missing stern section at some time in the near future.

The year 1968 was not good for two of the diving groups involved on the Gilstone site. A converted American minesweeper, the *Regency*, a 150-ton 'survey vessel' from Yarmouth, chartered by a London syndicate, sank off the Wolf Rock lighthouse that September, on passage to the mainland. Skippered by Bill Sutton, she carried a crew of nine, four of whom were divers, who like everyone else had found their share of 'treasure'. Friday the 13th October was certainly an unlucky day for the 'Blue Seas Divers.' At about 5 pm, their landing craft *Salvor* capsized and sank in heavy seas close to Trinity Rock, two miles east of St. Mary's, a crew of three being rescued by the Scilly's launch *Busy Bee II*, and landed at Hugh Town.

Jim Heslin(left) and Terry Hiron(right), salvors in possession of the wreck of the *Association* since 1973, shown here in 1987 in their shop 'Man o'war' in Hugh Town, St. Mary's, with coins from the 1707 wrecks and many others.
Acknowledgement: Paul Armiger, Daily Telegraph

In 1970 Terry Hiron, working for Blue Seas Divers found a very early ornate cannon that everyone else had missed, a bronze falconette made by Thomas Pitt in 1604. The events relating to this particular bronze gun make an interesting story. After cleaning it was shown to members of the local museum committee who had access to very limited funds. It was mutually agreed that the opportunity to acquire such an exceptional piece of British heritage could not be missed and the divers were offered £1,000. A wealthy retired engineer named Kenneth Leach, who had a holiday home on the Garrison, St.Mary's, then offered £3,000, which was countered by the museum who raised their offer to £5,000, whereupon Leach increased his offer to £6,000, which was finally accepted against a promissory note.

By coincidence, a Sotheby's valuer, on holiday in the islands, saw the gun and advised the finders that such an exceptional piece of ordnance would fetch at least £20,000 at auction in London. The news prompted the salvors to pack the cannon in a wooden box supplied by Humphrey Wakefield, one of the island's best known potters, place it in the back of a vehicle and drive poste-haste to London. Roland Morris heard of the impending sale from an unknown source, and contacted Kenneth Leach advising him of the situation. An immediate threat of a court injunction, should the salvors sell the gun to anyone else, saw its immediate return to the Isles of Scilly. Ironically, on becoming the owner of the gun, the late Mr Leach loaned it to the islands' museum for public display, where it remains to this day. The salvors admit that after all their expenses, they made a profit of exactly £350 on the transaction, narrowly avoiding expensive court proceedings for breach of contract.

Roland Morris's divers then commenced a search for the *Eagle* and *Romney* wreck sites, finding cannon on Tearing Ledge, near the Bishop Rock in 1969, and others off the Crim Rocks in 1970. Finally, the remains of the fireship *Firebrand* were found near St. Agnes by a team of RAF sports divers in 1982.

By 1973, although coins were still reasonably plentiful on the Gilstone reef, most of the original divers had departed for pastures new. Many of them were commercial diving in the North Sea, others invested their new found wealth in property or businesses, or took up diving for crayfish for a living around Lands End and South Wales, until the stocks were so depleted this was no longer viable.

In 1970, in an attempt to stop non-contract divers from working the *Association* site, Roland Morris applied for a High Court Injunction against two former 'Blue Seas' divers, Jim Heslin and Terry Hiron. The court turned down the application, confirming that the Admiralty contracts had no 'teeth'. By 1973, they were now well established in the islands, selling compressed air, running diving trips, and repairing cars etc. In addition Terry Hiron, a successful quantity surveyor and architect was hard at work preparing drawings and planning applications for many of the islanders. This was the year they discovered a considerable hoard of over 4,000 silver coins in an underwater 'cave' which attracted considerable media attention and provided them with a substantial coin stock for sale in their 'Man o' War' shop.

This latest find, in turn, brought news that another team of divers were coming to the Scilly's from London to work the wreck site. As a consequence Hiron and Heslin were motivated to seek legal means whereby they could protect their interest from intruders. Using a long established salvage position, they permanently buoyed the site and publicly established themselves as 'salvors in possession' through Thomas Cooper Lybrand, marine solicitors, which in law gave them exclusive rights to the site, a situation which holds good to this day. Although they were not the finders of the site and did not hold an admiralty contract when they took this stance, for a while rival divers were going in dense fog or at night to plunder the wreck in clandestine.

The situation eventually became so difficult that in 1979 they decided that the next person caught diving on the wreck without permission would be served with an injunction. It was ironic that the person on whom the first injunction was served was Chief Petty Officer Noel Pearce, one of the original Navy diving team, who was now out of the service and leading an unofficial team of service divers. The injunction was dated June 1979, issued by the Supreme Court of Judicatory in the Marine Division. Later a team of RAF sport divers attempted to gain access to the *Association* site, but fortunately for them were dissuaded from going to the Gilstone by HM Customs, and stayed away.

From the early 1970's each new season saw extensive underwater work carried out; air lifting, drilling rocks to fit lifting eyebolts with epoxy resin, removing boulders weighing up to ten tons or more, seeking what lay beneath. As late as 1983, sixteen years after the wreck site was relocated by the Navy team, the present salvors raised a small bronze signal cannon in perfect condition, and in 1984 a bronze breech loading gun was found and brought ashore.

Today, Jim Heslin, one time director of 'Scillonian Diving Services Ltd', operates a successful diving holiday business which grew out of the old company 'Divework'. He and his wife Lena give a great deal of pleasure to many hundreds of holiday divers who visit the islands, taking them out on their boat to dive the 'Big A' - the *Association*. The two diving directors have gone their separate ways, but remain good friends.

Terry Hiron and his wife Celia still run their Man o'War nautical gift shop, selling coins and artefacts. The large house in Church Street named 'Warleggan', where they accommodated generations of visiting divers, is now rented out as self-catering holiday accommodation, but the most successful side of their business is the architectural design practice Terry has built up over the years.

Divers come from all over the world, from the United States, from Germany and France, Australia and South Africa, simply to explore this fabled treasure wreck, and hopefully find for themselves a silver or gold coin. Many return home with a prized souvenir in the form of a piece of eight, a silver crown or a shilling. It is likely that the wreck site on the Gilstone will yield coins for the next fifty years, if not longer. Should these two adventurers, both of whom came to the Isles of Scilly with little more than a bed-roll and a diving cylinder on their backs, find the missing stern section of the *Association*, the 'salad days' may yet return.

Notes for Chapter 8
1. McKee A. *History Under The Sea.* (London 1968); Rule M. *The Mary Rose.* (London 1982); Bradford E. *The Story of the Mary Rose.* (London 1982)
2. Franzen A. *The Warship Vasa.* (Stockholm 1974)
3. See Chapter on the Herbert Expedition

The Isles of Scilly Receiver of Wreck, Eric Brown, watching Jim Heslin (left) and Terry Hiron (right) emptying a large quantity of silver Pillar Dollars onto his desk from the wreck of the *Hollandia,* in 1972. Jim and Terry became the 'salvors-in-possession' of the *Association* from 1973, and continue to exercise this right to date.

Acknowledgement: Frank Gibson

Chapter Nine

Tearing Ledge Shipwreck

'A cluster of great iron cannon stood proud of the seabed, some muzzle, others breech down, some at oblique angles, exactly as they must have cascaded, in an instant, over 250 years before'.

Edmond Gostelo's contemporary chart of the Isles of Scilly in the British Museum shows the *Association* on the Gilstone and the *Firebrand* close inshore to St.Agnes. Both sites have been positively identified in recent years by artefacts recovered by divers. He also placed the *Romney* on the Crebinnicks, which include the Tearing Ledge, just south-east of the Bishop and Clerks, and beyond these, to the north, the *Eagle* on the Crim. The source of information on which Gostelo based the relative position of each ship is not known, but some of the details are almost certainly in error.

An elaborate legend on the chart dedicates it to Lord Sydney Godolphin, Governor of the Islands, who held the exalted position of Lord High Treasurer of England. His warrant as Governor commenced in 1698 and he died in 1713, almost certainly confirming that the chart was contemporary. His ancestors had long held the title and as Governor he was entitled to half of all wrecks occurring in the islands.[1] Godolphin would have taken a particular interest in the contemporary salvage of Admiral Shovell's lost ships and Herbert's later expedition to the scene. It is possible that this chart was produced as the result of Herbert's investigation.[2]

The caption also asserts that of the forty-three islands comprising the Scilly's at the time, only seven were populated. This is confirmed by a census carried out in 1715, which shows several families resident on five of the smaller islands. The majority of the total population of 822 lived on St.Mary's (55%) and Tresco (17%).[3] A lighthouse was maintained on St.Agnes[4] and the Garrison on St.Mary's was staffed by a handful of pensioners from the Royal Regiment of Invalids (Chelsea Pensioners), a practice which continued well into the 18th century.[5] These figures add emphasis to the enormity of the tragedy and the effect it must have had on the population of the islands - the number of corpses resulting from the disaster being almost twice the number of current inhabitants.

Accounts from the various ships' logs are naturally vague and confused.

Section of the Gostelo Chart dedicating it to Lord Sydney Godolphin, Lord Treasurer of England and Governor of the Isles of Scilly. The Chart shows the assumed location of each of the wrecked ships from the 1707 disaster.

Acknowledgement: British Library Map Room

The disaster occurred at night throwing up a solitary survivor from the three offshore wrecks, a quartermaster from the *Romney*, totally unfamiliar with his surroundings, who was rescued later from a remote and unidentified rock. In the prevailing weather and circumstances Lawrence would have been able to give the vaguest of details.

The scene of the tragedy lay some seven hazardous nautical miles south-west from St. Mary's, as a consequence neither local boats nor those from the Welsh squadron anchored in the temporary haven, were able to get out amongst the rocks until some time after dawn the following day. Tentative identification of each ship could only therefore have been made from the tenuous account of the sole survivor, and the gathering of circumstantial evidence. The latter included tops of masts, spars and rigging attached to the wrecks, still showing above the sea, and information gained from the variety of flotsam distributed far and wide amongst the Western Rocks by the intervening tides.

In July 1969 divers employed by Roland Morris discovered a large number of iron cannon in close proximity to Tearing Ledge, which lies a short distance from the Bishop Rock. His team continued to work the site over the two seasons of 1969 and 1970, recovering enough artefacts and coins of the correct period to prove this was one of Shovell's ships. Among other divers who visited the wreck was Bob Rogers, who raised a number of iron guns. The most significant artifact that Morris's team discovered was a large bronze ship's bell, dated 1701, marked with a broad arrow signifying it was cast for the British government. On the basis of the Gostelo chart, and the bell, the wreck was perhaps prematurely identified as that of the *Romney*.

This last discovery meant that by 1970, only two of Sir Clowdisley's lost ships remained to be found, irrespective of actual identity; the fireship known to have gone down in the vicinity of St.Agnes, the other a ship of the line probably sunk near the Crim. As a consequence, early that year NAC-SAC planned yet another expedition for July to be led by Lieut. Roy Graham RN. with the intention of searching the Crim for the latter.

On arriving alongside the quay at St.Mary's that summer in the small minesweeper RNXS *Odiham*, the naval party was greeted by the frustrating news that they had been forestalled by Morris's team who had recently located a wreck, thought to be the *Eagle*, on the Crim. It transpired that in

April that year, Peter Grosch, a professional crayfish diver, who also worked for Morris on the *Association*, had located a deep water cannon site on the western side of the reef. An extended search of the area carried out later in the summer by Geoff Upton, Mark Horibin, Peter Grosch and Mike Hicks, covered by Paul Armiger, a Daily Telegraph staff underwater photographer, revealed two more areas of wreckage, possibly from the same ship. Naturally this was considered to be the resting-place of the *Eagle*.[6]

The well-equipped NAC-SAC team contacted Morris and subsequently carried out a pre-disturbance survey of the newly found site.[7] During the course of the work the late Eric Collins, a Penzance diver and RNXS member, found a small

A large bronze bell bearing the broad-arrow mark and the date 1701, recovered by the Roland Morris team from the Tearing Ledge site, and hence certainly the *Eagle*.

Acknowledgement: Peter McBride

The RNXS. inshore training minesweeper XSV. *Puttenham* (M.2784) manned by auxiliary service crew from Penzance, which was the main support vessel for the relocation of
the *Association* by divers of NAC-SAC for six seasons. Her skipper, the late Lieut.Cdr.
Ted Barter RN(Ret'd), an extremely competent and much respected seaman, can be seen
on the bridge, top left in this photograph. All the other individuals were members of the
diving team. Acknowledgement: Paul Armiger, Daily Telegraph

badly eroded bell. The size and design of the bell, which carried no
insignia, and the nature of the artefacts observed on site, were not typical of
those from a British warship. The guns recorded were of small calibre and
insufficient, numbering only thirty-four, for men o' war the size of the *Eagle*
or *Romney*. Until further excavation has been carried out there is a considerable element of doubt as to the origin and identity of this particular ship.[8]

The Navy team returned once again to the Scilly's in July 1971, and carried out a brief preliminary survey of the Tearing Ledge site under the guid-
ance of Richard Larn.[9] Realising that this important heritage site was being
neglected, and could well go the way of the *Association,* Rex Cowan, a
solicitor by profession with an enthusiasm for archaeology, applied, in
1973, for the wreck to be designated under the government's recently introduced Protection of Wrecks Act.

Cowan had earlier been instrumental in finding and salvaging the treasure from the historic Dutch East Indiaman *Hollandia,* also wrecked in the
Scilly Isles and had recently been appointed to the government's advisory

An iron cannon, probably a 24 pounder, recovered from the site on Tearing Ledge, thought to be the wreck of the *Eagle*. Clearly shown are the unusual double line of 'fins' found on many guns on this site, which are now known to be only concretion, but why they form naturally like this remains a mystery. Cannon from other sites around Gt. Britain have been found with the same feature.

Acknowledgement: Frank Gibson

Committee on Historic Wreck, chaired by Lord Runciman. A licence authorising him to carry out a survey of the Tearing Ledge site was duly issued. As director of the project, Cowan now assembled a team of divers, with all the skills and experience required, to carry out the necessary underwater tasks. Some of those chosen had already gained a wealth of experience on the *Association* site.

Throughout the seasons of 1974-76, the regular diving team, led by Roy Graham included the equally experienced Terry Hiron, Jim Heslin, and Roy's son Harry. Other helpers were the late Brian Ranner and Tony Pike, both divers from the RAF. The team was joined for periods each summer by Peter McBride, whose specific task was to measure and tentatively identify all the guns using specialised experience and techniques developed in the underwater survey of naval ordnance on other wreck sites of the same era. Recalling an earlier memorable dive that occurred in the early stages of the survey, Peter McBride recorded:

'The day was bright, clear and sunny, the azure sky broken by the occasional fleecy cloud. Our small diving vessel pitched and rolled steadily towards the Western Rocks. Overhead numerous gulls circled, swooping occasionally to hover noisily over our wake. Northwards the low grey silhouettes of the islands, with their myriad attendant rocks, studded the blue sea as far as the eye could see, merging into the haze on the horizon.

Nearing our destination, our experienced Scilly's pilot, David Stediford, reduced way and manoeuvred slowly ahead against the tide. At the bow a wet-suited diver picked up the orange coloured buoy deftly with a boat hook. As soon as the mooring line was secured the engine was cut and the boat fell back in the tideway, hauling taut the heavy rope which was firmly anchored to a large two and a half ton cannon lying on the seabed below. Less than a mile to the north, only recently crowned with a flat helicopter pad after 123 years service, a solitary sentinel, the Bishop Rock lighthouse, bore witness to our arrival. A stone's throw away, on our port bow, the long Atlantic swells broke periodically in a swirl of white foam briefly exposing the voracious reef which some ancient mariner had aptly named the Tearing Ledge many centuries ago.

On board, all was now activity, divers being briefed, checking their SCUBA equipment and kitting up, ready for the first dive of the day. Amidships, others were marshalling surveying equipment and preparing rope lines ready to delineate the wreck site. One was busy threading length's of cord, each sufficient to encompass the largest cannon, through the corner eyelets of large white perspex squares embossed with large black numerals. These were to be the guiding lights for those carrying out the survey, bright enough to reflect the limited light in the dense gloom of the deepest part of the site. As I prepared to enter the water I reflected on the only previous occasion I had dived the Tearing Ledge. I had been one of a pair of naval divers sent down on the last day of a previous NAC- SAC expedition to re-locate the wreck. We had been dropped off site into deeper water, and only as we had breathed the last of our air supply had we drifted onto the perimeter of the site spotting two cannon. We just managed to attach a buoy before surfacing. This time I was to be given

The ship's bell of the *Eagle* being recovered by divers from a depth of about 130 feet on the Tearing Ledge site. Acknowledgement: Paul Armiger

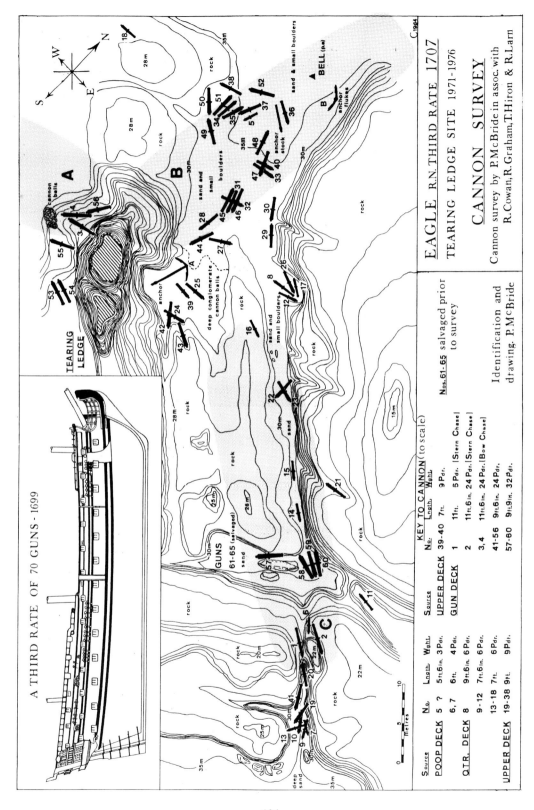

A THIRD RATE OF 70 GUNS - 1699

TEARING LEDGE

EAGLE R.N. THIRD RATE 1707
TEARING LEDGE SITE 1971-1976

CANNON SURVEY

Cannon survey by P.McBride in assoc. with
R.Cowan, R.Graham, T.Hiron & R.Larn

Nos.61-65 salvaged prior
to survey

Identification and
drawing, P.McBride

Source	No	Lngth.	Wght.
POOP DECK	5 ?	5ft.6in.	3Pdr.
	6,7	6ft.	4Pdr.
QTR. DECK	8	9ft.6in.	6Pdr.
	9-12	7ft.6in.	6Pdr.
	13-18	7ft.	6Pdr.
UPPER DECK	19-38	9ft.	9Pdr.

Source	No.	Lngth.	Wght.
UPPER DECK	39-40	7ft.	9Pdr.
GUN DECK	1	11ft.	5Pdr. [Stern Chase]
	2	11ft.6in.	24Pdr. [Stern Chase]
	3,4	11ft.6in.	24Pdr. [Bow Chase]
	41-56	9ft.6in.	24Pdr.
	57-60	9ft.9in.	32Pdr.

KEY TO CANNON (to scale)

104

a brief guided tour of the site by Roy Graham, the dive leader, before the more serious work of labelling the guns commenced.

After last minute diving equipment checks we dropped overboard almost simultaneously, finning against the tide to rendezvous on the surface, under the bow, on the mooring line. Exchanging the OK sign, we commenced our downward journey using the line as a guide, Roy's fins flashing a few feet ahead of me, illuminated against a blizzard of silver bubbles on their way to the surface in the reflected sunlight. Gradually the scene opened up below us and we dropped away from the rope, heading towards a bright plateau of rock exposed amongst a dark thick forest of waving kelp. In the centre the regular outline of the first small cannon became visible. Without pausing we followed the downward line of a cleft in the reef until the weed became sparse and then disappeared.

Suddenly there appeared below us, in twenty-two metres of water, two guns of extraordinary proportions, wedged in shallow recesses, on either side of a peak of rock. Lying beside one of the cannon I extended my diving fins to their maximum reach. I estimated that if I was 7'6" overall, these particular guns were at least 12ft long from button to muzzle and well worthy of a line of battle ship. One was much thicker than the other was and I surmised that they were almost certainly a pair of stern chase guns mounted on the gun deck, in the great cabin, near the rudder. The extraordinary length was necessary to extend the muzzle beyond the limit of the overhanging counter thus reducing the risk of damage when the powder and shot of the great guns were discharged.

Continuing our descent, the shallow clefts in which the two large guns were lodged, merged and then fell away in a deep wide crevasse on the opposite side of the reef. Roy disappeared abruptly into the chasm and a great mushroom of air ascended from below. Peering over the edge into the depths my eyes followed a scatter of guns. Together we pursued the trail downward into thirty-five metres. Gradually, through the gloom of the deeper water at the foot of the cliff, appeared the most amazing sight - a cluster of great iron cannon standing on end proud of the seabed, some muzzle, others breech down, some at oblique angles, exactly as they must have cascaded, in an instant, over 250 years before'.

Three years and many underwater hours later, the survey of the site was completed. Although the calibre of the guns can only be tentatively identified without actual recovery, the underwater survey, undertaken with callipers and measuring rod, strongly suggest that the wreck is that of the *Eagle* and not the *Romney*. (see Survey Plan, page 104 and list of guns, page 108)

There are three convincing arguments to support this conclusion. Firstly, the number of guns allowed to the *Romney*, a 4th rate of the smaller class, was fifty-four under any circumstance, the largest calibre being twelve-pounders. A total of sixty-five guns have been accounted for, on site to date, amongst which are four heavy thirty-two pounder demi-cannon and nineteen twenty-four pounders, guns far to heavy to have been carried on the main gun deck of the *Romney,* a vessel of only 683 tons.[10]

Secondly, a complete anchor found on site measured 10'6in, across the flukes, with a total length of 15'8in, is not relative to the size of the *Romney*. According to Sutherland, a contemporary expert, the rule for regulating the size of the largest anchor for a particular naval ship was that it should be, in length, two-fifths of the extreme beam or breadth of the ship. Although it cannot be proved easily that this is, in fact, the largest anchor in the vicinity of the wreck, since others may yet be found, it is interesting to calculate the beam of the ship for which this would have been suitable as the largest anchor. Whereas the beam of the *Romney* was only 34'4in, the anchor located would have been relevant to a ship of 39'0in beam or larger. The total beam of the *Eagle* was, in fact, 40'6in.[11]

Finally, the last and most convincing argument is the casting date of the large ship's bell recovered from the centre of the wreck site. The *Romney* was built in 1694, commissioned shortly thereafter, and never subsequently rebuilt. It is likely, therefore, that her bell would have carried the original date. Research has revealed that the *Eagle* was completely rebuilt in 1699, and recommissioned in 1701, which would clearly account for a similar date on the bronze bell recovered. Unless the *Romney* had previously damaged or lost her bell due to an accident, it is unlikely her bell would have carried the date '*1701*'.

The loss of the *Eagle* on a remote rock in the darkness of the night left not a single surviving witness from her total complement of 739 men. Despite these circumstances, analysis and comparison of the data recorded during the survey with contemporary records and deck plans of ships of a similar rate, throw a fresh and revealing light on the tragic sequence of events.

From the size and distribution of the guns, Peter McBride was able to deduce that the *Eagle* was probably on a south-easterly course when she struck the south-west side of Tearing Ledge with great force, bow on, breaching the forward part of her hull. With bow held fast and heavy breaking seas periodically lifting her stern in great surging swells, she then spilled several of her forward guns into shallow water below the Ledge. Her damaged hull taking in water fast, wind and tide now prevailed in turn on her stern, starboard quarter, and side, turning her 180 degrees in her own length, losing the above mentioned anchor in the process. Shortly after, presumably with some of her masts gone by the board, her upper deck a tangle of broken yards, sails and rigging, she slipped off the Ledge.

Now briefly afloat, with her head pointing NW by W, but unstable and heavily over-laden with the in-rushing sea, her pumps unable to cope, the *Eagle* quickly foundered. Her hull now bottomed temporarily, in 20 metres of water, bow downward, her keel athwart a high reef of rock, where she lay poised, stern overhanging a steep crevasse leading into deeper water to the east. Shortly after sinking, back broken across the reef in the surging seas, her hull was torn apart, cascading her after guns and long stern-chase cannon in a trail down to a depth of 35 metres. Simultaneously, the separated forward section of the hull slid into the deeper water of a wide descending rock and shingle bottomed ravine to the west of the reef, scattering the remainder of her cannon on route. Thus the *Eagle* met her tragic end.

Particulars of the three Wrecked Ships of the Line

Association (96 gun 2nd Rate)

Built ....Portsmouth.		**Guns**	
Date .... 1696.	Lower-deck	Demi-Cannon	26 - 9'9"
Builder...........Baggshott.	Middle-deck	Whole Culverin	26 - 9'6"
L/G Deck ....165ft.	Upper-deck	Demi-Culverin	26 - 9'0"
L/Keel ....132ft.			
Breadth ....45ft 5in.	Fo'castle	6 pounders	2 - 7'6"
Depth8ft 6in. Qtr-deck			2 - 9'6"
	6 pounders	12 - 7'6"	
Tons ....1459(bm)	Poop deck	6 pounders	2 - 7'0"

Eagle (70 gun 3rd Rate)

Guns [12]

Built ....Portsmouth.	Gun-deck	24 pounders	24 - 9'6"
Date ....1679.		*(4 x 32pdrs by survey)*	
Builder.....Daniel Furzer.		*(19 x24pdrs by survey)*	
L/G Deck ....15ft 6in.	Upper-deck	9 pounders	26 - 9'0"
L/Keel ....125ft.		*(22 x 9pdrs by survey)*	
Breadth ....40ft 8in.	Fo'castle	6 pounders	2 - 9'6"
Depth ....17ft 3in.			2 - 7'6"
Tons. . . . . . . .1065(bm)	Qtr-deck	6 pounders	12 - 8'6"
Rebuilt in 1699 -1099(bm)		*(11 x 6pdrs by survey)*	
	Poop-deck	3 pounders	4 - 5'6"
		(4 x 3pdrs by survey)	
		(3 x 4pdrs by survey)	

Romney (54 gun 4th Rate)

Built..............Blackwall.		**Guns**	
Date ....1694.	Gun-deck	12 pounders	22 - 9'0"
Builder..............Johnson.	Upper-deck	6 pounders	22 - 8'6"
L/G Deck ....31ft.	Fo'castle	6 pounders	2 - 9'6"
L/Keel ....109ft.	Qtr-deck	6 pounders	8 - 7'0"
Breadth ....34ft 4in.			
Depth ....13ft 7in.			
Tons ....683(bm)			

Notes for Chapter 9

1. JRIC, Vol 19, p292-8
2. See Chapter 6
3. Lilly C.L. *Survey and Census*, (1715)
4. A cresset erected on St.Agnes by Trinity House in 1680 after the loss of the English East Indiaman *Phoenix*
5. Gill, Crispin. *The Isles of Scilly*, p41 (Newton Abbot 1975)
6. Morris R. *Salvors Report on the Undersea Wreck of HMS Eagle.* (Penzance 1970)
7. NACSAC, Expedition Report (July 1970)
8. Ibid, p4
9. NACSAC, *Survey and Sketch Plan of the Wreck Site of HMS Romney.* (July 1971)
10. Ordnance Office Records, PRO, WO 55/1803.
11. Sutherland W. *Shipbuilding Unvail'd*, p22 (1717)
12. McBride P. & Cowan R. *Cannon Survey - Tearing Ledge Site* (1975-6) A total of 65 guns have been accounted for to date. There are many Admiralty references giving differing gun establishments for this period and the armament carried varied in war and peace. Additionally during the Toulon campaign, which immediately preceded the loss of the ships concerned, a great many guns were transferred between ships or landed by the fleet to fortify strategic positions. The *Eagle's* cannon were tentatively identified by external measurement underwater (since the critical fine measurement at the bore in nearly all cases was distorted by corrosion and the presence of concretion) and compared with researched lists and contemporary constructions. The range of guns on site appear to be nearest to the establishment for a 3rd rate shown in List Book 'B' for 1703 in the Admiralty Library. A major exception was the discovery of four additional 32 pounder demi-cannon, a size not normally carried even by a 3rd rate. Other establishments sometimes indicate 12 pounders on the upper deck but the presence of this calibre was not confirmed.

A selection of lead inkwells, sand shakers and lids, all recovered from the *Association* site over the years since its relocation.

Acknowledgement: Scillonian Diving Services.

Chapter Ten

Admiral Shovell's Family

'They knocked at the door, and out came a poor old woman, upon which Sir Clowdisley kissed her, and then fell down on his knees, begged her blessing, and called her mother'.

Abraham De la Pryme - 29 Dec 1697

Many of the biographies relating to Sir Clowdisley Shovell contain statements concerning his early life, which are unsubstantiated, and in many cases, completely untrue. These have been repeated and compounded over the past centuries to produce a family background, which is confused, to say the least.[1]

He was born on 20 November 1650[2] in the small Norfolk village of Cockthorpe situated one mile from the coast, and the parish register shows that he was baptised there on 25 November that same year.[3] His father was John Shovell (1625-1654), also of Cockthorpe, a man of some property, being the youngest son of Nathaniel Shovell, described as a 'gentleman', who was buried at Binham (one mile south of Cockthorpe) in 1636. This was probably the same Nathaniel who was baptised at St. Saviour's Church, Norwich, in 1601, the son of another John Shovell, Sheriff of Norwich in 1606-7.

The family appears to have settled in the Norwich area early in the 16th century, where a John Shovell was admitted as a citizen on 21 September 1554. There were many settlers from the Low Countries during this period, and Shovell may be an anglicised form of something like Schouvel. His mother Anne, was the daughter of one Henry Jenkensen of Cley, another small Norfolk coastal village, by his wife Lucy, eldest daughter of Thomas Clowdisley, also of the same village. North Norfolk parish registers for the 17th century contain numerous entries of births, marriages and deaths of both Shovell's and Clowdisley's, and the origin of the famous admiral's name now becomes obvious. During the latter part of the 17th and early 18th centuries, there were many men serving in the fleet with these surnames, but for the most part were in subordinate ranks.[4]

Accounts of Clowdisley Shovell's early years are various and conflicting. One source has it that: *'this great man was descended from parents who*

Bust of Sir Clowdisley Shovell, on display in Norwich Castle Museum.

Acknowledgement: Trustees & Curator, Norwich Museum

were in circumstances such as not to be able to make a better provision for him, than by binding him apprentice (as is reported by Dr. Campbell) to a shoemaker'. Of his entry into the navy, the same source continues: *'this mean occupation ill fitting to the nobleness of his disposition, he procured himself to be recommended exceedingly young, being at that time not more than 9 years of age, to the patronage of Sir John Narborough, who made him one of his cabin boys'.*[5]

Another reference cites Shovell as being *' - a native of Morson, near Clay, in Norfolk, where he lived at the Manor House. He was a cousin of Admiral Sir John Narborough'.*[6] Yet a third source states: *'- within a mile or two of Burnham Thorpe in Norfolk, the birthplace of Nelson, stands the obscure hamlet of Cockthorpe, a village of three houses or rather three hovels, each of which has produced from humble village life its individual admirals, those being Sir Christopher Mimms (Myngs); Sir John Narborough and Sir Clowdisley Shovell'.*[7]

Finally, it has also been claimed that Shovel was born in Yorkshire, and was for a time first ostler at an inn at Redford in Nottinghamshire,[8] or else that he came from Hastings.[9]

One must turn to the Dictionary of National Biography to obtain a clearer picture, since the information given for each of the admirals must be pieced together to establish their relationships. This confirms that Vice Admiral Myngs (1625-66) came from Norfolk, and is said by Samuel Pepys to have been: *'- of very humble origin, his father being always and at this day, a shoemaker, and his mother a hoymans daughter, of which he used to frequently*

boast'.[10] Sir John Narborough is con-
firmed as the son of Gregory
Narborough of Cockthorpe, bap-
tised in the village 11 October 1640.
Sir John first went to sea under
Myngs, being promoted to
Lieutenant of the *Portland* (1664).
He continued to serve under him in
successive ships, ie. *Royal Oak*;
Triumph; *Fairfax* and *Victory* and
was in the latter when Myngs was
mortally wounded on 4 June 1666.[11]

Reference to Sir Clowdisley
asserts that he first went to sea in
1664 under *'his probable kinsman Sir
Christopher Myngs, after whose death
he closely followed the fortunes of
another kinsman, Sir John
Narborough'.* A brief account of the
admiral's early life, which has a ring

Memorial to the Narborough's in Knowlton
church on the family estate, Deal, Kent.

Acknowledgement: Brian Turner

of authenticity about it, is to be found in *'A Consolatory Letter to Lady
Shovell'*[12] published shortly after Sir Clowdisley's death, as a long rambling
booklet written by the Rev Gilbert Crokkat, Rector of Crayford. It was in
the Kent parish of Crayford that Sir Clowdisley's residence 'May Place',
purchased in 1694, was located. The letter relates:

*'As to the Admiral, he was born in 1650, in the county of Norfolk of an
ancient family, chiefly considerable for loyalty and downright honesty, which
was therefore natural and hereditary to Sir Cloudesly; nor was it inconsiderable for estate, though that was lessened by their faithful adherence to King
Charles I of ever blessed memory. However the good old gentlewoman, Sir C's
mother, being still alive enjoys no contemptible competency, which has been
transmitted for many years from father to son; and being by her son, Sir C.
redeemed from some encumbrances was by his natural affection, continued
entire to his mother. Cloudesley was the second son of the family, which was
a numerous one but the rest all died young, when he was about thirteen'.*

Crokkat continues:

*'- Sir Christopher Myngs being then an Admiral and most famous in his
time, coming to visit his family to which he was related, desired to have the*

education of one of their sons under him in the Royal Navy; and as he was an excellent judge of persons, soon observed something extraordinary hopeful and promising in young Cloudesley, who readily and cheerfully agreed to go under him as a gentleman volunteer in the fleet: and Gt. Britain being quickly after engaged in a bloody war with the Dutch our young hero soon found occasion to distinguish himself in battle; and so became remarkable for valour, as he had been before for virtuous and modest deportment. His parents having carefully trained him up to such learning as their country schools afforded, Sir Christopher quickly saw that there was a foundation fit enough to receive and bear a noble superstructure, which Sir Christopher began to raise, and afterwards completed by (the never enough to be commended) Sir John Narborough, who upon the experience of Shovell's eminent courage, conduct and sweet temper, soon advanced him from one post to another, until he became one of the most considerable captains in the fleet'.

The will of John Shovell, Clowdisley's father, made 22 March 1654, proved at Westminster 12 June 1654, contains these words:

'I give and bequeath unto Anne my wife all the singular my real and personal estate whatsoever upon condition that she shall pay or give unto Nathaneall John and Clowdsley my three sons one hundred pounds a piece to be paid to them at there several ages on one and twen-

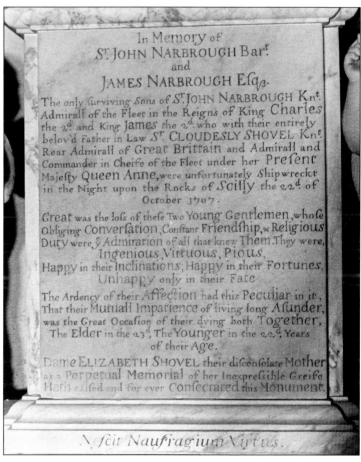

The inscription on the Narborough memorial. Knowlton Court was the seat of Sir John Narborough, father of John and James, whose widow later married Clowdisley Shovell, making him their step-father.

Acknowledgement: Brian Turner

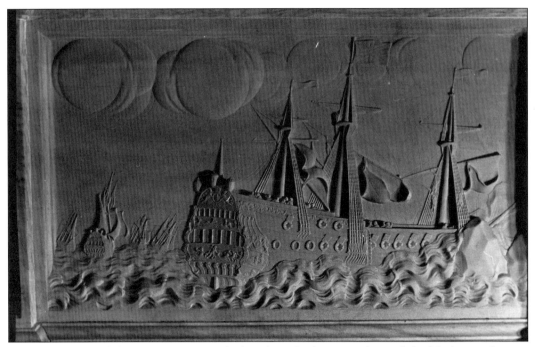

The shipwreck of the *Association* as depicted on the base portion of the Narborough memorial. Whilst it may be a pure coincidence, with a degree of artistic licence, the starboard stern gallery of the carved man o'war clearly shows a coat of arms, with a rampant lion and unicorn. This closely matches a similar carved wooden coat of arms which now hangs in the Magistrates Court in the town of Penzance. Tradition has it that this came from the *Association,* having been preserved by the islanders since 1707 and presented to the residents of Penzance in 1818 as a token of appreciation for food supplied to the islands during a period of hardship and famine. If there was a coat of arms on the starboard side, then it is reasonable to assume it was mirrored on the port side.

Acknowledgement: Brian Turner

tie years. And upon this Condition I make her my Executrix'.

Marsham also succeeded in finding the registration of the second marriage of the widow Anne Shovell to John Flaxman of Walcot, at Gimmingham (north Norfolk) on 8 February 1659. The Walcott (modern spelling) registers record the burial of John and Nathaniel Shovell, young Clowdisley's two brothers on 2 and 10 February 1664 respectively.[13]

Assessing the evidence from these various sources, it is most improbable that Clowdisley Shovell was ever apprenticed to a shoemaker, this story probably being a corruption attributable to Myngs' background. Nor did Clowdisley go to sea as a cabin boy at nine years of age. His father *'a man of property,'* and the grandson of a *'gentleman'*, died when Clowdisley was four years of age, leaving his mother Anne in reduced circumstances until she remarried when the boy was nine, to John Flaxman. The nature of the tragedy which caused the death of Clowdisley's two brothers, one older the other younger, within a week of each other in 1664, we may never know. These were pestilent times and the plague ravaged Europe, reaching its peak in England in 1665. It is possible they were victims of this or some other disease.

Without doubt, the Shovells were related, albeit distantly, to both the Myngs' and Narborough. Admiral Myngs' visit to the family may have been provoked by the death of his brothers, since Clowdisley went to sea that same year. No doubt Anne Flaxman was distraught at losing her only surviving son to the sea, but possibly acceded to Myngs' suggestion for her son's health and well being.

Clowdisley Shovell joined the *Portland*, a 4th rate, 50 gun ship, as a 'gentleman volunteer' or midshipman at thirteen years of age in 1664 [14], just before the outbreak of the Second Dutch War. He served on the same ships under both Lieut. Narborough and Admiral Myngs until the latter's death, in the great battle off North Foreland, on board the *Victory* in 1666. At that time it is probable that the responsibility for nurturing young Shovell fell to Narborough, only ten years his senior. Throughout the rest of his career he showed the utmost consideration for Clowdisley, providing the opportunity, patronage and influence that was necessary for a successful naval career of the period.

Little is known of Sir Clowdisley's later private, or family life until the early 1660's. In the meantime he had served continuously on board the same ships with Narborough for some thirteen years, and even after achieving command of the *Sapphire* in 1677, continued as part of Narborough's Mediterranean Squadron. They obviously became close friends, which is reflected in the fact that in March 1691, three years after the death of Sir John, Clowdisley married Narborough's thirty-two year old widow, Elizabeth, at All Hallows Church, Staining, London. In doing so, Shovell, now 41 years of age, took upon himself the responsibility for bringing up Sir John's three young children, (Sir) John, aged six; James, five and Elizabeth, eight years.

Narborough had commanded three very successful expeditions to the Mediterranean against the corsairs of Tripoli and Algiers, and had amassed considerable prize money by the time his active career ended in 1679. He then became Commissioner of the Navy, with a special responsibility for the

Victualling Department, a very lucrative position, which Clowdisley was to hold some twenty years later.

In 1681, at the age of forty-one, Narborough married Elizabeth, the twenty-one year old daughter of Captain John Hill, of Shadwell, Middlesex (Narborough's first marriage to Elizabeth Calmady in 1677 had ended tragically with her death nine months later).[15] On his death, Captain Hill, a man of considerable wealth and a Navy Commissioner (1691-1706), left the enormous sum of £100,000 to his second son-in-law, Sir Clowdisley.[16] Shortly after his marriage to Elizabeth Hill, Sir John bought the manors of Knowlton Northcote, Southcote and Southborne, all in Kent, at least £5,000 of the cost coming from the dowry of his young bride. His family seat became Knowlton Court, near Deal, which was still in the family at the beginning of the present century. Their town residence was a house near St. Olaves church, Hart St, London, and each of their children were baptised there, two of whom died in infancy.[17]

In 1686, Sir John Narborough shared in the celebrated venture of Sir William Phipps, which succeeded in salvaging a great deal of treasure from a Spanish treasure wreck near Hispaniola, in the West Indies. Narborough's meagre investment of £400, giving him a one seventh share, in fact brought him the welcome windfall of £21,766.[18] Two years later, King James, the principle shareholder in the venture, provided a frigate, and gave personal command of a second salvage attempt to Narborough.

Unfortunately, Sir John was to die of a fever on board the *Foresight*, actually moored over the wreck on 27 May 1688. He was buried at sea, his bowels being brought home and interred with great ceremony in Knowlton church that July. In the following November, his eldest son John, then four years of age, was created a baronet in recognition of his father's outstanding service for his country.[19] Long after her marriage to Sir Clowdisley Shovell, and even after his death, Dame Elizabeth was still engaged with the widows of other shareholders in litigation concerning the ill-fated second treasure hunt and the estate of the deceased Duke of Albemarle.[20]

The year after he had been knighted and appointed Rear Admiral of the Blue, Sir Clowdisley, who had also acquired some wealth in his campaign against the corsairs, married Elizabeth Narborough. His eligibility for her hand had been increased by his good fortune. Their first daughter, Elizabeth, was born on 3 November 1692, and baptised at St. Mary's, Whitechapel. She was eventually to marry twice; first in the Chapel Royal,

Whitehall in 1708, Sir Robert Marsham, created the first Baron Romney in 1716, who died in 1724, and secondly; John Lord Carmichael, later the third Earl of Hyndford. The latter was the English Minister at the Court of the Hague when Elizabeth passed away in 1750.

In 1694, Sir Clowdisley now aged 44, purchased May Place, a large house in Crayford, Kent, which became his country-seat. He also owned a town house in Frith Street, Soho, both properties being still in the family when he died.

His second daughter Anne Shovell was born 14 November 1696, baptised at St. Olaves, Hart St, London, and later married the Hon. Robert Mansell at St. Annes, Blackfriars, in 1718. He died in 1723, and all three of their children died in infancy. Anne married again in 1726, to John Blackwood, at Charlton, Kent, and had three children by him. She died in 1741, and was buried at Crayford.[21]

As to Sir Clowdisley's stepchildren, Sir John Narborough had made ample provision for them prior to his death. £5,000 and his manors in Kent went to the eldest son, John, with reversion to daughter Elizabeth if John died unmarried. James and Elizabeth both inherited £10,000 each, which was a considerable sum at the time.[22] Elizabeth Narborough married in 1701, Thomas D'Aeth, who was created a baronet in 1716, and died in 1724, to be buried a Knowlton. It is obvious that Shovell showed every consideration to his step-children, as Narborough had to him in his younger days, arranging and supervising their education and progressing their careers. In 1707, still unmarried, they were both tragically lost with their step-father, the great admiral, in the *Association.*

In 1691 Shovell was granted his own coat of arms, '*viz Gu. a chevron arm in chief two crescents arg, in base a fleur-de-lis or*', these being symbolic of his victories over the Turks and French. In 1698, Sir Clowdisley became Member of Parliament for Rochester, which was not far from his country-seat at Crayford, a position he held until his death. He is said to have taken a great interest in civic affairs, and endowed the then new Rochester Guildhall with an ornate plaster ceiling. Resplendent with its gilded arms (both those of the town and Sir Clowdisley) and carved trophies of war, the latter remains an impressive memorial to the Admiral's memory, as does the nearby Corn Exchange, built in 1706 to house the butcher's market.

He also presented the town of Rochester with a large clock, which can still be seen on the front of the Corn Exchange, its original square face having been replaced with a round one in 1771. During his infrequent visits to the town, the records show the mayor often entertained him. In 1701 he was wined and dined to the tune of £15.2s.0d, the meal including such things as: '- *six fowls with bacon and sprouts, a pedgione pye, legge of muttone and turnipps, and a large apple pye and cheese'*. The food in fact accounted for only one third of the bill, the other £9.11s.0d being the cost of the wine.[23]

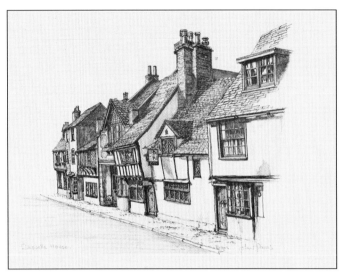

The historic & picturesque cottage at No.125-6 All Saints Street, Hastings, known locally as 'Mrs. Shovell's House', today marked with a plaque and a hanging sign. Acknowledgement: John Adams

As to Anne Shovell, Sir Clowdisley's mother, referred to by Crokatt as the *'good old gentle-woman,'* mention has already been made that she married a John Flaxman. They seemingly had two children, but only Anne's details survive, she being born in 1672. John Flaxman died in 1687 leaving Sir Clowdisley's mother a widow for a second time, now aged 59, her husband not living to see his daughter's marriage to Thomas Shorting of Morston three years later, nor any of their eleven children. Letters written by Clowdisley Shovell to Thomas in 1695-6 show that he was very close to both his mother and his step-sister, and sent *'his duty to his mother and love to his sister',* signing himself as *'your Loving Brother Clow Shovell'*.[24]

Some time after her second husband's death, Clowdisley's mother appears to have moved to Hastings, in Sussex where according to a strong local tradition, she took up residence in a small picturesque cottage now known as 125-6 All Saint's Street. This is known to this day as *'Mrs. Shovell's House'* and bears a wall plaque and hanging sign, rather like an inn, which states the details of this previous occupant and her son. The Hastings Cottage Improvement Society purchased the cottage in 1857, at which time it was said to be 250 years old.[25] Whether or not Anne Flaxman had relatives in the Hastings area is not known; certainly the names of both Cloudesly and Shovell appear in the Corporation's records as early as 1590, the former for a person living in All Saints' Street.

An extract from the diary of an Abraham De la Pryme, dated 29 December 1697, offers the following interesting account:

'I heard a Gentleman say (this was in fact a Captain Russell) that was in the ship with him about six years ago that, as they were sailing over against Hastings in Sussex, says Sir Cloudesley, 'Pilot, put near, I have a little business on shore here', so we put near, and him and this gentleman went a land in the boat, and having walked about half-a-mile ashore, Sir Cloudesley came to a little house; 'Come', says he, to the gentleman, 'my business is here, I came on purpose to see the good woman of this house'. Upon which they knocked at the door, and out came a poor old woman, upon which Sir Clowdisley kissed her, and then fell down on his knees, begged her blessing, and called her mother (she being his mother that had removed out of Yorkshire thither).[26] *He was mighty kind to her and she to him, and after that he had paid his visit, he left her ten guineas, and took his leave with tears in his eyes, and departed to his ship'.*[27]

In Sir Clowdisley's will, his lands at Morston were bequeathed to his mother, Mrs. Anne Flaxman: *'with remainder to his sister Mrs. Anne Shorten'*. In an account book or ledger, kept with considerable neatness by Sir Clowdisley himself, now in the possession of his descendant the Earl of Romney, there are several entries dated 29 July 1703. These include: *'To Joseph Jacobs, for a Calash (small light carriage with a folding top) for my mother Fflaxman, fourteen pounds'*. After the admiral's death there are entries by his widow Lady Shovell: *'several Legacies paid in Norfolk, to Mother Flaxman, Brother Shorting, etc, making together as per little book £640'.*[28]

Three months after receiving her legacy she died aged eighty-one, being buried at Morston on 17 June 1709. Presumably she had returned to her inherited estate from Hastings, if indeed the tradition of Hastings is correct. Her will, proved before the Surrogate at Cockthorpe 11 July, the year she died, mentions Thomas and Anne Shorting and their children, but makes no allusion to any other surviving children of her own, nor to Lady Shovell or her grand daughters Elizabeth and Anne.[29]

A pamphlet published shortly after Shovell's death bears testament to his humble family origin and the prestige within which he was held:

'The memory of Sir C. Shovell does most deservedly claim a place amongst the greatest worthies that ever the British Nation was honoured with; and as there have been so very few whose lives are worthy to be compared with his,

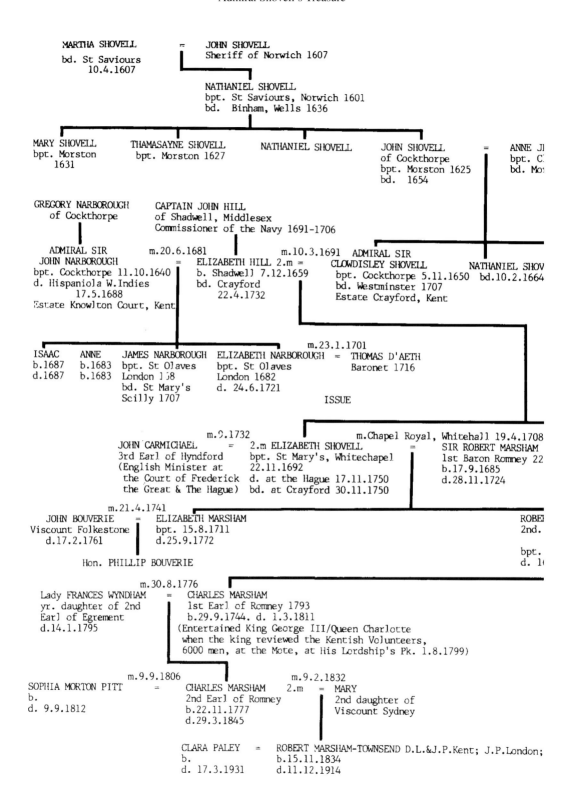

MARTHA SHOVELL
bd. St Saviours
10.4.1607

= JOHN SHOVELL
Sheriff of Norwich 1607

NATHANIEL SHOVELL
bpt. St Saviours, Norwich 1601
bd. Binham, Wells 1636

MARY SHOVELL
bpt. Morston
1631

THAMASAYNE SHOVELL
bpt. Morston 1627

NATHANIEL SHOVELL

JOHN SHOVELL
of Cockthorpe
bpt. Morston 1625
bd. 1654

= ANNE JI
bpt. C
bd. Mo:

GREGORY NARBOROUGH
of Cockthorpe

CAPTAIN JOHN HILL
of Shadwell, Middlesex
Commissioner of the Navy 1691-1706

ADMIRAL SIR
JOHN NARBOROUGH
bpt. Cockthorpe 11.10.1640
d. Hispaniola W.Indies
17.5.1688
Estate Knowlton Court, Kent

m.20.6.1681
=

ELIZABETH HILL 2.m =
b. Shadwell 7.12.1659
bd. Crayford
22.4.1732

m.10.3.1691

ADMIRAL SIR
CLOWDISLEY SHOVELL
bpt. Cockthorpe 5.11.1650
bd. Westminster 1707
Estate Crayford, Kent

NATHANIEL SHOV
bd.10.2.1664

ISAAC
b.1687
d.1687

ANNE
b.1683
b.1683

JAMES NARBOROUGH
bpt. St Olaves
London 158
bd. St Mary's
Scilly 1707

ELIZABETH NARBOROUGH
bpt. St Olaves
London 1682
d. 24.6.1721

m.23.1.1701
= THOMAS D'AETH
Baronet 1716

ISSUE

JOHN CARMICHAEL
3rd Earl of Hyndford
(English Minister at
the Court of Frederick
the Great & The Hague)

m.9.1732
=

2.m ELIZABETH SHOVELL
bpt. St Mary's, Whitechapel
22.11.1692
d. at the Hague 17.11.1750
bd. at Crayford 30.11.1750

m.Chapel Royal, Whitehall 19.4.1708
= SIR ROBERT MARSHAM
1st Baron Romney 22
b.17.9.1685
d.28.11.1724

JOHN BOUVERIE
Viscount Folkestone
d.17.2.1761

m.21.4.1741
=

ELIZABETH MARSHAM
bpt. 15.8.1711
d.25.9.1772

ROBE1
2nd.

bpt.
d. 1(

Hon. PHILLIP BOUVERIE

Lady FRANCES WYNDHAM
yr. daughter of 2nd
Earl of Egrement
d.14.1.1795

m.30.8.1776
=

CHARLES MARSHAM
1st Earl of Romney 1793
b.29.9.1744. d. 1.3.1811
(Entertained King George III/Queen Charlotte
when the king reviewed the Kentish Volunteers,
6000 men, at the Mote, at His Lordship's Pk. 1.8.1799)

SOPHIA MORTON PITT
b.
d. 9.9.1812

m.9.9.1806
=

CHARLES MARSHAM
2nd Earl of Romney
b.22.11.1777
d.29.3.1845

m.9.2.1832
2.m =

MARY
2nd daughter of
Viscount Sydney

CLARA PALEY
b.
d. 17.3.1931

= ROBERT MARSHAM-TOWNSEND D.L.&J.P.Kent; J.P.London;
b.15.11.1834
d.11.12.1914

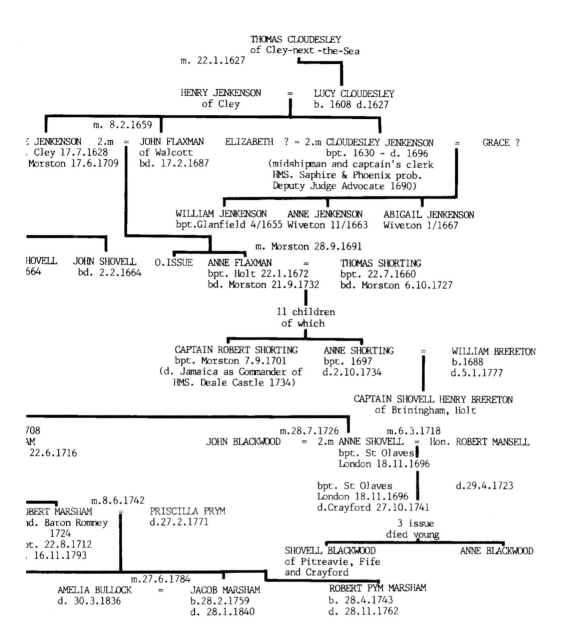

SHOVELL FAMILY
TREE

on; MA.Oxford; FSA; FRGS; FGS; (in Diplomatic Service 1855-1859)

so likewise the singularity of his death will enhance the Glory of his famous exploits. The character of his parents held amongst their neighbours was that of honesty rather than riches, and they are hardly conspicuous for anything else'.[30]

Notes for Chapter 10

1. Marsham-Townsend R. (we are indebted to Marsham-Townsend, a descendant of Shovell's, for rectifying many of the published inaccuracies, and recording many revelations, concerning the Admiral's life through extensive research carried out in the 19th century. (see Chapter 6)
2. Styles S. *Admiral of England,* p174
3. Marsham-Townsend states that the entry is a *'manifest interpolation'* inserted after the event ascribed to turbulent times, the Shovell's being Royalist sympathisers. The entry was probably made after he became famous.
4. It would appear that at least some of these were related to Shovell, since they frequently served in the same ship. e.g. Clowdsley Jenkinson was a Midshipman and Captain's Clerk in the *Sapphire* and *Phoenix* and is probably the uncle mentioned in the will of CS. A Clowdsley Jenkenson was also Deputy Judge Advocate in 1690 and is probably the same person. Thomas Shouell, an Able Seaman, served under CS in the Edgar in 1689 and later became Quarter-Gunner. On board the *London* in 1692 at the Admiral's request was the Thomas Shewell, Chaplain; and in 1692-3 John Shouell was Captain of the *Royal William* when carrying Sir Clowdisley's flag. Marsham-Townsend Notes and Queries 6th Series Vol X (27.12.1884)
5. Charnock J. *Biographia Navalis,* Vol II p16 (London 1795); Campbell R. *The Lives of the Admirals,* p235 (London 1812). Charnock misquoted Campbell, since Campbell qualified his statement, *'I think that of a shoemaker',* which is entirely unsubstantiated.
6. Spelt today and probably then as Morston and Cley. *History of Ships,* Pt 36 p713
7. *Naval Gazetteer,* Pt II p404 (1827)
8. De La Pryme. *Diary* (1697)
9. *Sussex Archaeological Collections,* Vol XIV p109
10. DNB, Vol 40 p10
11. Ibid, p89
12. BL, (BM) 4406 bb33
13. Marsham-Townsend, N& Q's 8th S. VII p42 (1895)
14. The great majority of *'young gentlemen'* who entered the navy in the hope of rising to commissioned rank began their career in ratings which were neither specifically intended for, nor entirely occupied by them, the most common being as a captain's servant. A captain was allowed four servants for every 100 men in his ship, but very few of these were actually domestics. They were boys growing up in a career either as seamen or officers, depending on their education, background and good fortune. Clowdisley was probably a *'servant'* for a time, an apprentice to Myngs, from whence grew the story that he went to sea as a cabin boy.
15. The Calmady's were a notable Plymouth family with a manor at Langdon Court, Wembury. Narborough's young wife, Elizabeth Calmady was only 19 years old and

with child when she died of a fever. She was interred in a fine monumental tomb that can still be seen within the Wembury parish church of St.Werburgh close to Wembury beach.

16. Dyer F. *Life of Sir John Narborough*, p207 (London 1931)
17. bid, p207-8
18. Earle P. *Wreck of the Almirante*, p201 (London 1979)
19. Marsham-Townsend, N & Q's 7th S. Vol VI (1888)
20. Earle P. *Wreck of the Almirante*, p218; House of Lords' MSS 1714-18 Vol XII No 4058
21. Smith F. *A History of Rochester*, p299
22. Dyer F. *Life of Sir John Narborough*, p241
23. Pinder A. *A Kent Life*, p41 (Nov 1978)
24. Marsham-Townsend, N & Qs 8th S VII (1895)
25. Cousins H. *Hastings of Bygone Days-and the Present*, p74-84 (1911)
26. *Sussex Arch. Coll*. Vol XIV p109
27. Cousins H. *Hastings and St. Leonards Pictorial Advertiser and V. List* (1914)
28. Cousin H. *Hastings of Byegone Days-and the Present*, p76 (1911)
29. Marsham-Townsend, N & Q's 8 S. VII p42 (1895)
30. Brown D. *Secret Memoirs of the Life of the Honourable Sir Cloudsley Shovell* (London 1708) BM 615 a.6

Chapter Eleven

Admiral Shovell's Early Career

'Our men employed in the boats in this particular action were 157, they all behaving themselves as becometh Englishmen'.

Sir John Narborough - 18 Feb 1675-6 (Lt. Shovell's action at Tripoli)

Admiral Sir Clowdisley Shovell's long and successful naval career spanned the reign of four successive English monarchs, during which he appears to have taken part in almost every naval affair of consequence in a long series of wars. As the admiral's career developed he saw the navy rise and prosper under the patronage of Charles II and his brother James, Duke of York, Lord High Admiral, who later became James II, despite the reluctance of the restoration parliaments to grant sufficient funds for the navy's needs. The navy increased in size, ship design improved and large numbers of new keels were laid down. More important, under the firm influence of Samuel Pepys, the seemingly tireless Clerk and later, Secretary to the Admiralty, the whole sphere of naval administration was progressively reorganised gradually becoming more efficient, and much less open to corruption.

During this period the States of Holland, England's principal maritime and commercial adversaries in Europe, were mastered in three short, but major wars commenced during the Commonwealth. These involved a series of sea battles fought with incredible ferocity and exceptional bravery on both sides and provided a generation of valuable experience and tradition. On this firm foundation successful naval campaigns against both the French and Spanish were fought during the reigns of William and Ann, Admiral Shovell succeeding by merit to see the English fleet emerge as the largest and most powerful in the world. At the time of the Restoration, England possessed seventy six ships of the line of 4th Rate or larger, until shortly before Shovell's tragic death in 1707, there were 129 such ships in commission, as well as an increased variety and number of smaller vessels.[1]

Clowdisley Shovell went to sea as a midshipman in 1664, serving continuously under his patron Sir John Narborough, throughout the Second Dutch War, probably remaining with him during the South Seas and West Indies voyages (1669-71).[2]

At the outbreak of the Third Dutch War in January 1672, young Shovell was still a midshipman, having joined the 1st Rate *Royal Prince*, flagship of the Duke of York, seventeen days after Narborough became a lieutenant in the same ship.[3] Both saw considerable action that following May, when the *Royal Prince* was so severely damaged the Duke was forced to temporarily shift his flag to the *St. Michael*. Narborough, as second Captain, was left in command after Sir John Cox, first captain, was killed. His account of this action shows his esteem for the Duke, and the degree of personal danger they shared:

'His Royal Highness went fore and aft in the ship and cheered up the men to fight, which did encourage them very much. The Duke thought himself never near enough to the enemy, for he was ever calling to the quarter master which cunded the ship to luff her nearer, giving me commands to forbear fighting till we got closer to them. Between 9 and 10 o'clock Sir John Cox was slain with a great shot, being close by the Duke on the poop. Several gentlemen and others were slain and wounded on the poop and quarterdeck on both sides of the Duke. Presently when Sir John Cox was slain, I commanded as Captain, observing his Royal Highness's commands in working the ship, striving to get the wind of the enemy. I so absolutely believe no prince upon the whole earth can compare with his Royal Highness in gallant resolution in fighting his enemy and with so great conduct and knowledge of navigation, as never any General understood before him. He is better acquainted in these seas than many masters which are now in his fleet; he is general, soldier, pilot, master, seaman; to say all, he is everything that man can be, and most pleasant when the great shot are thundering about his ears.

Between 11 and 12 o'clock our ship was much disabled in the masts and rigging. A great shot from the enemy cut our maintop mast clear asunder, that it fell down on the deck and put us past the use of our mainsail, so that we would not work the ship to keep the wind, nor use our guns on the upper deck for rigging; neither could any man work aloft about mending the rigging for shot flying so thick, we being got so near the enemy's great ships and fireships, that out ship was in more than ordinary danger'.

The following day, in recognition of his obvious ability to command, the Duke personally presented Narborough with his commission as captain, on board the *Royal Prince*.[4]

Such battle dangers intimately shared and the mutual recognition of courage and skill between the Duke, Narborough and Clowdisley Shovell probably created the basis for the high regard and patronage later shown by James towards both officers. Later, when the Duke became King James II, he promoted Shovell to the 4th rate *Dover,* despite the fact he was unsympathetic towards his monarch's catholic religion.

Shovell joined the *Fairfax* as Master's Mate under Narborough on 17th September 1672, along with 210 other men all described as *'volunteers'.*[5] With Shovell on board this ship went on to serve in the Mediterranean, and during the return voyage narrowly missed being wrecked on the Bishop and Clerks rocks, in the Isles of Scilly, the self same rocks on which Shovell was to die some thirty-four years later.(see pages 2-3). Shortly after leaving the *Fairfax*, Narborough was appointed to the *St. Michael*, taking with him young Shovell, still master's mate.[6]

Later that same year, Narborough was given the command of the 3rd Rate *Henrietta*. Again Shovell followed him, both men seeing action in the battle of the Texel in August 1673. As a direct result of his conduct in this battle, John Narborough was promoted to Rear Admiral of the Red in September, and later knighted by the King at Whitehall. It was probably no coincidence that Clowdisley also received promotion, being made 2nd Lieutenant of the *Henrietta* on 23 September,[7] and yet again followed his patron to the Mediterranean in 1675 on board the *Harwich*. The first substantiated proof of Clowdisley Shovell's personal qualities of leadership and courage came in January 1676, as Lieutenant, still aboard the same ship. Sir John's orders were to use his squadron to put down the piratical state of Tripoli, which was allowing the port to be used as a base for a fleet of marauding corsairs or pirates. These were capturing merchant vessels and carrying their crews to slavery, either in the North African markets, or in the galleys.

Shovell was chosen by Sir John Narborough to negotiate with the Dey of Tripoli, in an attempt to settle the matter by peaceful means. Despite having delivered the terms with great spirit, the Dey treated him with disrespect and he returned on board with an indefinite reply. Back he went again, with a second message, and instructions to establish the positions of the local defences. Shovell managed to delay his return, and hence could reassure the Admiral that it was practicable to burn the shipping within the harbour despite the commanding batteries. In returning, he was given command of a small task force of boats with which the harbour was attacked, the resulting action being considered so important that Narborough's account of it was made a special supplement to the London Gazette newspaper, which read:

'Friday, 14 January 1675-6. I being before Tripoli in Barbery with his Majesties ships under my command, namely these, Harwich, Henrietta, Portsmouth, the Anne, Christopher and Holmes fireships, and two merchant ships, Guiney and Martin, attending on me for convoy to Scanderoone. I hoped to have made an honourable and lasting peace, but the Dey and government of Tripoli refusing to make restitution for the injuries done to his Majesty and his subjects, I seeing four of the Tripoli ships of war of considerable force in the Port of Tripoli, preparing to go out to cruise, I then having the fireships with me with fireworks, I fitted a fire boat accordingly out of them, commanding that all the boats of my squadron being 12 in number should be manned, armed and fitted with fireworks: Also I commanded a considerable officer to be commander in every boat, and my Lieutenant Cloudesley Shovell to be my Commander-in-Chief of them all, I, being resolved by God's permission that night to attack the enemies ships in their port, gave directions requisite to such a design.

About 12 of the clock in the night, my boats resolvedly entered the Port, seized the guardboat, boarded the ships, fired them, and utterly destroyed them all; some Turks and Moors slain, the rest fled to save themselves . These four ships lay under the deep castle walls, which were all that were in that port, excepting a Tunis merchant ship, which I ordered should not be meddled with, so escaped firing. This action was performed in less than an hours time without sustaining the least damage on our part, more than the expense of some ammunition, fireworks and fireboats which effectually were bestowed as designed, to the great astonishment of the Turks, that endeavoured to impede our design by plying several great and innumerable small shot at our boats and men, which were within pistol shot of the Dey's own castle and palace.

Such was the wonderful mercy of the Almighty God towards us, that not one man of ours was killed, wounded or touched, nor a boat anyways disabled, but all our men returned in safety, bringing the guard boat, two Moors and the Turkish colours of the two ships in triumph along with them, to my ship. Our men employed in the boats in this particular action were 157, they all behaving themselves as becometh Englishmen. And for present reward of their good service I caused this day 1,956 pieces of eight to be distributed among them. Names of the Tripoli ships of war that were burnt with their guns; White Crowned Eagle - 50 guns; Looking Glass - 34 guns; Sancta Chiaro - 24 guns; a French petach - 20 guns; a guard boat brought off with one pedreroe and two Moors in her.

From on board His majesties Ship Harwich at Maltha,
Febr.18th 1675-6   (Signed) John Narborough'[8]

Shovell's share of this generous reward was eighty pieces of eight; worth about £20, and sometime later application was made on his behalf to the

The largest of the bronze cannon recovered from the wreck site of the *Association* in 1967, showing the markings of the French crown. The breech carried a later incised addition of an English *'broad-arrow'*, the weight of '45 (cwt) 8(qtrs)' and the word *'Vigo'*, indicating that it had been captured by Shovell after the Battle of Vigo Bay and retained on board as a trophy.

Acknowledgement: Richard Larn

King, who personally granted him a medal and chain, to the value of £100.[9]

As a result of continuing good service, he was promoted to captain of the *Sapphire*, a 5th Rate, in 1677,[10] and remained in the Mediterranean for the next nine years continuing the fight against the Barbary Corsairs. In November 1679, with a squadron under Admiral Herbert, Captain Shovell was one of fifteen officers sent on shore with a party of seamen, to assist in the defence of Tangier against a besieging Moorish army. The enemy made desperate, but fruitless, attempts to storm the lines of defence, with heavy losses. The English suffered only minor casualties amongst who was Clowdisley Shovell, who was temporarily withdrawn with a wound.

Between 1681 and 1686, he was involved in several actions on board the *James Galley*, 30 guns, destroying and capturing Corsair vessels, two of which were taken into service as prizes, being the *Half Moon* and *Schiedam*. The former was captured after a long chase and fierce battle, in which the ships lay alongside for periods totalling five and a half hours at night. The Turk yielded only when they had lost fore, main and mizzen masts. Shovell reported:

> *'We found him to be the Half Moon, 32 guns, and come out from Argier, with 240 men of which 39 were christians, of which 20 English. They took a small English ship bound to Barmoodus, with seven English, which they have and burnt the vessel. The captain of the said Half Moon was a Turk and the lieutenant an English renegado, whom I caused to be hanged from the yardarm. The damage we received was 18 men killed and 30 wounded, and both main and foremast spoiled; we took him 45 leagues SW by W halfway from Cape*

Spartell.

There were killed upon him 93 Turks and Moors, and most of the living wounded, and they positively inform me that except the White Horse and 'Canaries' ship, there was not a better than she in Argier. The Sapphire had 17 men killed and 30 wounded (n.b. she was only briefly involved before losing her foremast and bow sprit), and by destroying the ablest of the Turks on the quarter-deck, much disposed them to surrender, though not able to come aboard her'.[11]

In 1683 the *Schiedam*, a Dutch flyboat captured by the Moors with her cargo of timber, was re-taken as a prize by the *James Galley*, under Shovell's command, near Gibraltar. At this time the adjacent port of Tangier was a centre of conflict. Given to Charles II as dowry on his marriage to Henrietta Maria, the city had become a severe financial embarrassment to the king due the hostility of the local moors and the marauding Sallee pirates. As a consequence Lord Dartmouth was employed in command of a major British naval and military expedition to evacuate the city, in which there were a great many English merchants, and not inconsiderable military force. The evacuation plan included the destruction of the harbour mole and city's defences, in order to prevent its future use as a haven by the pirates. The *Schiedam*, once named the *Great Schiedam* of Hoorn, was therefore laden with ordnance, horses and property belonging to English merchants, and sent home. On 4 April 1684, she was wrecked at Gunwalloe, in Mount's Bay, Cornwall, when her master, Gregory Fish, mistook the coast for part of France.[12] The wreck of the *Scheidam,* with its obscure connection with Shovell, was discovered by Tony Randall, a local diver from Helston in 1971. The site was later excavated by a team of local diver archaeologists, including the authors, under the protection of the 1973 Act for the Protection of Historic Wreck.

Returning to England in 1686, Shovell was appointed to the *Dover*, 48 guns. By the following year he had been appointed to the *Anne*, a third Rate of 70 guns, in which in June 1687, he was made temporary custodian of the treasure recovered from the Spanish treasure ship in the West Indies, and brought back by the celebrated Sir William Phipps. The Calender of State papers gives the following information:

'Warrant to Captain Clowdisley Shovell, Commander of the Anne, or in his absence to the officer on board the said ship riding at anchor in the Hope - after reciting that by warrant dated 8th Day of this instant he was directed to detain the ship James & Mary, Wm Phipps, Commander, and to put such sea-

men on board as judged necessary for securing her and preventing the taking out or other disposal of any of the plate on board her - forthwith upon receipt to take off the said guard and leave the said ship and cargo in the custody of the said William Phipps, notwithstanding any former order to the contrary'.[13]

This task was probably allocated to Shovell as the trusted friend of Sir John Narborough who, as one of the prime instigators of the salvage expedition, had a direct interest in the eventual proceeds of the treasure. It appears that the *Anne* later went into refit, Sir Clowdisley rejoining the *Dover* in which he was in command at the landing of King William in 1688, to whom he transferred his allegiance. From now on, the honours and acclaim came thick and fast. He distinguished himself at the battle of Bantry Bay, under Admiral Herbert on board the *Edgar*, for which he was knighted, the ceremony taking place on board the *Elizabeth* in Portsmouth, when the King also awarded ten shillings *'to every private sailor in the battle'*.[14] In June 1690, Sir Clowdisley was given the task of convoying William and an army to Ireland in 280 transports, having been given command of a squadron of six men o'war.

Title page of a commemorative booklet published in 1707, concerning the life of Sir Clowdisley Shovell.

Acknowledgement: British Library

The King, again impressed by Shovell's diligence and devotion to duty, not only appointed him Rear Admiral of the Blue, but also delivered him his commission with his own hands.[15] That same autumn, Shovell gave naval support to General Kirke at the siege of Waterford, in Ireland.[16]

One year later, in September 1691, in his capacity as a flag officer, he was part of a combined Anglo/Dutch fleet patrolling the English Channel under the command of Admiral Russell. Faced with a severe SE gale and in difficulties, the fleet ran for the shelter of Plymouth Sound. A number of the ships narrowly missed striking the Eddystone reef, others had difficulty in weathering Penlee Point, and a number ran foul of each other off Mount Edgcumbe, attempting to enter the Hamoaze, where the *Harwich*, a 3rd Rate, was totally wrecked. Amongst the men o'war that anchored off Rame Head in an attempt to weather the storm were the *Duchess*, *Coronation* and Sir Clowdisley Shovell's flagship, the *London*, all 2nd Rates. From her poop deck he personally witnessed, from only a few cables distance, the *Coronation* cut away all her masts, capsize and founder with the loss of over 600 men, including two companies of the newly formed regiment of Marine, less than one mile from the cliffs of Rame head.[17] Sir Clowdisley was, in fact, nominated major of the First Regiment of Marines in 1691, Lieutenant Colonel in 1692, and a full colonel of the Second Regiment in 1698, appointments which were lucrative sinecures, bearing in mind his almost constant sea service.

Further personal service to the crown took place in the October following the *Coronation* disaster, when Shovell's squadron escorted the King, on board the yacht *Mary,* from Holland to England. Next spring, having been appointed Rear Admiral of the Red, he was given command of the squadron that escorted the King back to Holland. On his return to England, he joined Russell's fleet in time to play a major role in the famous victory of Cape Barfleur and La Hogue. Unfortunately, a sudden bout of illness prevented his completion of the victory.[18] He was to have commanded the flotilla sent inshore to burn the capital ships stranded in the shallows of the Bay of La Hogue, but Admiral Rooke took his place. In this battle, the French were utterly defeated, losing sixteen warships burnt or totally destroyed. Amongst them were several flagships and the great *Soleil Royal*, the 104 gun flagship of Count de Tourville, Admiral of the Fleet, which *'occasioned infinite mortification to the French king and the utmost degree of despondency to King James.'*[19]

In 1694, Sir Clowdisley was promoted to Vice-Admiral of the Red and given the command, initially under Lord Berkeley, of the abortive expedition to Camaret Bay, at the entrance to Brest harbour. Although the attack with frigates, bomb vessels and fireships was unsuccessful, no blame was attached to Shovell. His behaviour in this instance has been described as follows:

'Sir Clowdesley Shovell, however, took care to demonstrate from his con-

duct, that there was no fault lay in him: for he went with a boat within the enemy's works, and so became an eye witness of the impossibility of doing what his orders directed to be done; and therefore on his coming home, he was perfectly well received, and continued to be employed as a man who would command success, where it was possible; and omit nothing in his power, where it was not'.[20]

In October 1696 whilst blockading Brest he was promoted to Admiral of the Blue and for the remainder of that war against France, which ended with

Sir Clowdisley Shovell, as Rear Admiral of the Red, painted in oils when on board the *Royal William*, circa January 1692, and reproduced as a lithograph.

Acknowledgement: Terry Hiron

the Treaty of Ryswick in 1697, he was employed principally in commanding the bombardment of French ports and their blockade. He was appointed Extra Commissioner of the Navy on 20 April 1693. This was followed two years later with an appointment to the position of Comptroller of Victualling, in March 1699. He held this office until Christmas Day 1704.[21]

In 1702, William III died as a result of a riding accident, to be succeeded by Queen Anne, who in alliance with the Dutch, opposed Spain and France in the War of the Spanish Succession. This year Shovell was appointed Admiral of the White, command of the English Grand Fleet having gone to Sir George Rooke. Rooke initially attempted to take Cadiz but managed only to capture the poorly defended Rota. Receiving intelligence that the treasure fleet from the West Indies had put into Vigo Bay under convoy of a French squadron, he sailed north with his fleet and launched a brilliant action against stiff resistance. Although successful, the English suffered many casualties (the *Torbay*, 80 guns, for example, having over 100 killed). The combined English/Dutch fleet forced the defence boom, and captured or burned twenty-one French men o'war with no less than 960 guns.[22] They also captured eleven of the treasure ships and sank five others, bringing home money and merchandise to the value of some 7,000,000 reales of eight (£1,750,000).

Unfortunately, Sir Clowdisley, who was at sea with a small squadron specially fitted and patrolling with orders from the cabinet to intercept the treasure fleet, did not arrive at Vigo until 16 October, by which time fighting had ceased. Rooke then departed for England with the bulk of the fleet. Shovell remained behind, tasked with bringing home as many prize ships as he could put into sailing order, burning the remainder after salvaging as many guns and as much merchandise and silver as he could carry. In a quite remarkable display of zeal and organising ability, but remembering that there was a considerable amount of personal prize money at stake, Sir Clowdisley took only one week to collect sixty iron cannon from the forts and batteries around the harbour. A further sixty bronze guns, most of which weighed between 50 and 60cwt, were gathered from the French ships run onshore and transported, before he departed on the 24th. (This was obviously the source of the French bronze cannon carried on board the *Association*, and salvaged in the Isles of Scilly following the discovery of the wreck in 1967.) A petition was made on his behalf later, to the Queen, for a Royal Bounty as a reward for his diligence, citing the sixty brass guns recovered.[23]

The year 1703 saw Shovell promoted to Commander-in-Chief of the Confederate fleet, comprising thirty-five English and fourteen Dutch warships, stationed in the Mediterranean. This expedition was ill conceived, Sir Clowdisley having been given an inadequate force, insufficiently victualled, and sent too late in the season to achieve the task ordered by the Admiralty. The fleet did not depart until the end of June, with orders to return by the end of September, and Shovell rightly protested. Nevertheless, in the limited time available, he managed to acquit himself well, and was not blamed for the limited results.[24] One incident of note, which serves to illustrate his character, concerned the refusal of the Governor of Leghorn to accord a royal salute on entry of the fleet into the Roads. Sir Clowdisley peremptorily ordered the salute to be made, *'or to expect all the guns of the fleet to ask the same question.'*[25] Needless to say, the threat sufficed.

With his flag in the 96 gun *Barfleur*, in June 1704, Shovell reinforced the fleet which successfully bombarded and captured Gibraltar under Sir George Rooke. That August, in the sea battle that followed off Malaga, the Anglo/Dutch fleet managed to put up a considerable fight, despite a very limited supply of shot, against a French force of slightly superior strength. Once again Admiral Shovell proved his

Illustration of Sir Clowdisley Shovell and title page of a commemorative book, published in London in 1708.

Acknowledgement: British Library

ability as a seaman, by maintaining such heavy and accurate fire, that his squadron prevented part of the English fleet from being cut off. At one point he ordered the ships of his squadron to deliberately set their sails aback, so that they went astern, much to the surprise of the enemy.[26]

The loss of life on both sides was considerable, Sir Clowdisley's squadron of nine ships, the *Barfleur, Eagle, Orford, Assurance, Warspite, Swiftsure, Nottingham, Tilbury* and *Lenox*, suffering 106 killed and 303 wounded.[27] Summing up the battle, Sir George Rooke, Commander-in-Chief on board the *Royal Katherine*, which bore the brunt of the fight in the centre of the line, losing twenty-seven dead and ninety-four wounded, had this to say in his report:

'Sir Clowdesley and other flag officers of our van and rear do say the

enemy did not behave themselves well in those stations, but I'm sure those in the centre did their duty very valiantly; and I must say that every officer in our line did his duty without the least umbrage for censure or reflection, and I never observed the English spirit more prevalent and apparent in our seamen than on this occasion'.

At the other end of the scale, Matthew Bishop, a seaman on board the *Swiftsure*, part of Shovell's division, remarked: '- *all the officers behaved with gaiety, and their actions were gallant. The sailors were very diligent in observing their commands'.*[28]

Both sides claimed a victory at Malaga but the French, for the remainder of the war, which was to last seven years, never again attempted to face a Confederate fleet in battle. Although only second in command, Sir Clowdisley won the principal credit for the victory, and on his return to England was given the honour of being presented to the Queen by Prince George, the Lord High Admiral. On Boxing Day 1704, Shovell was promoted to Rear Admiral of the Fleet of England, and eighteen days later, on 13 January 1705 was made Admiral and Commander-in-Chief of the Fleet, '*to wear the Union flag at the Main'.*[29]

That same year saw the campaign against Barcelona, in which Sir Clowdisley jointly commanded the fleet with the Earl of Peterborough, until the latter disembarked with his troops, leaving the conduct of the ships entirely to the admiral. The following extract of a letter, written by Sir Clowdisley Shovell to Prince George of Denmark, shows the degree to which the fleet contributed to the venture:

'The 17th, our battery of thirty guns was opened, and fourteen of them began to play, with very great execution, upon that part of the wall where the breach was designed: the Earl of Peterborough came aboard, and represented to us the great necessity he laboured under for want of money for subsisting the army, and carrying on the siege of Barcelona, and the services of Catalonia, and in very pressing circumstances, desired the assistance of the fleet: upon which our flag officer came to the enclosed resolution: To lend the Earl of Peterborough forty thousands dollars out of the contingent and short allowance-money of the fleet. The 19th, we came to these resolutions; viz. To remain longer before Barcelona than was agreed on at first; to give all the assistance in our power, and to lay a fireship a-shore with 200 barrels of powder; and a further demand being made for guns for the batteries, we landed fourteen more, which made up in all 72 guns, whereof 30 were 24 pounders that we landed here, with their utensils and ammunition.

We continued to bombard the town from the sea, as our small store of shells and the weather will permit. The 20th, a demand was made for more shot, and we called together the English flag officers, and came to a resolution to supply all the batteries with all the 24 and 28 pound shot, except a very small quantity, which was accordingly done. The 22nd, the Prince of Liechenstein and the Earl of Peterborough having desired, at the request of his Catholic Majesty, that the town of Lerida might, for its security, be furnished with about 50 barrels of powder, and a further supply of shot being demanded from the batteries a-shore, it was considered at a council of war, and we came to the enclosed resolution, viz. to furnish 50 barrels of powder for Lerida, and to send so many more 24 and 18 pound shot ashore, as would reduce the English to 30 rounds, as likewise to be farther assistant upon timely notice. The 23rd, at night, our breach being made, and all things prepared for an attack, the town was again summoned, and they desired to capitulate, and hostages were exchanged; on our side, Brigadier Stanhope, and on the enemy's, the Marquis de Rivera; and all hostilities ceased'.

Sir Clowdisley's shrewd counsel and personal endeavours, including the landing guns and seamen to man them, encouraged the Council of War to continue the siege. His contribution ultimately led to the success of the expedition, and the capture of the city.[30]

Notes for Chapter 11

1. Archibald E.H. *The Wooden Fighting Ship*, p124-133 (London 1968)
2. *DNB,* Vol 40 p89 & Vol 52 p159
3. ADM 33/103 Ticket No 55; Le Fevre P. Mariner's Mirror, Vol 70 Pt 1 p92 (Feb 1984)
4. Anderson. *Journals -Narratives of the Third Dutch War*, p97 & 102 (NRS 1946)
5. Ibid, p154; ADM 33/91 Ticket No 1076; Le Fevre P. MM, Vol 70 Pt 1
6. ADM 33/104 Ticket No 1398; Le Fevre P. MM, Ibid. Note. Young gentlemen who were candidates for commissioned rank passed through a number of ratings, one of which was master's mate. As implied he was an assistant to the ship's master, learning navigation and seamanship under his tuition and perhaps aspiring to a master's warrant. Hence, potential lieutenants served for a while as master's mates.
7. ADM 33/98 Ticket No 680; Le Fevre P. MM, Ibid; DNB, Vol 40 p89
8. Dyer F.E. *The Life of Sir John Narborough,* p151 (London 1931); Campbell R. *Lives of the Admiral's,* Vol IV p239 (London 1812); Charnock J. *Biographia Navalis*, Vol II p16 (London 1795); Nav. Chr. Vol 33 p178
9. *Pepys MSS,* Vol 33 p398 (NRS)
10. Nav.Chr. Vol 33 p179
11. Charnock J. *Biographia Navalis,* Vol II p17-18
12. Fish was held to be incompetent, but Samuel Pepys, employed on the expedition as an observer, returning home on another vessel in the same fleet made some interesting comments on the difficulties of deep sea sounding and navigation in the approaches. (see Chapter 1) *'Strange the disagreements in so fair a weather with so fair a wind immediately on a fair observation and clear soundings at 65 fathom and 49°34' latitude*

among our navigators about the entrance to the channel, My Lord (Dartmouth) and Mr. Phillips being very positive that we were shot to the eastward of Scilly whilst Sir William Booth and the master and mates were of the opinion that we were yet to the westward and one part of them being apprehensive of our running upon the French coast, and the other upon the English, some being for lying by all night, others for sailing boldly forward as we did, due east'. Chapell E.(Ed) *The Tangier Papers of Samuel Pepys,* p248 (NRS 1935); Dartmouth MSS, HMC Report Vol II p115

13. CSP Dom. 1687 44/337 p287
14. Nav.Chr. Vol 33 p181
15. Ibid, Vol 33 p182
16. Ibid
17. Finch MSS, HMC Reports Vol IV p251; ADM 52/57 Master's Journal, *London* (Charles Brittish)
18. This may have been gout, since a London newspaper dated 14th March 1690 stated *'he was indisposed with gout, and went not with his squadron on a previous voyage'.* HMC 12th Report Pt VII p320
19. Nav. Chr. Vol 33 p183-91; Campbell. *Lives of the Admirals,* Vol IV p244; DNB, Vol52 p159
20. Charnock, Vol II p20
21. DNB, Vol 52 p160
22. Nav. Chr. Vol 33 p195
23. CSP Treasury 1702-7 Vol LXXXIX Entry 87; Nav. Chr. Vol 33 p196
24. Nav. Chr. Vol 33 p197-8
25. Styles S. *Admiral of England* (1978)
26. Laird-Clowes W. *The Royal Navy, A History,* Vol IV p397-402 (London 1897)
27. Campbell, Vol IV p249-50
28. Owen J.H. *The War at Sea under Queen Anne,* 1702-1708, p96 (Cambridge 1938); *House of Lords* MSS No 2058 p173
29. Campbell, Vol IV p250; DNB Vol 52 p160
30. Nav. Chr. Vol 33 p206-7

Chapter Twelve

The Siege of Toulon

The siege of Toulon was the last campaign of Sir Clowdisley Shovell's long and distinguished career. Since all the ships destined to be involved in the Isles of Scilly disaster took part, the siege is worthy of a full account. The capture of Toulon had been the prime objective in the naval war, ever since Savoy joined the Grand Alliance in 1703. Such a project if successful, would spell the ruin of French sea power in the Mediterranean. For want of a suitable base within the Straits, from which the allied fleet could operate the whole year round, the English men o'war were forced to run the gauntlet of bad weather, in going out early and returning home late each year. (see page 5) With Toulon in Allied hands the vital problem of a suitable base for the Confederate Fleet would be solved once and for all.

With this grand strategy in mind, Shovell, Admiral of the White and Commander in Chief, arrived off Nice and Antibes with his squadron of warships in June 1707, assisted by Sir George Byng and Sir John Norris. Shovell's orders were to co-operate with the land forces of the Imperial Army, commanded by the Duke of Savoy and his brother, Prince Eugene, with the capture of Toulon the prime objective.

From June until the end of September, the great cabin of the *Association* was the setting for numerous councils of war, attended by many high-ranking officers and officials. The first of these took place on 29 June. A surviving account offers an interesting insight as to the admiral's accommodation on board, and possibly offers an explanation as to why the *Association*, a 2nd Rate ship, was frequently employed as a flag ship in preference to one of the larger 1st Rates. On this occasion, those attending the meeting included the Duke of Savoy, Prince Eugene, most of the general officers, as well as English and Dutch ministers.

Sir Clowdisley, although perhaps not the politest of senior officers, was very rich in his own right and *'showed a great deal of prudence and address, in the magnificent entertainment he made upon this occasion'*. Having boarded the *Association*, the Duke found a guard of halberdiers, all in new livery, at the great cabin door. At the upper end of the table, set with no less than 'sixty' covers, was an armchair with a crimson velvet canopy. Everything was so well ordered and managed that his Royal Highness, commenting on the

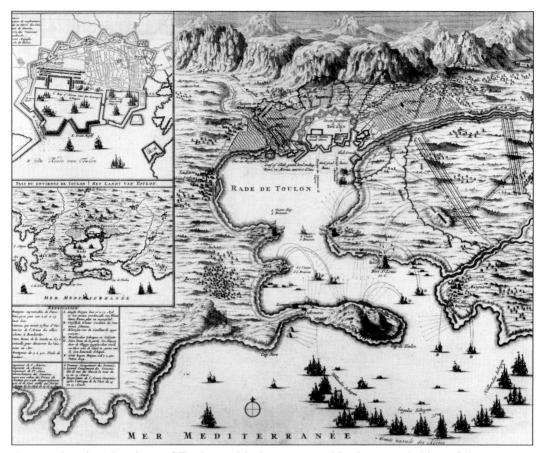

A map showing the siege of Toulon, with the town, and harbour, and ships of the Confederate fleet blockading the entrance and carrying out a bombardment of the shore batteries.

Acknowledgement: National Maritime Museum

sumptuous dinner that followed the conference, said, '*If your Excellency had paid me a visit at Turin, I could scarcely have treated you so well*'.[1]

Shovell's earliest endeavours were directed at obtaining sufficient supplies and ammunition for the army. To this end he sent two ships to Gibraltar for 12,000 rounds of shot, purchased more on private credit from Italy, and offered to reduce the fleet's stock to thirty-five rounds per gun.[2] The passage of the Duke's army to Toulon was blocked by an enemy strongly entrenched along the line of the River Var with 800 dragoons and six battalions of foot soldiers. Realising the vulnerability of the seaward defences, Shovell ordered the *Monmouth, Panther, Tilbury, Romney, Rye, and Landskroon,* with the two bomb vessels *Basilisk* and *Blast,* and the yacht *Isabella*, to the mouth of the river, to commence a bombardment.

One of the three bronze guns recovered from the *Association* site by the Roland Morris diving team. Measuring some 9ft.6in (3.05m) in length and weighing in excess of 2 tonnes, each bore the arms of various French nobles. This gun carries the mark of *'Le Comte de Vermandois'*. One such gun can be seen in the Tower of London Collection; another stands on a replica gun-carriage as part of the Valhalla Collection, Tresco. Others are to be found in the Museum of Nautical Art, Penzance, and one is in private hands.

Acknowledgement: Roland Morris

Simultaneously, Sir John Norris landed with 600 seamen and marines in open boats. By this action, the enemy was out-flanked with few casualties occurring on the allied side, but further up river, where the Duke had attacked and crossed with 8,000 troops, over 100 were swept away by the fierce current and drowned.[3]

From intelligence sources, Sir Clowdisley learnt that Toulon was still only weakly defended, manned by a limited garrison consisting mainly of some 2,000 seamen from the blockaded French fleet. Realising the vulnerability of the town to attack, he urged the Duke to press on, but the army was weary from the long march, and for that and other reasons the Duke delayed. He arrived at Toulon in twelve days, instead of the planned six, by which time fortifications had been strengthened, and the town had received considerable military reinforcement. He now faced a determined enemy.[4] To the north of the town lay the heights of Mont Faron, with a crest running east/west for two miles, and it was from here, with five companies of grenadiers, that the Duke was able to dislodge the garrison.

From Mont Faron Admiral Norris reported:

'The town has ten bastions, a shallow dry ditch, but no palisadoes or out-works to the bastions and curtains. In the two basins lay their ships without masts or anything, I believe, on board them. I endeavoured to count them, but could not distinguish them; but I judge the number of men-of-war to be upwards of forty sail; they seem to lay lashed on board of each other, and most-ly in the West Basin. The front of the basins to the water is walled as high as a ship and has an entire range of cannon placed upon it; and at each end of the town are placed a three deck ship to help flank any attack that should be against the town. Between the two land gates of the town towards the moun-tain (Faron) their army lay encamped in two lines; but the tents looked thin, our officers did not judge them above 7,000 men, and they had made entrench-ments and were working them. There are many fine forts and batteries that command the two roads (harbours) and they seemed to be so narrow that a ship cannot anyways ride, but it is commanded by one shore or the other'.

Nearly all the ships Norris saw were preparing to scuttle, it being the intention that the three deck ships would lie with their upper decks out of water, the rest to be completely submerged, so that they could not be set alight by shells or other incendiary shot. The two, three-decked ships men-tioned in the report were *Le Tonnant* and *Le Saint-Philippe*, both of 90 guns, turned into floating batteries, protected overhead and on their sides by mantlets of rope and planks, and screened from attack by fireships with floating booms or stockades. Both ships were later moved to the eastern flank of the harbour and performed gallant service. Seamen and gunners, organised in eight brigades of 300 men each, manned the fixed defences of the port and new batteries of naval guns taken on shore.[5]

The Allies prepared their defences by digging two parallel lines running north and south, one from the eastern edge of Mount Faron, through the plateau d'Artigues and Fort St. Catherine, to the hill of Malgue, and a sec-ond line from La Valette to the foreshore. But these preparations all took time, during which the French opposition and strength increased with every passing day, so that by the end of August they numbered some 30,000 assorted troops.

Towards the end of July the first of the Allied batteries were ready, and the Duke requested that the gunners be sent on shore, and by the end of July Sir Clowdisley had provided over 100 heavy guns with sufficient men to man them. He also suggested the assault on Fort St. Louis and St. Margaret's Castle, and promised help by cannonading from the sea.[6]

Throughout the preparations and subsequent siege, Sir Clowdisley acceded to every request from the Duke and particularly the Prince, '- *in order to engage Prince Eugene to go vigorously on with this affair here, for I believe it stops most on his account*', he told Norris. Unfortunately, it would seem the Prince was never fully committed, wishing to give up the attempt, fearing attack from the rear.[7] Acting almost as an advisory, Shovell, with great diplomacy, not only encouraged them all, but offered counsel and placed the fleet almost entirely at their disposal. When finally the Duke's resolve began to fail in the face of successful French attacks, coupled with the low moral of his own troops, Sir Clowdisley delayed their departure whilst he attempted the destruction of the French fleet which was trapped within the harbour.[8]

The intention was to destroy first the shore batteries that kept the Allied fleet at bay and then attack the French ships where they lay. Unusually severe weather hampered progress, but on 30 July the marines landed at Cape Brun and overset a battery of thirteen guns. St. Margaret's Castle with a garrison of 130 seamen surrendered on 4 August. The next day another battery of nine guns were destroyed by the English men o'war *Tryton*, *Milford* and *Falcon*, and a further three guns by the *Somerset* and *Lancaster* the day after.[9]

On 7 August, three days before the siege ended and the army withdrew, Fort St. Louis fell:

'- *the seamen having made a practicable breach in the fort, a detachment of the army was ordered to storm it, but at their approach they found the enemy had abandoned the fort; there were 22 cannon, most of which they spiked up*'.[10]

Two days of bad weather followed, but this did not prevent Sir Thomas Dilkes from going ashore, accompanied by the captain of the bomb-vessel *Blast*, to take '*a view of Toulon and set marks how to bombard*'.

Shortly after dawn on the 10th, the *Basilisk*, *Blast*, *Granado* and two Dutch ketches sailed close in, and anchored in the bight between the Grand Tower and the ruins of Fort St. Louis. Dilkes then shifted his flag to the *Romney*, and took the flotilla, reinforced with the *Centurion, Aldeborough*,

Enterprise and two Dutch frigates, closer inshore. To their surprise they came under quite heavy fire, the French having already mounted a new battery on shore, to replace one destroyed three days earlier.[11]

The bombardment commenced at 2pm, and went on right through the night until the morning of 11 August. The Allied fleet fired a number of carcass shot, setting fire to ships and storehouses, besides over 500 rounds of shell, about 100 from each ketch. They also succeeded in setting on fire and destroying *Le Sage*, 58 guns, *and Le Fortune*, 52 guns, both of which had been afloat, whilst the scuttled *Le Diamant* had her upper deck burnt, and the frigates *L'Andromede* and *La Salamandre* were badly damaged.

The following morning Dilkes was forced to withdraw, since under cover of darkness, the French had mounted another larger battery, using main armament cannon from the bigger vessel, so that the ketches in particular were much damaged as day came on. Shovell then called a council of war, which resolved that any further bombardment was impracticable and unsafe. *'I would we had more time'*, he told Byng,'*but they brought the big guns to the waterside and mauled our bomb vessels'*.[12] This was the last naval action of the expedition.

The Allied fleet sailed from Toulon next morning, covering the retreat of the army along the coast to the river Var, where 3,000 sick and wounded men were taken on board the ships.[13] There was no hiding the fact that Sir Clowdisley was very disappointed with the limited success of the campaign, but Marlborough took a different attitude:

> *'This diversion has been one of great use to the King of Spain (an ally at that time), and likewise put a stop to the successes of the French in Germany by the detachments they were obliged to make from all parts of the Province'.*

In fact, the achievements were substantial, Shovell having taken every step within his power to ensure that the French Mediterranean fleet was no longer an effective one. *'Toulon est sauf; mais notre flotte est defunte,'* wrote M. de la Ronciere, the French historian. Several of the warships had broken their backs lying aground in the basins, others were too leaky or damaged to repair, many had been sacrificed as barriers to protect the others, and of course, many had been destroyed by the bombardment. In point of fact, only a small part of this once fine fleet ever sailed out of Toulon again.[14]

One of the reasons advanced for the failure of the capture of Toulon was the Duke of Savoy's suspicion of the zeal and activities of the fleet from the outset. This was possibly due to some seed of jealousy sewn by the Earl of

Peterborough. Norris wrote to Shovell:

'- the Duke asked me if the fleet when Rook commanded did not stay in the Mediterranean until September; I told him I did not remember, but I believed if he was necessitated, you would endeavour to serve his commands to that time; if I have slipped too much I pray pardon for the same, but my meaning was he should have no jealousy of our leaving him; after this he said My Lord Peterborow had told him that the fleet would only embarrass by councils of war and do nothing. I told him my Lord had little reason to blame us, and that I could wish we were of that force we was with him at Barcelona, where I might modestly say the Sea contributed more than my Lord's Land to the taking of that place'.[15]

Clearly the Earl of Peterborough's tactlessness had had far reaching results.

Sir Clowdisley Shovell then sailed for Gibraltar, leaving only a few ships behind to act as transports in case the Duke decided to send reinforcements to Spain. The remainder of the fleet divided again at Gibraltar. A few were ordered to delay their departure and escort the homeward bound trade convoys in December. Others were to remain on station in the Mediterranean under the command of Dilkes and Convent, while the rest, under the command of Shovell, Byng and Norris, left for England, to face the tragic and fatal consequence of their very late departure, which the capture of Toulon might have avoided.[16]

Notes for Chapter 12
1. Campbell, Vol III p516
2. Captain's Journal, *Panther*; Shovell to Marlborough 3/14th July, Owen J.H. *The War at Sea under Queen Anne, 1702-1708*
3. Captains' Journals, *Monmouth & Blast; Byng Papers,* Vol I p220; Owen, p169-70
4. Shovell to Marlborough 3rd July; Eugene to Marlborough 2/13 July; *Byng Papers,* Vol I pp204, 219, 223; Murray, Gen Sir G. J. *The Letters of John Churchill - First Duke of Marlborough,* Vol III p281-2; Owen, p167
5. Ronciere De La C. *Histoire de la Marine Francais,* p391-4 (Paris 1899); BM Add MSS 28141; Brun V. *Guerres Maritime de la France,* Vol I p119-21 (Paris 1861); Owen, p173-4
6. Owen J.H. *The War at Sea under Queen Anne, 1702-1708*, p174-7(Cambridge 1938)
7. Captain's Journal, *Royal Anne; Byng Papers,* Vol I p199-207, 228; Owen, p176
8. Owen, p181
9. Ibid p182, 185-7
10. Norris's Journal, 7th Aug 1707
11. Captain's Journals, *Basilisk, Chichester, Centurion & Aldeburgh;* Brun, p124; Jonge J.C. *Geschiedenis Van Het Nederlandsche Zeewesen,* Vol IV p10 (1853/62); Owen,

   p188.
12. Captain's Journals, *Basilisk, Blast* & *Aldeburgh*; Norris's Journal; Lieut's Journal, *Enterprise;* Byng Papers, Vol I p213-4; La Ronciere, p394; Owen, p189
13. Captain's Journal, *Royal Anne*; Master's Journals' *Somerset, Newark*; Norris's Journal; Byng Papers, Vol I p210, 213; Owen, p191
14. Marlborough to Shovell, 17/28 Sept. 1707, Murray; La Ronciere, p395; Owen, p191
15. Byng Papers, Vol I p235; Norris to Shovell, 23 July 1707, BM, Add MSS 28141
16. Owen, p190.

Chapter Thirteen

The 'Great Storm' of 1703 and Other Historic Events.

'The Lord hath his way in the Whirlwind and in the Storm, and the Clouds are the dust of his Feet'.

D. Defoe - 1704 (Epigraph to the 'The Storm' - Nahum 1:3)

All four of Admiral Shovell's ships, lost in the Scilly's disaster, fought or participated in historic engagements at sea whilst British maritime power and prestige was in its ascendancy in the successive reigns of William and Anne. Additionally the *Eagle* and *Association,* together with Admiral Shovell in the *Russell,* experienced the greatest of jeopardy in an earlier epic maritime disaster in 1703 caused by the greatest gale ever to sweep the shores of Britain. The events were dramatically catalogued by Daniel Defoe in a pamphlet the following year.

At the battle of Barfleur in 1692, the *Eagle*, commanded by Captain (later Admiral) John Leake, was in the centre or Red Squadron of the combined Anglo/Dutch fleet. After the action on 20-21 May, in which the smaller French fleet was decisively beaten, Vice-Admiral Rooke was ordered to destroy the surviving French ships, which ran into the shallow waters of the Bay of La Hogue. Rooke had flown his flag in the 2nd Rate *Neptune*, but for this part of the action transferred into the smaller, shallow draught *Eagle*, in order to get closer to the French ships, some of which had hauled themselves ashore, the larger vessels grounding in an attempt to avoid capture. Boats of the fleet were employed in burning thirteen French men o'war, amongst which were eight three-deckers, including *Le Merveilleux*, 96 guns, and *Le Ambiteux*, 104 guns, both flagships. Although the French fought bravely throughout, they were utterly defeated by a superior force at the end of a six-day operation.[1] The *Eagle* was later rebuilt in 1699 at a slightly higher tonnage, and subsequently recommissioned in 1701.

The 12 August 1702, saw the *Eagle* as part of the Confederate fleet which captured Rota, near Cadiz, for the Archduke Charles, but she took no part in the subsequent battle involving the famous capture of the Spanish treasure galleons at Vigo. On the other hand, the *Association* played a very prominent part in the Vigo affair, being assigned with the *Barfleur* to engage Forts Corbeyon and Rande respectively, being the north and south batteries commanding the entrance to Redondela harbour. The attack created a diversion, during which time the main boom was forced, and the harbour and shipping attacked by the fleet. As described in Chapter 12, the operation was a total success and Shovell was destined to bring home the captured booty, including the bronze cannon retained as war trophies on board the *Association*.[2] That same year, the *Romney* took part in protecting the routine convoy to Russia.

The year 1703 saw the event that history has described as the 'Great Storm', a disaster of major proportions for the British fleet, in which Sir Clowdisley, on board his flagship *Russell*, along with the *Association* and the *Eagle,* were in desperate trouble. This was the worst storm in Britain's recorded history, which began at 11pm Thursday, 27 November and continued unabated for several days.

In London, the Thames overflowed reaching a great height inside Westminster Hall, and Queen Anne was taken into the cellar of St. James Palace to protect her from the danger of being injured by falling chimney-stacks and tiles. London Bridge was stopped up with the wrecks of ships and small craft, of which there were 700 recorded in the Thames alone.

At Plymouth, three merchantmen were wrecked and the newly built Eddystone lighthouse was completely destroyed. When the gale abated nothing of the lighthouse remained above water and its renowned engineer-designer, Henry Winstanley, together with all his workers and keepers had completely disappeared. In London the havoc wrought was estimated at around £1m, and in the City of Bristol, in excess of £150,000.[3]

The navy suffered the greatest damage and tragic misfortune. Thirteen ships were either lost or destroyed, resulting in the death by drowning of over two thousand seamen.

Sir Clowdisley Shovell, returning from the Mediterranean late in the season, had left the Downs for the River Thames with part of the fleet which included the 2nd Rates; *Association, Triumph, St. George*, and the 3rd Rates *Revenge, Cambridge, Dorsetshire* and *Royal Oak*. As they anchored at the Gunfleet they caught the full fury of the storm. Sir Clowdisley with his flag in the *Russell*, 80 guns, commanded by Captain Isaac Townsend, was forced to veer out three cables on the best bower anchor, but even so it parted in the gale and she began to drift. Her main sheet anchor and several small anchors were then let go, with all the available cable attached in an attempt to stop her dragging onto the Galloper Sands.

At 4pm Friday the 28th, the crew was obliged to cut away her long boat, which was being towed astern. Soon afterwards the tiller of the rudder gave way, and before it could be secured, the entire rudder was torn completely away, starting a severe leak at the stern post and allowing water to enter the bread and fish rooms. Four hand-pumps and the main chain-pump were manned continuously in a desperate attempt to keep the water level under control. In a last ditch attempt to lighten the stern to make up for the loss of weight in the bow and draw water forward to the pumps, her poop and quarter-deck guns were thrown overboard. Finally, in a desperate attempt to save the *Russell,* Sir Clowdisley ordered her main mast to be cut down. The ship miraculously managed to ride out the storm all night, but continued to drive towards the Dutch coast all the following day.

Burchett continues the account:

'On Sunday the wind was at WNW and NW and it being judged that the s*hips drew near to Goree, it was concluded that she must unavoidably drive on shore by midnight. The Captain therefore ordered two guns to be slung with the top chains, and made them fast to the Sheet Cables, that so her d*int to the l*and might be slower. At six at n*ight *falling into twelve and fourteen f*athom *of water, he had sight of a light, which he took to be either the Island of Goree, or of Schowen.*

At half an hour past ten the ship came into seven fathoms of water, and then her commander let go his stream, and strapped it to a kedge anchor, in hopes the cable which the guns were made fast to, and this veered to the bitter end, would ride her in so shoal water, but she came head to wind in five fathom and dragging all home tailed into four, when she struck twice, but not violently. The water deepened to five, six, seven and eight fathom and it was very smooth, but the stream cable soon broke, and cast the ship northward so that she drove with the wind on the beam, and a great breach was seen to the leeward; whereupon they cut away the cables, and set her foresail and foretopsail with all possible diligence, by which they were in four fathom and a half and immediately the ship struck, but swimming still by the stern, the blow put her right before the wind, and so she miraculously got over the shoal, after she had touched several times.

The water soon deepened from four to twelve fathom, and then became gradually lower, until they pitched her on shore on the ooze, about two miles below Helvoet-Sluys, a little after three in the morning; from whence, by the great pains and particular industry of her commander, she was gotten off, and

A large bronze bell, bearing the broad-arrow mark of the British Government, recovered from the wreck site of the fire-ship *Firebrand,* near Menglow Rock, St. Agnes, by Mark Horobin, a member of the Roland Morris team.

Acknowledgement: Peter McBride

put in a condition to come to England in little time'.[4]

After the gale four vessels were missing, namely the *Russell, Association, Revenge* and *Dorsetshire.* Sir Stafford Fairborn, Vice-Admiral of the Red, with his flag in the *Association,* also got into difficulties. Her anchor cable parted at 4am, when the pilot had the sheet anchor let go, veering out a cable and a half:

'*- But the ship not looking towards it, she drove about seven in the morning over the north end of the Galloper, in eight fathom of water, where there broke against her so great a sea, that it made her lye along for some time, without any of her righting again. The ship soon drove into deeper water and dragged her small bower anchor, with the best bower and sheet cables; but at length, by the help of a piece of spritsail, (the wind being too violent for more) they wore her and brought her to with her head northward'.*

The other ships were driven clean to the coast of Holland, whilst the *Association* was given up for lost. In driving over the Galloper, her rudder was unshipped, and the great seas, which broke against her, smashed in her entry port, allowing the sea to enter between decks. The *Association* was driven north all the way to Gothenburgh, where she arrived on 11

December, having lost her longboat, pinnace, three anchors, and all her cables. She was also in dire need of fresh water and provisions. She did not arrive back in England until 15 January, after obtaining assistance in Copenhagen. Elsewhere off the English coast many other warships were wrecked or had disappeared in the same storm.

On the Goodwin Sands there was a catalogue of disaster; Rear Admiral Beaumont was lost with the *Mary*, 60 guns and the *Northumberland*, *Restoration* and *Stirling Castle*, all 70 guns, were also total wrecks with some eighty survivors between them. The 'Great Storm of 1703' and Sir Clowdisley Shovell's disaster of 1707, rate as the greatest tragedies in the long history of the Royal Navy.[5]

In 1704, the *Eagle*, commanded by Lord Archibald Hamilton, took part in the siege of Gibraltar, being one of the ships detailed to attack the South Bastion. As she anchored with the fleet in the bay, heavy gunfire from the many forts forced her, along with other ships, to lay further offshore. Despite this initial opposition, the allied bombardment was a success, and 1,800 marines were landed by the fleet, and captured the city.[6]

In the resultant battle with the Franco-Spanish fleet off Malaga a month later, *Eagle* as part of Shovell's squadron, was one of three men o'war left isolated, outnumbered and heavily engaged by the enemy. Two hours before nightfall on 13 August, the *Eagle* had to be towed out of the line when she ran out of shot, her casualties being seven killed, and fifty-seven wounded. The *Firebrand*, commanded by Captain Henry Turvill, was also involved in this battle, and Captain Hancock, later appointed to the *Eagle* and lost with her in the Scilly's, was captain of *Assurance*, part of Shovell's squadron, which was commended for its vital contribution to that battle.[7]

The *Romney* was cruising to the Elbe and Norway in 1705, returning home before the winter set in, whilst that September the *Eagle* took part in Shovell's expedition which played a major role in the capture of Barcelona.[8] Both were also involved in the reduction of Ostend in 1706, and sailed with the Grand Fleet to Lisbon under Shovell's command.

In December, Captain Coney, commander of the *Romney*, distinguished himself by capturing a valuable French privateer of sixteen guns, which was lying under the protection of the Malaga Roads forts. On board, in her hold, were thirty bronze guns, recently salvaged from the *Magnamine*, a French warship driven on shore some twelve leagues away.

On Boxing Day 1706, in company with the *Milford* and the *Fowey*, the

Romney attacked and blew up the *Content*, a French man o'war of sixty-four guns. Sometime later, they also captured the *Mercury*, a forty-two gun ship, lent to the French king by merchants for use as a privateer.[9]

Finally, during the summer of 1707, the *Association, Eagle, Romney* and *Firebrand* were continually employed in the preparations and ensuing attempt to capture Toulon with the Confederate fleet and the Duke of Savoy's army. The *Romney*, Captain Coney, was involved in the two principal actions; the first being the successful skirmish at the crossing of the River Var, and later, as flagship of Admiral Sir Thomas Dilkes, she escorted the flotilla of bomb vessels into Toulon Roads. Anchoring between Fort St. Louis and the Grand Tower, she assisted in the final bombardment of the harbour in the face of intense gunfire from many shore batteries.[10]

Shortly after this episode, his last as Admiral in command of the Confederate Fleet in the Mediterranean, and following his tragic death with the loss of all four ships, a glowing tribute was paid to Sir Clowdisley's memory:

'He was one of the greatest sea commanders of our age, or indeed that ever this island produced; of undaunted courage and resolution, of wonderful presence of mind in the hottest engagement and of consumate skill and experience. But more than all this, he was a just, generous, honest and good man. He made his own fortune by his personal merit alone, and from the lowest raised himself to the highest station in the navy'. [11]

Notes for Chapter 13

1. Lecky H.S. The Kings Ships, Vol I p321 (London 1913); Nav. Chr. XXXIII p184-90
2. Burchett J. The Complete History of Transactions at Sea, p630 (London 1720); Laird-Clowes, Vol II p382-4; Nav. Chr. XXXIII p194-7
3. Defoe D. The Storm. (London 1704); Nav. Chr. XXXIII p198
4. Burchett, p656-60
5. Ibid; Nav. Chr. XXXIII p198-9
6. Nav. Chr. XXXIII p200; Laird-Clowes, Vol II p238-402; Lecky, Vol I p321
7. Ibid, p201-2; Laird-Clowes, Vol II p398-402
8. Lecky, Vol II p322
9. Charnock, Vol III p291 (Coney)
10. Owen, p169-70 & 188-9
11. Anon, The Life and Glorious Actions of Sir C. Shovell, Admiral of the Confederate Fleet in the Mediterranean Sea (London 1707) BM 10815 c.5

Notes to Appendix I to IV - Crew Lists

The personnel listed in the appendices are those recorded as being aboard each ship at the time of her sinking. Details have been extracted from the Admiralty Treasury Neat Books for each vessel and are listed alphabetically for ease of reference. The last three columns of the Neat Book indicate the Neat Sum paid in settlement to the beneficiary, often the next of kin or executor, but sometimes an agent, attorney or creditor. Payments to the few survivors are also recorded. The following abbreviations are used to indicate relationship in the Next of Kin column:

(A) Aunt   (F) Father   (M) Mother   (W) Widow
(B) Brother   (G) Grandfather   (S) Sister

Other abbreviations are clarified in the table below which also shows the total of each rank or rating on board each ship. It is apparent that amongst the commissioned officers there were vacancies, whilst some ranks were duplicated. It is assumed some of the latter were promoted to fill the vacant positions but the appointment had not been officially confirmed.

Summary of Ranks/Ratings Borne - October 1707

Abbrev.	Full Title	Assoc	Eagle	Romny	FBrand
R. Adml	Rear Admiral	1			
Capt/Comdr	Captain/Commander	1	1	1	1
2nd Capt	2nd Captain	1			
1st Lt	1st Lieutenant	1			1
2nd Lt	2nd Lieutenant		1	2	
3rd Lt	3rd Lieutenant		2		
4th Lt	4th Lieutenant	1			
5th Lt	5th Lieutenant	2			
Mastr	Master Mariner	1	1	1	
Boats	Boatswain	1	1	1	1
Gunr	Gunner	1	1	1	1
Carpr	Carpenter	1	1	1	1
Chyr	Chyrurgeon(Surgeon)	1	1	1	1
Pursr	Purser	1	1	1	
Chaplain	Chaplain	1	1		
Ck	Cook	1	1	1	
Schl Mstr	Schoolmaster		1		
Tchr Mthmtc	Teacher of Mathematics			1	
Sailmr	Sailmaker	1		1	

Abbrev.	Full Title	Assoc	Eagle	Romny	FBrand
Arm^r	Armourer	1	1		
Chyr M^t	Surgeon's Mate	2		1	
Marshall	Marshall	1			
M^r M^t	Master's Mate	3	1	4	1
Pyl^t	Pilot	1			
Pyl^t Ext^{ra}	Pilot Extra	1			
Mids	Midshipman	20	13	9	2
Capt Clk	Captain's Clerk		1	1	
2nd Capt Clk	2nd Captain's Clerk	1			
Secr^{ty}	Secretary	1			
Q^r M^r	Quarter Master	8	4	3	1
Q^r M^r M^t	Quarter Master's Mate	7	4	2	1
Bo^s M^t	Boatswain's Mate	4	1	2	1
Bo^s Yeo	Boatswain's Yeoman	2			
Cox^n	Coxswain	1	1	1	1
G^r M^t	Gunner's Mate	4	2	1	2
G^r Tayl^r	Gunner's Tailor			1	
Yeo Pwd^r	Yeoman of the Powder	2	1	1	
Q^r G^r	Quarter Gunner	17	14	7	
Carp^r M^t	Carpenter's Mate	1	1	1	
Stw^d	Steward	1	1	1	
Ck M^t	Cook's Mate		1		
Corp^l	Corporal	1		1	
Trump^r	Trumpeter	1	1	1	
Carp^r Cr^w	Carpenter's Crew	3	3	3	
Gunsth	Gunsmith	1			
Coop^r	Cooper	1	1		
Mr Swab^r	Master Swabber	1			
Chyr 2nd M^t	Surgeon's 2nd Mate		1	1	
Chyr 4th M^t	Surgeon's 4th Mate	1			
Adm^l Ret^n	Admiral's Retinue	5			
AB	Able Seaman	388	143	75	21
Ord	Ordinary Seaman	140	125	74	6
Capt Sv^t	Captain's Servant	30	21	11	4
1st L^t Sv^t	1st Lieutenant's Servant				1
2nd L^t Sv^t	2nd Lieutenant's Servant			2	
3rd L^t Sv^t	3rd Lieutenant's Servant		3		
4th L^t Sv^t	4th Lieutenant's Servant	1			
M^r Sv^t	Master's Servant		1	1	
Bo^s Sv^t	Boatswain's Servant	2	1	1	
Carp^r Svt	Carpenter's Servant	1	1		
Chap^l Sv^t	Chaplain's Servant	1			
Chyr Sv^t	Surgeon's Servant	1	1	1	
Purs^r Sv^t	Purser's Servant	1	1	1	

Abbrev.	Full Title	Assoc	Eagle	Romny	FBrand
G^r Sv^t	Gunners Servant		1	1	1
Ck^s Sv^t	Cook's Servant	1	1	1	
Vol	Volunteer		5		
VPO	Volunteer per Order		1	3	
Pen^s	Pensioner	1	2		
Cable	?			1	
Arc	?	1			
	Total	**676**	**372**	**225**	**48**
Abbrev.	**Full Title**				
Serj	Sergeant, Royal Marines	1			
Corpl	Corporal, ...	1		1	
Drumr	Drummer	1			
Mne	Royal Marine	23	5	11	
	Total	**26**	**5**	**11**	

The actual Neat Book entries are chronological, irrespective of rank, rating or occupation and begin in July 1705. Columns on the left hand page show the date entered, ticket number and pay in arrears on joining, and movements from, or too, other ships. They also include dates of promotion and other miscellaneous information. Columns on the right hand page show various deductions under the column headings of; Tobacco, Slops (clothing etc.), Beds, Deadman's Clothes, Chest (pensions), Greenwich Hospital, Chyrurgeon, Chaplain, Full Wages and Neat Sum due after the various deductions. The final column is used for recording payment to the individual, his agent, beneficiary or executor. Each payment in the latter categories are signed and verified by an independent witness.

Dates are as shown and it should be borne in mind that the calendar year at that time was from 1st April to 31st March so that payments made in the January, February and March after the disaster are still dated 1707.

The covering page of the Neat Book of the *Association* reads as follows:

'Began Sea Wages 1st July 1705. Ended do 22nd October 1707 Being then cast away of Scilly on the Rocks called the Bishop and Clerks. Being paid at Broadstreet 1st March 1707/8.

Present: Sir Richard Haddock. Kt.

Clerks; Wm. Hogg, Roger Webb - Navy, W. Wahisp, Tho. Bluett - Treasury Made up on 21st July 1712. Neat Sum, £22339.15.9 1/2

The next few pages record the considerable sums payed to chaplains, pursers, slopsellers and surgeons, their beneficiaries or agents, in respect of deductions from the pay of each member of the crew or royal marine.

In the case of a chaplain, he was allowed 4p per month (28 days) for every person on board, whilst the surgeon received 2p per month per person. Over a long commission this could amount to a considerable sum. As a consequence of his services, from 1st July 1705, to the date of his death, the widow of Humphrey Foster, surgeon of the *Association* received £164.18.8 in respect of the crew on 20th March 1707. On 6th January 1709, and 3rd November 1710, further payments of £4.4.7 and £0.17.4 were paid in respect of royal marines carried.

Three categories of discharge are shown in the *Association*'s Neat Book over the 26 month period to the end of the Toulon Campaign, September 1707. The numbers of each category are as follows:

<pre>
'D'------------Discharged-------------661
'DD'--------- Discharged Dead-------70
'R'------------Run (ie.deserters)---- --76
</pre>

The number of captain's servant's on board, which in fact were mainly young gentlemen entered as potential officer's under patronage, is surprising, no less than thirty are named on the *Association* plus twenty midshipmen.

Other interesting aspects are that Sir John Narborough, who joined the *Association* the same day as Sir Clowdisley Shovell, was entered as an able seaman and James Narborough, ordinary seaman, then rated captain's servant on 19th October the same year. There was also a John Shovell in the admiral's retinue, who must have been related to Sir Clowdisley, since Dame Elizabeth Shovell was named as his executor/beneficiary. She was also named in this capacity for several others, whose names are highlighted in the table.

The closing entry of the Neat Book reads:

His Royal Highness having by his late order of ye 10th Nov last directed ye payment of ye Wages due for ye Service of ye Officers and Company of her Majesty's late ship the Association to ye 22nd October preceeding (the day she was unhappily lost on ye Rocks of ye Island of Scilly). The foregoing book has in pursuance thereof been collected from the several muster books remaining in the Ticket Office so far as they have been received either from ye Captain and Officers, Clerks of ye Cheque and Muster Master as is set down in ye front thereof, with respect to ye Entries, Names, Qualities, Discharges, times of Death, Runs, with ye Deductions of slops, under ye several Vendors heads, as also Beds, Divers Cloaths and Tobacco so far as *the same is Charged on any or all of ye said Muster books and this Collection is made as perfect and correct as ye said Muster books will admit of.*

2nd February 1707/8

APPENDIX I A

ASSOCIATION - NAVAL CREW - OCTOBER 1707

Surname	First	Rank	Amount	NOK/Beneficry	D. Paid
Ackett	Jam.	Ord	13. 6. 2	R[d] Farrington	4. 3.1707
Adamson	Fra.	Ord	6.16. 3	Arthr Delgarn	9. 3.1707
Akins	John	Q[r] M[r]	25.17. 3	(W) Mary	4. 3.1707
Allen	W[m]	AB	33.18. 0	(F) Rich[d]	1. 3.1707
Allenson	W[m]	AB	22.10.11	(M) Alice	2. 3.1707
Amy	John	AB	16.12. 8	Giles Cleaves	9. 3.1707
Anderson	Jo[s]	AB			
Angers	Pet[r]	Pyl[t] Ext[ra]	17. 2. 2	(U) Pet[r]	3. 3.1707
Archer	Henry	Mids	25. 9. 7	(F) John	4. 3.1707
Ariston	Leon[d]	Pyl[t]			
Arnold	E[d]	Ord	15.15. 4	Abra. Cornwall	2. 3.1707
Ascott	Sam[l]	Ord	12.16. 8	Jam. Roy	4. 3.1707
Atwood	W[m]	AB	17. 9.10	Anth[y] Conning	9. 3.1707
Avery	Sam[l]	AB	21. 0. 6	Eliz[th] McBright	9. 2.1708
Aylmer	Ed.	5th Lt	56.11. 0	(F) Matthew	8.10.1708
Babidge	Alex[r]	Cap[t] Sv[t]	7. 2. 0		6. 3.1707
Bagglehole	Tho[s]	Q[r] M[r] M[t]	21.13. 6	(W) Kathrine	3. 3.1707
Bale (1)	Jn[o]	AB	33. 5. 6	(W) Ann	1. 3.1707
Banister	Tho[s]	AB	16.15.10	(F) Wm	3. 3.1707
Baregraft	Sam[l]	AB	8.12. 7	(W) Jane	9. 3.1707
Barker	W[m]	AB	16. 0. 8	?	3. 3.1707
Barker	John	AB	17. 2. 2	(W) Kathrine	5. 3.1707
Barker	Hen.	AB	17. 2. 2	Thos Cook	5. 3.1707
Barker	Rob[t]	Cap[t] Sv[t]	6.16. 3	Benj Dwbrry	2. 3.1707
Barley	Tho	AB	23. 8.11	Jn[o] Leaf	10. 2.1708
Barnaby	Edw[d]	Qr Mr	25.17. 3	(W) Sarah	3. 3.1707
Barnett	W[m]	Ord	16.18. 0	(B) Sylvester	3. 3.1707
Barron	Jere.	AB	15. 4. 8	W[m] Bachelour	4. 3.1707
Bartholomew	Hen.	AB			
Bastard	Pet[r]	AB	23.12.10	(W) Elizabeth	1. 3.1707
Bateman	Jam.	Cap[t] Sv[t]	6. 9. 3	Benj Dwbrry	2. 3.1707
Bayley	Elias	Ord	33.18. 0	(W) Mary	1. 3.1707
Beane	Js[ph]	AB	16.12. 8	Eliza Reynolds	3. 3.1707
Beare	W[m]	Q[r] G[r]	18.12. 7	(W) Alice	3. 3.1707
Beaver	Jn[o]	AB	31.15. 0	(S) Eliz[th]	1. 3.1707

Surname	First	Rank	Amount	NOK/Beneficry	D. Paid
Belcham	John	G^r M^t	25. 9. 7	(F) Samuel	4. 3.1707
Bell	Jams	Pen^r	18.11. 6	(W) Ann	3. 3.1707
Bellingham	Saml	AB	16. 7. 0	(M) Mary	5. 3.1707
Bellingham	Saml	Capt Sv^t	13. 6. 2	Tho Coleby f Capt	6. 3.1707
Berne	Tho	Ord			
Berry	Magn^s	AB	16.12. 8	Mary Dewitt	4. 3.1707
Berry	John	AB	15.13. 2	(M) Joan	10. 2.1708
Bethell	Ben.	AB	17. 2. 2	Geo Burgiss	4. 3.1707
Bevis	John	Mids	29.13. 3	(W) Judith	2. 3.1707
Bevis	Jam.	Ord	13. 6. 2		6. 3.1707
Bews	Robt	Q^r G^r	18. 3. 1	(W) Judith	27. 3.1707
Bile	Jno	Ord	21.15. 0	(W) Ann	1. 3.1707
Bindham	Ja^s	AB	22.16. 6	(S) Elizth	2. 3.1707
Blake	Jno	AB	33. 9. 6	(M) Mary	1. 3.1707
Blake	Edwd	Bo^s M^t	25. 9. 7	(W) Sarah	4. 3.1707
Blewit	R^d	Ord	25.17. 4	Sarah Thatcher	1. 3.1707
Bliss	Ja^s	Ord	22. 1. 3	(W) Margaret	2. 3.1707
Bloss	John	Capt Sv^t	6.16. 3	Benj Dwbrry	2. 3.1707
Bollard	Edwd	Q^r G^r	19. 0. 3	James Lanson	4. 3.1707
Bolton	Allex	AB	18. 3. 6	(W) Margaret	2. 3.1707
Bondy	John	Q^r G^r	18. 8. 1	(W)	4. 3.1707
Booth	John	AB	16. 0.10	Ann Plumb	4. 3.1707
Booth (P)	Sol^o	Ord	15.17. 7	Ja^s Watson	2. 3.1707
Boswell	Thos	AB	17. 9.10	(W) Elizabeth	5. 3.1707
Bothel	W^m	AB			
Bowes	Tho	Ord	14. 8. 1	Chas Dewis	10. 2.1708
Bowles	Ja^s	AB	23. 6. 6	(W) Bridgett	2. 3.1707
Boyd	Dav^d	AB	16.19. 0	Lanc^t Robinson	10. 2.1708
Bradford	W^m	AB	16.11.10	(W) Sarah	3. 3.1707
Bradshaw	Thos	AB	17. 2. 2	(W) Susan	3. 3.1707
Bragg	Thos	AB	15.17. 6	(F) Thos	9. 3.1707
Brand	John	AB	17. 2. 2	(W) Ann	3. 3.1707
Brice	Jno	AB	16.19. 0	Jno Slater	3. 3.1707
Brittain	Dan^{el}	AB	16.12. 8	(W) Judith	3. 3.1707
Britting	Geo.	AB	17. 2. 2	(B) John	3. 3.1707
Brook	Allist^r	AB	16. 8. 4	(F) R^d	9. 3.1707
Brothery	Jno	Q^r M^r M^t	21.13. 6	(W) Kathrine	3. 3.1707
Brown	W^m	AB	16.12. 8	(F) W^m	3. 3.1707
Brown	Hen.	AB	15.15. 9	(M) Rebecca	5. 3.1707
Brown	John	Capt Sv^t	6.16. 3	Benj Dwbrry	2. 3.1707
Browne	Hen.	AB	28. 0. 7	Elizth Humphreys	1. 3.1707
Browne	Ja^s	AB	22.19. 7	Tho Williams	2. 3.1707
Browne (4)	John	AB			
Bryant	John	AB	16. 9. 6	(W) Amey	6. 3.1707
Buck	W^m	Ord	25. 8. 4	(W) Elizth	1. 3.1707
Burley	W^m	AB	19.10. 2	(W) Elin^r.	9. 2.1708

Surname	First	Rank	Amount	NOK/Beneficry	D. Paid
Burny	Edm^d	AB	17. 2. 2	(W) Jane	6. 3.1707
Burrow	Jno	AB	23.15. 1	Tho Rogers	1. 3.1707
Burrow	Mich^l	AB	17. 2. 2	(M) Rebecca	4. 3.1707
Bushell	Ste	Ord	18. 2. 5	(F) Isaac	3. 3.1707
Butland	Guilb^t	AB	17. 2. 2	(M) Mary	6. 3.1707
Butler	Saml	AB	23. 8. 7	? Palmer	2. 3.1707
Byllingsley	Lewis	1st Lt	50.16. 4	Dor^{ty} Hancock	5. 3.1707
Cable	Cary	Mids	25. 3. 2	(W) Susan	3. 3.1707
Cady	Jas.	Ord	22.17. 1	(F) Nich^o	5. 3.1707
Calcot	John	Capt Sv^t	6.16. 3	Benj Dwbrry	2. 3.1707
Catree	Alex^r	AB	16.12. 8	Kath^{ne} Catree	4. 3.1707
Caneby	Hen^y	AB	19.19.11	Tho Forrester	10. 2.1708
Carter	Th^o	Ord	25. 5.10	Geo. Chapman	1. 3.1707
Carter	W^m	Ord	17.11. 1	Cornel^s Clarke	2. 3.1707
Carter	Robt	Ord	16. 6. 7	Seth Lollis	9. 3.1707
Carter	Danl	AB			
Carter	Jam.	AB	15.17. 4	(W) Jane	4. 3.1707
Cartwright	Jno	M^r M^t	44.17. 7	(F) Jonathan	1. 3.1707
Cawes	Jno	Q^r M^r	25.17. 3	(W) Susanah	4. 3.1707
Cawes	John	Ord	13. 6. 2		6. 3.1707
Chalas	Elias	AB	16.19. 0	Susan Choloer	6. 3.1707
Chambers	Robt	AB	17. 9.10	(W) Mary	2. 3.1707
Chapman	Sim^n	AB	17. 2. 2	(F) Symond	5. 3.1707
Charton	Mor^s	Ord	17.10. 5	Jos Arden	2. 3.1707
Cheek	Robt	Capt Sv^t	6.16. 3	Cpt's (W) Mary	2. 3.1707
Cherbroke	W^m	Ord	11.17. 8	(W) Susan	6. 3.1707
Christopher	Saml	AB	16.15.10	Jno Bryan	5. 3.1707
Chubb	John	Bo^s M^t	19 15. 8	(W) Kath^{ne}	9. 3.1707
Clare	Pet$^{r.}$	AB	33.15. 6	(F) Jno	9. 2.1708
Clarke	Saml	AB	15. 8. 0	Wm French	3. 3.1707
Clarke	Ste	AB	17. 9.10	(W) Mary	3. 3.1707
Clarke	Robt	Ord	9. 0. 0	(W) Joan	9. 3.1707
Claypitt	Jos.	Ord	12. 4. 8	Wm Bachelour	4. 3.1707
Clerke	Jno	Yeo Pwd^r	51. 4. 9	(W) Ann	1. 3.1707
Clifton	Jno	AB	31. 2. 2	Elizth Holines	1. 3.1707
Cload Vickett	**Edm^d**	**Adm^l Ret^n**	**13. 6. 2**	**D.Eliz Shovell**	**6. 3.1707**
Cobnall	John	AB	7. 0. 2	(W) Mary	9. 3.1707
Cobnell	Jam.	Capt Sv^t	6.16. 3	Benj Dwbrry	2. 3.1707
Cock	John	AB	16.12. 4	(W) Elizth	4. 3.1707
Coffield	Mich^l	Ord			
Collins	Jno	AB	23.11. 1	(S) Mary	2. 3.1707
Collins	Tim.	Ord	6.14. 3	Hugh Collins	9. 2.1708
Colly	Pet^r	AB	17. 2. 2	(S) Mary Tinsly	4. 3.1707
Colson	And^w	AB	23.11. 9	Elin^r Lawrence	3. 3.1707
Comander	Hercu^l	Ord	6.16. 3	Elinor Bagnell	9. 3.1707
Combe	Dav^d	AB	22. 8. 6	(W) Judith	3. 3.1707

Surname	First	Rank	Amount	NOK/Beneficry	D. Paid
Comden	Robt	Ord	18.18. 3	(F) W^m	23. 3.1707
Compion	Thos	AB	17. 2. 2	Edwd Bembridge	6. 3.1707
Conolly	Pet^r	Ord	14.15. 0	(B) R^d	9. 2.1707
Coomer	W^m	Ord			
Cooper	Corn^s	AB	21.12. 5	Mary Cooper	2. 3.1707
Copping	Saml	Ord	12. 4. 8	Elin^r Lipsey	4. 3.1707
Coriana	Angel^a	AB	21. 6. 9	Thos. Williams	2. 3.1707
Corick	W^m	AB	34.13. 2	(W) Alice	1. 3.1707
Cornwall	Rich^d	Ord	24.19. 6	(W) Anne	5. 3.1707
Cornwall	Thos	Mids			
Cornwall	Thos	Mids	29.13. 3	(S) Caroline	9. 3.1707
Coyle	Sam$^{l.}$	AB	33. 6. 0	(W) Mary	1. 3.1707
Coyle	Jno	AB	33.11. 8	Mary Burgoin	10. 2.1708
Craven	Tho	AB	19.13. 2	Jno Davis	2. 3.1707
Crews	John	Ord	9. 0. 0	Jno Luke	9. 3.1707
Cross	W^m	Ord	6.14. 3	Eliza Parsons	9. 3.1707
Crow	John	Ord	7. 6. 9	(W) Susan	9. 3.1707
Culley	W^m	AB	33.12. 4	Jno Cook	1. 3.1707
Curry	Anth^o	AB	22. 6.10	(S) Marg^t	2. 3.1707
Curtis	Math	Ord	6. 2. 6		
Cutless	W^m	Ord	21.12. 4	(M) ?	3. 3.1707
Danzy	R^d	Ord	13. 6. 2	(G) Elizth Danzy	4. 3.1707
Darby	Thos	AB	19. 1. 6	Marg' Avery	3. 3.1707
Davis	Hen	AB	22. 1.11	Tho Attwood	8.10.1709
Davis	John	Bo^s Yeo	19. 0. 3	(W) Elizth	6. 3.1707
Davis (2)	W^m	AB	33.18. 0	(W) Rebecca	1. 3.1707
Davison	Thos	AB	16. 9. 6	Tom^{sn} Cornish	9. 3.1707
Dawson	Geo	AB	20.14. 2	? Athcrton	10. 2.1708
Dawson	John	Q^r G^r	18.12. 7	(B) Robert	4. 3.1707
Deberth	W^m	AB	16. 9. 6	(W) Mary	6. 3.1707
Dee	Jam.	Bo^s Sv^t	26. 7. 4	(W) Ann	1. 3.1707
Delier	Jos	Qr Mr	25.17. 3	(W) Rebecca	3. 3.1707
Demires	W^m	AB	17. 2. 2	Mary Kemp	6. 3.1707
Dodson	Sim^n	Mids	25. 9. 7	(F) William	5. 3.1707
Doleman	R^d	Q^r G^r	35.12. 5	(W) Elizabeth	1. 3.1707
Doyle	Allex	Ord	15.12. 7	Wm Morley	8.10.1709
Draper	W^m	AB			5. 3.1707
Drew	R^d	AB	17. 9.10	(W) Mary	3. 3.1707
Drew	John	Ord	13. 6. 2		6. 3.1707
Dunbar	Jno	AB	31.10. 9	? Matthews	10. 2.1708
Dunn	Tern^{ce}	AB	8.11. 3	(W) Elizth	9. 3.1707
Dyer	John	G^r M^t	25. 9. 7	(W) Ann	5. 3.1707
Dyer	Thos	AB	16.13. 4	(W) Ann	5. 3.1707
Dyer (2)	John	AB	12 18.10	Ann Freeman	9. 3.1707
Easten	W^m	Q^r G^r	17.19.11	(M) Mary	5. 3.1707
Edwards	Jam.	AB	17. 2. 2	Susan Banks	4. 3.1707

Surname	First	Rank	Amount	NOK/Beneficry	D. Paid
Elliott	W^m	AB			
Elliott	Abr^m	AB	16.12. 8	(M) Mary	9. 3.1707
Elmott	Jack	AB	32.10. 4	(W) Elizabeth	1. 3.1707
Elphinston	Pet^r	AB	16.19. 0	Wm Smith	10. 2.1708
Elven	Thos	AB	15.17. 6	(M) Elizth	9. 3.1707
Elwing	Thos	AB	15.17. 6	(M) Elizth	4. 3.1707
Emerson	Phill	Bo^s Yeo	20.16. 6	(W) Anne	4. 3.1707
Evans	Hugh	AB	28.16. 2	(M) Ann	1. 3.1707
Evans	Math	AB			
Evans	R^d	AB	16.15.10	(W) Katherine	6. 3.1707
Fairley	W^m	AB	16. 0. 8	(W) Philodelph	20. 3.1707
Fanwich	W^m	AB	22. 4. 0	(W) Mary	2. 3.1707
Farrington	Ralph	Mids	29.13. 3	(W) Mary	4. 3.1707
Fatcot	Jam.	AB	16.19. 6	(S)Mag^{dn} Leonard	6. 3.1707
Faulkner	Jno	AB	13.15. 7		9. 3.1707
Faulkner	Jno	AB	13.15. 7	(B) Jam.	9. 3.1707
Fell	Jos.	Ord	5.13. 1	Wm Grayham	9. 2.1708
Ferrabosco	Mos^{tn}	Sec^{rty}			3. 3.1707
Ferres	Thos	Mids	29.13. 3	(W) Elizth	4. 3.1707
Flaggett	John	AB	15.13. 2	(W) Dianah	5. 3.1707
Fleek	Mich^l	AB	13 8. 6	R^d Grace	9. 3.1707
Flemming	Jam.	AB	16. 2.10	(M) Kath^{ne}	5. 3.1707
Fletcher	R^d	AB	30.13. 4	(B) Jno	1. 3.1707
Flowers	Chas	Ord	18.19. 3	Marth Hutchins	2. 3.1707
Fobby	Jos	AB	21.18. 1	Thos Williams	10. 2.1708
Foden	Rand^l	Stew^d	36. 3. 3	Elizth	1. 3.1707
Fogwell	Sim^o.	AB	31.17.10	(W) Mary	1. 3.1707
Foster	Humph	Chyr	148. 8. 9	(W) Deborah	2. 3.1707
Foster	Thos	AB	17. 2. 2	(W) Marg^t	2. 3.1707
Foulks	Th^o	AB	33.15. 6	Jno Chapman	1. 3.1707
Fox (1)	Th^o	AB	33.14.10	(M) Joan	1. 3.1707
Frame	Jenkin	Ord	24.19.11	(B) William	2. 3.1707
Franklin	W^m	Mids	29. 5. 7	(F) W^m	4. 3.1707
Frazer	Danl	AB	15.13. 2	Margt Hurs^t	5. 3.1707
Frederick	Isaac	Coop^r	34.13. 2	(W) Rebecca	1. 3.1707
Freeman	Jno	Ck Sv^t	26. 7. 4	(W) Elin^r	1. 3.1707
French	R^d	AB	8. 9. 7	(W) Sarah	4. 3.1707
Frenoe	Jam.	AB	16.19. 0	Jno Frenoe	5. 3.1707
Frizle	Jno	AB	33. 3. 0	(W) Maudlin	1. 3.1707
Froloan	Hen.	Ord	13. 6. 2	Jans Lover	1. 7.1708
Frost	Jos.	AB	32. 1. 4	(W) Elizabeth	1. 3.1707
Gable	R^d	AB	16.12. 8	(W) Sarah	4. 3.1707
Garbett	John	AB			
Gardner	Thos	Ord	6.16. 3		9. 3.1707
Garnam	W^m	AB	8. 7.10	(U) Hen^{ry}	9. 2.1708
Gascon	Tho	AB	22.12. 4	(B) Ben^j	6. 3.1707

Surname	First	Rank	Amount	NOK/Beneficry	D. Paid
Gauntlett	Jn[o]	Ord	15.16. 7	(W) Jane	2. 3.1707
Giles	Rob[t]	Cap[t] Sv[t]	6.16. 3	Benj Dwbrry	2. 3.1707
Gill	Jos.	AB	8. 5. 7	(M) Mary	20.10.1708
Gilson	John	AB	16.19. 0	Mary Bourne	5. 3.1707
Glandnning	Rob[t]	AB	16. 1. 8	(M) Ticy	3. 3.1707
Goodman	R[d]	AB	33.18. 0	(W) Julia	1. 3.1707
Goodray	Fra.	AB	32. 7. 0	Susan Dou?	1. 3.1707
Goodridge	W[m]	Cap[t] Sv[t]	6.16. 3	Cpt's (W) Mary	2. 3.1707
Goodwin	Jn[o]	AB	17. 2. 2	(B) Nath[l]	3. 3.1707
Gore	Tho[s]	Ord	13. 6. 2	(F) Hen[ry]	2. 3.1707
Goslin	W[m]	AB	17. 2. 2	(W) Elizabeth	5. 3.1707
Gosling	Hen[r]	AB	31. 3.10	W[m] Pope	11.11.1708
Gosling	Jn[o]	AB	32. 7. 4	(M) Jane	1. 3.1707
Gover	Jn[o]	AB	33.13. 0	Jane Ruth?	1. 3.1707
Grant	Ed.	AB	31.10.10	(M) Alice	1. 3.1707
Grant	Th[o]	AB	31.14. 8	(W) Anna	1. 3.1707
Green	W[m]	AB	22. 8. 0	Tho Groose	3. 3.1707
Green	Tho[s]	AB	16. 0. 8	Alex[r] Grigg	4. 3.1707
Grigg	Jn[o]	AB	32.13. 0	(W) Mary	1. 3.1707
Grimstock	Jos.	Mids	25. 9. 7	Margt Barker	9. 2.1708
Grumblestn	Tho[s]	M[r] M[t]	31.11. 5	(W) Eliz[th]	1. 3.1707
Gullen	John	4th Lt	54. 1. 1	(W) Ann	1. 3.1707
Gullen	John	4th Lt Sv[t]	6.15. 7	(M) Ann	1. 3.1707
Gulling	W[m]	Ord	4.14.11	(M) Ann	1. 3.1707
Hailey	R[d]	AB	16.14. 4	(W) Jans	2. 3.1707
Hale	Sam[l]	AB	17. 2. 2	(W) Sebinah	9. 2.1708
Hamond	John	Ord			
Hancock	Wes	AB	30.17. 6	(W) Joyce	1. 3.1707
Hanger	Dv[d]	Ord	24. 4. 2	(M) Patience	9. 3.1707
Harding	Jacob	AB	16. 5. 2	(F) David	4. 3.1707
Harman	Geo.	AB	8.11. 3	(F) Geo.	9. 3.1707
Harrington	Jn[o]	Chyr 4th M[t]	24.19. 9	? Mary	3. 3.1707
Harris	John	AB	15. 7. 6	(W) Emblin	4. 3.1707
Harris	Tho[s]	Q[r] G[r]	18.13. 1	(W) Anne	4. 3.1707
Harrison	Rob[t]	AB	16. 3.10	Mary Dallister	5. 3.1707
Harrison	Tho[s]	Chap[l] Sv[t]	13. 6. 2	(W)Tho D'Aeth	2. 3.1707
Harrop	John	AB	16.19. 0	(W) Eliz[th]	5. 3.1707
Hart	Tho[s]	2[d] Cap[t] Cl[k]	14.19. 9	(F) Paul	4.12.1708
Harvey	Dan[l]	AB	17. 2. 2	(F) Joseph	4. 3.1707
Harvey	Ben.	AB	16.11.10	(F) Jos.	4. 3.1707
Hatch	R[d]	Ord	20. 6. 8	Eliz[th] Creed	1. 3.1707
Hayes	Dav[d]	AB	33. 2.10	(B) John	3. 3.1707
Hayes	Math[w]	AB	15.10.10	(F) Ste	27. 3.1708
Hedgecock	W[m]	Ord	13. 2. 6		3. 3.1707
Henson	**Rob[t]**	**Adm[l] Ret[n]**	**13. 6. 2**	**D.Eliz Shovell**	**6. 3.1707**

Surname	First	Rank	Amount	NOK/Beneficry	D. Paid
Hickman	R^d	M^r M^t	44.17. 7	(F) Obediah	3. 3.1707
Hill (3)	John	AB	16.12. 8	(F) John	5. 3.1707
Hills	John	AB	16. 9. 6	(W) Elizabeth	4. 3.1707
Hills (1)	Jno	AB	16.12. 8	(M) Joan	3. 3.1707
Hogg	John	Capt Sv^t	6.16. 3	Cpt's (W) Mary	2. 3.1707
Holeyman	Christ^r	Carp^r Cr^w	35. 9.11	(W) Ann	1. 3.1707
Holland	Spencer	AB	17. 2. 2	Edwd Southell	5. 3.1707
Holland	Edwd	Mids	29. 5. 7	(W) Jane	6. 3.1707
Hollier	John	Capt Sv^t	6.16. 3	Benj Dwbrry	2. 3.1707
Hollowmore	And^w	AB	32. 4. 1	(F) Jno	1. 3.1707
Holton	Thos	Q^r M^r	48.18. 1	(W) Susan	1. 3.1707
Horden	W^m	AB	17. 2. 2	Wm Jolly	6. 3.1707
Hornby	W^m	AB	8. 5. 7	(W) Elin^r	9. 3.1707
Horsey	Th^o	AB	33.18. 0	(F) Abendigo	9. 3.1707
Horton	Ben	Ord	12.16. 8	Mary Barracle	4. 3.1707
Howard	Jno	AB	33.15. 8	(W) Sarah	1. 3.1707
Howard	Jno	Arm^r	23. 9. 1	Jno Hamm	6. 3.1707
Hudson	Edwd	AB	16. 9. 6	(M) Sarah	3. 3.1707
Huff	W^m	Trump^r	20.10. 9	(W) Mary	5. 3.1707
Humphreys	Jno	Ord	23. 3. 2	(M) Jane	1. 3.1707
Hunteridge	Jam.	AB	17. 2. 2	Chas. Green	5. 3.1707
Huntridge	Jacob	AB	25.18. 4	Tho Forrister	10. 2.1708
Hurd	Job	AB	16. 1. 8	(F) Job	4. 3.1707
Hutsfield	W^m	AB	16.12. 8	(M) Elizth	6. 3.1707
Hyde	Jo^s	AB	18. 7.10	(F) Benjn	11. 3.1707
Innocent	R^d	Ord	13. 6. 2	(B) Jno	6. 3.1707
Jackson	Th^o	AB	33.10. 6	Tho. Lyng	1. 3.1707
Jackson	Geo.	AB	16.15.10	(F) Thomas	4. 3.1707
James	Henry	Capt Sv^t	6. 9. 3	Benj Dwbrry	2. 3.1707
James	Sim.	AB	16. 7. 0	Wm Smith	6. 3.1707
Jeckall	Jno	AB	25.15. 2	(W) Anna	9. 3.1707
Jefferson	Robt	G^r M^t	25. 7. 9	(W) Barbara	4. 3.1707
Jeffridges	W^m	Ord	14.15. 1	(W) Ann	9. 2.1708
Jenkins	John	AB	17. 2. 2	(W) Frances	4. 3.1707
Jenning	John	Bo^s M^t	25.10.11	(W) Sarah	5. 3.1707
Jervin	Jam.	AB	17. 2. 2	Marth Nwborne	5. 3.1707
Jespor	John	Ord	6.14. 3	(B) R^d	9. 3.1707
Johnson	W^m	AB	32.14. 8	Alice Tremain	1. 3.1707
Johnson	W^m	AB	8. 1. 4	J? Long	10. 3.1707
Johnson	Erasm^s	AB			
Johnson	Math	AB	16. 6. 0	? Johnson	4. 3.1707
Johnson	Jam.	AB	15. 5.11	Danl Campbell	23. 3.1707
Johnson	W^m	AB			
Johnson (2)	Jno	AB	20.14. 9	Thos Rice	10. 2.1708
Jolly	W^m	Capt Sv^t	6.16. 3	Benj Dwbrry	2. 3.1707
Jones	Owen	AB	32.11. 6	Mary Brittain	3. 3.1707

Surname	First	Rank	Amount	NOK/Beneficry	D. Paid
Jones	Saml	AB	19.18. 4	Norman Phelps	23. 3.1707
Jones	Gab.	AB	17. 2. 2	R^d Thorne	3. 3.1707
Jones	Jenk^n	AB	15.17. 6	Blandina Cole	9. 2.1708
Jones	Pet^r	Ord	13. 6. 2	Arth^r Morgan	6. 3.1707
Jones	W^m	AB			
Jones	Robt	AB	8. 5. 7	Marg^t Boucher	9. 3.1707
Jones (1)	Jno	AB	31.18. 2	Ann Attwood	1. 3.1707
Jones (5)	John	Ord	13. 4. 2	(M) Kath^{ne}	8.10.1709
Jordan		AB	17. 2. 2	(W) Martha	20. 3.1707
Judge	Tho	AB			
Julius	W^m	Capt Sv^t	6.16. 3	Cpt's (W) Mary	2. 3.1707
Keeling	Wal^t	AB	14.16. 5	Wm Flood	6. 3.1707
Kelly	Danl	AB	17. 2. 2	(F) Jno	3. 3.1707
Kelsal (1)	Jam.	AB	17. 7. 4	(W) Mary	5. 3.1707
Kelsal	Jam.	Capt Sv^t	6. 9.11	(M) Charity	4. 4.1709
Kent	Sebast^n	Ord	13. 6. 2	(B) Clemens	19. 8.1709
Kerslake	Robt	AB	33. 5. 6	(W) Elizabeth	1. 3.1707
Kestle	John	Mids	20. 5.11	(M) Martha	9. 3.1707
Kinbow	John	AB	17. 2. 2	Norman Phelps	23. 3.1707
King	Pet^r	Bos Sv^t	26. 7. 4	(W) Ann	1. 3.1707
King	W^m	AB			
King	Saml	Ord			
King (2)	Pet^r	AB	16. 9. 6	(M) Susan	3. 3.1707
Kitmore	John	Ord	11.14.10	(M) Elizth	4. 3.1707
Kneebone	R^d	AB	16.19. 0	Reb^{ca} Deleer	3. 3.1707
Knight	Jam.	AB	17. 2. 2	(W) Mary	3. 3.1707
Lahce	W^m	AB	18. 6. 4	(M) Ellen	10. 2.1707
Lamb	Jos	Q^r M^r M^t	19. 9. 9	(W) Elizabeth	5. 3.1707
Lambert	R^d	AB	17. 9.10	(M) Jane	5. 3.1707
Lambert	W^m	Capt Sv^t	6. 9. 3	Benj Dwbrry	2. 3.1707
Lamming	Jno	AB	21. 1. 4	?	2. 3.1707
Landen	John	AB	17. 9.10	Jno Wright	3. 3.1707
Lands	Jno	Ord	24.19.10	(B) W^m	1. 3.1707
Larry	Mich^l	Ord	16. 1.10	Joan Falcon	3. 3.1707
Lashley	Jam.	Ord			11. 9.1710
Lawrence	R^d	AB	16.12. 5	(F) William	5. 3.1707
Lawrence	Tobias	Carp^r Cr^w	36. 0. 7	(W) Kathrine	1. 3.1707
Lay	Saml	AB	8. 5. 7	(F) Saml	10. 2.1708
Leaker	W^m	Ord	17. 1.10	Susan^h Waite	10. 3.1707
Lear	Bart	Ord	26. 3. 0	(S)Marg^t Grace	1. 3.1707
Lebat	Saml	AB	16. 0. 8	(W) Elizth	4. 3.1707
Lee	Geo	AB	16. 8. 8	(W) Ann	3. 3.1707
Lenvost	W^m	Ord	24.11. 6	Elizth Hollyer	1. 3.1707
Lewis	Jno	AB	17. 2. 2	Jos Lewis	3. 3.1707
Lewis	W^m	Q^r G^r	17.19.11	(W) Isabella	5. 3.1707
Lewis	Edwd	Q^r G^r	18. 3. 1	Marg^t Briggs	5. 3.1707

Surname	First	Rank	Amount	NOK/Beneficry	D. Paid
Linton	Robt	AB	16.15.10	(W) Mary	6. 3.1707
Lisson	Jno	Ord	23.18. 0	Mary Warriss	3. 3.1707
Littlewood	Th^o	AB	30.19. 8	(W) Avis	1. 3.1707
Loades	Edwd	2nd Capt	208. 0. 0	Thos Coleby	3. 3.1707
Lockeor	Rich^d	Yeo Pwd^r	49.19. 7	(B) Henry	1. 3.1707
Lornes	Thos	Q^r M^r M^t	10. 7. 7	(W) Mary	10. 3.1707
Londale	Phile	Ord	17. 0. 6	(W) Mary	2. 3.1707
Longman	Thos	Marsh^l	13.13.10	(S) Bridgett	9. 2.1708
Love	W^m	AB	17. 2. 2	Hen. Cairnes	9. 3.1707
Love	**James**	**Adm^l Ret^n**	**13. 6. 2**	**D.Eliz Shovell**	**6. 3.1707**
Loveday	W^m	AB	23.16. 0	(M) Elizth	2. 3.1707
Lowd	John	AB	16.12. 8	Geo Saynon	4. 3.1707
Lucas	Hen	AB	20.10. 1	Mary Moore	2. 3.1707
Lund	Lewis	Capt Sv^t	6.16. 3	Benj Dwbrry	2. 3.1707
Lutton	W^m	AB	33.18. 0	(W) Susan	1. 3.1707
Lyon	Jam.	AB	17. 2. 2	(W) Susanah	5. 3.1707
Mackey	Danl	AB			
MacKnolly	Jas	AB	19. 6. 7	(W) Alice	3. 3.1707
Maclain	John	AB	16.12. 8	Jno Stoker	9. 3.1707
Macorell	Dunk	AB			
Magnus	Rowl^d	AB	22.13. 9	(W) ?	2. 3.1707
Mann	John	Ord	13. 6. 2	(W) Kath^{ne}	13. 3.1707
Mansfield	John	AB	17. 2. 2	(W) Mary	2. 3.1707
Maplesdon	R^d	AB	17. 2. 2	(B) Jarvise	4. 3.1707
Marks	John	Ord	13. 6. 2	?	6.12.1708
Marsh	Th^o	Ord	25.14. 8	Edwd Sharp	10. 3.1707
Marshall	Pet^r	Ord	17.16.11	(F) James	2. 3.1707
Martin	W^m	AB	24. 7. 2	(W) Jayne	1. 3.1707
Martin	W^m	Ord	15. 9. 8	Hugh Lattin	3. 3.1707
Martin	John	Mids	23. 9. 0	(M) Eliz Jackson	28. 6.1708
Martinson	Nic^h	AB	33. 1. 8	(W) Kathrine	5. 3.1707
Mason	W^m	AB	21. 0. 8	Jno Formby	10. 2.1708
Matthews	Pet^r	AB	32.15.11	(W) Ann	1. 3.1707
Maugridge	W^m	Chyr M^t			
Merriman	Saml	Ord	13. 6. 2	(M) Sarah	5. 3.1707
Midling	Jno	AB	32. 3. 4	(W) Sarah	6. 3.1707
Milborn	Jonas	AB	20. 4. 2	Elizth Gunner	10. 2.1708
Miles	Jam.	Ord	25.17. 4	Jam. Corbin	1. 3.1707
Mills	Robt	AB	16. 9. 6	Elizth Robb	6. 3.1707
Missonett	Sim$^{n.}$	Ord	33. 6.10	(W) Ann	1. 3.1707
Mitchell	Ogleby	AB	17. 2. 2	(F) Thos	4. 3.1707
Mitchell	W^m	AB	8. 5. 7	(W) Mary	
Monery	Jos.	AB	9. 0. 0	(W) Mary	
Mony	John	AB	16.19. 0	(M) Mary	4. 3.1707
Moon	Robt	AB	17. 2. 2	(B) Jos.	3. 3.1707
Moone	Th^o	AB	32.15. 4	(W) Frances	1. 3.1707

Surname	First	Rank	Amount	NOK/Beneficry	D. Paid
Moore	Step	AB	32.12. 2	(F) And^w	30. 3.1708
Moore	Robt	AB	17. 2. 2	(W) Frances	3. 3.1707
Morgan	Thos	AB	17. 2. 2	(W) Hester	2. 3.1707
Morgan	Thos	AB	17 2. 2	(F) Jno	19. 8.1709
Morris	R^d	AB	18. 7. 2	(W) Mary	3. 3.1707
Morris	Robt	Ord	11.14.10	(W) Blanch	6. 3.1707
Mortimer	Edm^d	Mids	25. 9. 7	Susan Countss of Newport	5. 3.1707
Morton	Th^o	AB	32. 8. 2	(W) Mary	1. 3.1707
Moss	Jam^s	AB	23.17. 8	Jno Thompson	1. 3.1707
Mountstephen	Jno	Ord	17.10. 1	(M) Ann (F) Jno	2. 3.1707
Mountsteven	W^m	AB	33.11. 8	(W) Marg^t	1. 3.1707
Mundey	Thos	AB	17. 2. 2	Hen. Jevon	4. 3.1707
Murfy	Pat^k	AB	17. 2. 2	(W) Jane	5. 3.1707
Murrion	Pet^r	AB	16. 9. 6	(F) Josua	6. 3.1707
Murry	Dennis	Ord	13.15. 8	(M) Mary	10. 2.1708
Napp	Ed^{wd}	Ord	24.19.10	John Poll	1. 3.1707
Narborough	**Sir Jn^{tn}**	**AB**	**17. 2. 2**	**D.Eliz Shovell**	**6. 3.1707**
Narborough	**John**	**Ord**	**6. 16. 3**	**(F) Robert**	**9. 3.1707**
Neach	R^d	Sailm^r	19.13. 7	(F) Jos	4. 3.1707
Neagle	Jer^{my}	AB	22.12. 1	Eliz. Williams	2. 3.1707
Newcomb	Jno	Ord	22. 6. 6	(W) Mg^t	1. 3.1707
Nicholes	Isaac	AB	32.19. 0	(W) Mary	1. 3.1707
Nicholes	R^d	Ord	15. 0. 6	(F) Rich^d	2. 3.1707
Nicholes (1)	Jno	AB	31. 0. 5	(M) Joan	1. 3.1707
Nicholls	Rd	Corp^l	23.11. 7	(W) Elizth	4. 3.1707
Nicholson	Hen.	Ord	13. 6. 2	(M) Dorothy	5. 3.1707
Nixon	Danl	Q^{r}M^r	16.12. 8	(W) Mary	27. 3.1708
Norman	John	Ord	6.16. 3		9. 3.1707
Norris	Hugh	Cox^n	21.13. 6	(W) Mary	3. 3.1707
Northam	Thos	AB	17. 2. 2	(M) Hannah	9. 3.1707
Norton	Jno	Ord			
Nowell	Nic^s	AB	20.18. 0	Jno Roveen	9. 2.1708
Nutking	R^d	AB	19.19. 7	(W) Amy	3. 3.1707
Oliver	Geo	AB	30. 7. 3	(W) Mary	1. 3.1707
Osborn	Saml	Q^{r}G^r	12.12.7	(W) Xlian	6. 3.1707
Osborne	Saml	Capt Sv^t	6.16. 3	Benj Dwbrry	2. 3.1707
Page	Abra	AB	23. 0. 5	Elias Armand	2. 3.1707
Pain	Jno	AB	33.18. 0	(W) Grace	1. 3.1707
Painter	Th^o	Ord	22. 4. 5	(F) Geo.	1. 3.1707
Pankherst	Jos.	Ord	13. 6. 2	Judith Bevis	2. 3.1707
Paralow	Jam.	Q^r M^r M^t	25. 3. 3	(W) Hester	3. 3.1707
Parkes	Saml.	AB	33.18. 0	(W) Elizth	1. 3.1707
Partridge	Step.	AB	34. 3. 8	R^d Smith	12. 7.1708
Patten	Geo	AB	20. 1. 5	(M) Isabella	2. 3.1707
Patty	Edwd	AB	15.19. 6	(W) Anne	3. 3.1707

Surname	First	Rank	Amount	NOK/Beneficry	D. Paid
Payne	Jos.	Capt Sv^t	6.16. 3	Cpt's (W) Mary	2. 3.1707
Peak	Robt	Q^r G^r	15. 7.10	(W) Elizth	9. 2.1707
Peake	Robt	AB	16.15.10	(F) W^m	9. 2.1708
Pearce	Jno	AB	16. 6.11	(W) Paskew	3. 3.1707
Pearce	Thos	AB	15.15. 9	(W) Alice	3. 3.1707
Pearce	Thos	AB	15.17. 8	(M) Rebecca	3. 3.1707
Peare	W^m	Q^r M^r	25. 9. 7	(W) Rebecca	5. 3.1707
Pearey	John	AB	16. 9. 6	Mary Bare	3. 3.1707
Peary	Ed^{wd}	Ord	26. 7.4	Jno Smith	11. 3.1707
Peck	Saml	Capt Sv^t	6.16. 3	Cpt's (W) Mary	2. 3.1707
Pellet	John	Ord			
Penny (al Pury)	Pet^r	Chap^l	13. 6. 2	(W) Mary	2. 3.1707
Penry	Thos	Q^r M^r M^t	21. 7. 2	(W) Kathrine	4. 3.1707
Penry	R^d	Ord	13. 6. 2		6. 3.1707
Perkins	Is^h	Mids	29.13. 3	(W) Mary	5. 3.1707
Persons	Cha	Ord	17.10. 9	(S) Jans	22. 3.1707
Peters	Gowen	Ord	16.15. 5	(M) Joan	2. 3.1707
Phillip	**Luke**	**Adm^l Ret^n**	**13. 6. 2**	**D.Eliz Shovell**	**6. 3.1707**
Phillips	Arth^r	Ord			
Pike	Ben.	AB	15.10.10	(W) Deborah	6. 3.1707
Pincott	Thos	AB	16. 2. 0	And^w Rye	9. 3.1707
Pinsons	Jno	AB	22. 3. 4	Jos. Harrion	2. 3.1707
Pitt	Thos	Mids	23. 9. 0	(M) Mary	3. 3.1707
Pocock	Ja^s	AB	17. 0. 4	(W) Barbara	3. 3.1707
Poett	Saml	AB	13.14. 6	(M) Martha	5. 3.1707
Poole	John	AB			11. 9.1710
Pooley	Thos	AB	16. 9. 6	(W) Ann	4. 3.1707
Poor	Ja^s	Ord	17. 7.11	Ann Ward	2. 3.1707
Pope	W^m	AB	16.19. 0	(M) Agnes	11. 3.1707
Pope	John	AB	17. 2. 2	(B) Edmund	4. 3.1707
Pope	John	Ord	9. 0. 0	Jno Luke	4. 4.1709
Potter	Thos	Capt Sv^t	6.16. 3	Cpt's (W) Mary	2. 3.1707
Powditch	R^d	Mids	25. 9. 7	Thomas Olden	5. 3.1707
Powell	Robt	AB	33.18. 0	(W) Mary	1. 3.1707
Priest	R^d	AB	20. 9. 1	(F) R^d	1. 7.1708
Prosper	W^m	AB	17. 2. 2	Elizth Atkins	10.10.1709
Pruce	Wal^t	AB	15.11. 9	Jno Hartup	6. 3.1707
Pullister	John	Q^r M^r	21. 9. 5	Mary Pallsoir	27. 3.1708
Purse	Ed.	AB	32.12. 4	(W) Hanah	1. 3.1707
Pury	Robt	Ord	13. 6. 2	Thos Death (M)	2. 3.1707
Ralph	R^d	AB	16.12. 8	(W) Ann	4. 3.1707
Ratcliffe	Ste	Ord			
Rawlins	Geo.	Carp^r Sv^t	2.19. 3	Carp^r Smith's (W)	17. 8.1708
Raynolds	Th^o	AB	33.12. 4	(F) Jno	1. 3.1707
Read	Thos	AB	19. 8. 8	(W) Jans	2. 3.1707
Redman	Ste.	AB	17. 9.10	(W) Mary	4. 3.1707

Surname	First	Rank	Amount	NOK/Beneficry	D. Paid
Reed	Jno	Ord	25. 2.10	(W) Sarah	1. 3.1707
Reeder	Saml.	AB	32.15.10	(W) Susan	1. 3.1707
Reign	Ja^s	AB	20.13. 4	Jno Willis	2. 3.1707
Rice	Allen	AB	17. 2. 2	(W) Susan	3. 3.1707
Roase	Jno	Ord	17.10. 2	(F) John	2. 3.1707
Roberts (2)	John	AB	17.19. 7	(M) Ganor	10. 2.1708
Robertson	Ralph	AB	16. 9. 6	(W) Abigail	28. 3.1708
Robins	Jno	AB	16.10. 2	(W) Elizabeth	3. 3.1707
Robinson	Dan^{el}	Q^r G^r	18.12. 7	(W) Ann	3. 3.1707
Robinson	W^m	AB			
Rose	Robt	AB	16.19. 0	(M) Elizth	9. 3.1707
Ross	Jno	AB			
Row	Hugh	Q^r G^r	18.12. 7	(M)?	4. 3.1707
Rowen	Robt	Ord	6.10. 7	Mark Potts	9. 3.1707
Rowlandson	Tren	AB	17. 9.10	(W) Mary	5. 3.1707
Royston	Jno	AB	33. 8. 0	(W) Elizabeth	1. 3.1707
Rudd	Geo	Ord	17. 2. 2	Jno Giles	2. 3.1707
Russell	Isaac	AB	33.18. 0	(B) Abram	1. 3.1707
Rust	Roger	Ord	23. 6. 8	Ann Ward	8. 3.1708
Rye	Arth^r	AB	16.12. 8	(W) Lydia	4. 3.1707
Salter	Nic^o	AB	19.18. 3	(W) Betty	3. 3.1707
Samford	Jno	AB	33. 8. 6	(W) Susanah	1. 3.1707
Saul	Nic^o	5th Lt	54. 1. 1	(B) Jno	9. 3.1707
Saunders	Phil^p	AB			
Saunders	Alex^r	AB	17. 2. 2	(W) Elizth	4. 3.1707
Scadon	W^m	AB	23.12. 2	Robt Elliott	11. 3.1707
Seal	Danl	Ord	5.13. 1	(W) Ann	9. 3.1707
Sebby	Saml	AB	17. 2. 2	(W) Elizath	2. 3.1707
Sexton	Thos	Ord	13. 6. 2	(M) Sarah	6. 3.1707
Sharpe	John	AB	17. 2. 2	(W)	4. 3.1707
Sheeter	Chas	Purs^r Sv^t	16.18. 1	Ann Plumb	20.10.1708
Sheppard	Thos	AB	16.17. 2	(W) Elizabth	3. 3.1707
Sheppard	Thos	Ord	13. 6. 2		6. 3.1707
Sherlock	Ge^o	Ord	24. 4. 6	(W) Ellen	9. 4.1708
Shewcrift	John	AB	16.19. 0	(W) Ann	5. 3.1707
Shiter	W^m	Ord	17.19. 4	Jno Tildersley	23. 4.1708
Shovell	**Cloud^y**	**R. Adm^l**			
Shovell	**John**	**Adm^l Ret^n**	**13. 6. 2**	**D.Eliz Shovell**	**6. 3.1707**
Sidwell	Hen.	AB	16.12. 8	Ann Evans	6. 3.1707
Silcock	Jno	AB	29.10. 6	(W) Kathrine	1. 3.1707
Silver	Tob^s	Ord	24. 6.10	(M) Isabella	1. 3.1707
Simmonds	Israel	Mids	25. 9. 7	(S) Mr^y Salmon	5. 3.1707
Simms	James	AB	30.18.10	(W) Mary	1. 3.1707
Simpson	W^m	AB	16.14. 8	(B) John	4. 3.1707
Simpson	Coll	AB			
Skelton	Saml	Carp^r Cr^w	21. 3. 1	(W) Sarah	3. 3.1707

Surname	First	Rank	Amount	NOK/Beneficry	D. Paid
Skinner	Fran	Capt Sv^t	6.16. 3	Benj Dwbrry	2. 3.1707
Slade	Thos	Q^r M^r M^t	21.13. 6	Is^a Stidson	10. 2.1708
Smaldrig	Thos	AB	17. 2. 2	(W) Mary	3. 3.1707
Smith	Jno	Boats	52.11. 3	Har^{ld} Masters	9. 3.1707
Smith	Phile	Ord	19. 5. 5	Hugh Pain	2. 3.1707
Smith	Jno	Ord	16. 7. 3	Saml Scutt	2. 3.1707
Smith	Nic^s	AB	16.19. 0	(W) Joan	9. 3.1707
Smith	Jam.	Carp^r	11.14. 0	(W) Lydia	17. 8.1708
Smith (1)	W^m	AB	16.19. 0	(F) Thomas	5. 3.1707
Snow	Saml	AB	15. 4.10	(W) Kath^{ne}	9. 3.1707
Spareman	W^m	Ord	17. 0. 4	(B) Rich^d	2. 3.1707
Speciall	Math.	G^r M^t	25. 9. 7	(S) Mary	3. 3.1707
Spence	John	Ord	6.16. 3	(F) George	18. 3.1707
Spragg	Thos	AB	16.15.10	Elizth Smith	6. 3.1707
Spurr	Hen.	Mids	29. 10. 9	(W) Anne	4. 3.1707
Squibb	James	Ord	13. 6. 2	(F) W^m	4. 3.1707
St. John	W^m	Ord	18.14. 7	(M) Sarah	1. 3.1707
Stains	W^m	Ord	24. 7. 2	(W) Tomasin	1. 3.1707
Stanley	Fra^s	AB	16.15.10	(W) Mary	3. 3.1707
State	Jno	Ord	17. 5. 6	(W) Elizabeth	2. 3.1707
Steele	W^m	Mr Swab	32. 2. 6	(W) Abigail	2. 7.1707
Stegg	R^d	Cook	35. 8. 1	(W) Elin^r	1. 3.1707
Stevens	W^m	Ord	22.16. 0	Jno Hill	11. 3.1707
Stevens	W^m	AB	16.12. 8	(W) Sarah	4. 3.1707
Stevens	Ant^y	AB	17. 2. 2	(W) Kathrine	5. 3.1707
Stevens	W^m	Ord	13. 6. 2	(M) Sarah	6. 3.1707
Stockman	John	AB			
Stringer	Gilb^t	AB	16.11.10	Ann Davis	4. 3.1707
Sturgeon	John	AB	17. 2. 2	(F) James	4. 3.1707
Summrfield	Perciv^l	AB	14.12. 7	(W) Ann	5. 3.1707
Summers	John	Capt Sv^t	6. 16. 3	Cpt's (W) Mry	2. 3.1707
Surle	Edwd	AB	17. 2. 2	Thos Searle	5. 3.1707
Swinny	Den^s	AB	15.17. 6	Wm Stocker	5. 3.1707
Tar	John	AB	16.15.10	Fra. Cartor	5. 3.1707
Taylor	Jno	Chyr Sv^t	26. 7. 4	Chyr^s (W) Deb	2. 3.1707
Taylor	W^m	Ord	16. 2. 4	(W) Sarah	20. 3.1707
Taylor	Chas	AB	17. 2. 2	(W) Mary	2. 3.1707
Taylor	Henry	AB	16. 3.10	(F) Hen^{ry}	5. 3.1707
Taylor	John	Capt Sv^t	6.16. 3	Cpt's (W) Mry	2. 3.1707
Taylor	W^m	Ord			
Taylor (2)	John	Ord	16.10. 3	(F) William	3. 3.1707
Tead	Jos.	Ord	12. 8. 8		9. 2.1708
Terry	Phill	AB			
Thackery	Rich^d	Ord	23.13. 4	(F)Geo	1. 3.1707
Thankam	Thos	AB	16. 9. 6	Nic^o Wright	10. 2.1708
Thompson	Jno	AB	18. 0. 8	(W) Grace	2. 3.1707

Surname	First	Rank	Amount	NOK/Beneficry	D. Paid
Thompson (2)	W^m	Arc	23. 0. 6	(W) Elizabeth	1. 3.1707
Thorne	Jno	AB	18.17. 6	Mary Thorne	3. 3.1707
Thwaites	Thos	Ord	6.16. 3	(F) Thoms	30. 3.1709
Tico	Thos	AB	17. 2. 2	(W) Rebecca	2. 3.1707
Tilham	Jno	AB	30.17. 8	(W) Elizabeth	1. 3.1707
Tilderly	Jno	Purs^r	69. 9. 7	Mg^t Alderson	20.10.1708
Till	John	AB	17. 2. 2	(W) Jane	2. 3.1707
Timms	Rich^d	AB	34. 3. 0	(W) Mary	1. 3.1707
Tinkerson	Arth^r	Capt Sv^t	6. 9. 3	Benj Dwbrry	2. 3.1707
Tinkerson	Arth$^{r.}$	AB	34.13. 2	(W) Elizabeth	1. 3.1707
Tippett	Rich^d	AB			
Tompion	John	AB			
Tovey	R^d	AB	17. 2. 2	(F) Richard	5. 3.1707
Tratlet	R^d	AB	8. 5. 7	(F) R^d	12. 7.1708
Trefrey	Cha	Gun^r	68.10. 3	(W) Mary	1. 3.1707
Tregnall	Pet^r	AB	18. 6. 5	John Mulliott	3. 3.1707
Trifrey	Caesr	Q^r G^r	16.13. 7	(W) Mary	2. 3.1707
Trodd	Th^o	AB	30. 4. 2	(W) Margaret	1. 3.1707
Trood	Chas	Ord	18. 0. 5	(F) Edmund	9. 2.1708
Truman	Thos	AB	33. 8. 0	(W) Elizabeth	1. 3.1707
Trussing	Dav.	AB	33.18. 0	(W) Elizabeth	1. 3.1707
Tucker	Matt.	Gunsth	34.18. 7	(W) Susannah	1. 3.1707
Tuk	Ben.	AB	15.10.10	(W) Elizth	9. 3.1707
Tumbar	John	AB	16.15.10	(W) Susannah	5. 3.1707
Turner	Jno	AB	19. 7. 7	Mart^n Watson	2. 3.1707
Turno	Hen.	AB	16.12. 8	Elias Armand	3. 3.1707
Twiford	Jam.	Ord	13. 6. 2	Saml Laver	5. 3.1707
Urion	Curson	AB			
Urling	Geo.	AB	16.12. 8	Thos.	4. 3.1707
Urquahart	Jam.	AB			
Ush	Rich^d	AB	31.14. 8	(M) Agnes	1. 3.1707
Vandale	John	AB	17. 2. 2	(W) Ann	4. 3.1707
Veal	E^d	AB	33. 8. 6	(W) Elizth	6. 3.1707
Visando	Is^c	AB	18.12. 9	Fra Guering	5. 3.1707
Vittle	Jno	Ord	15.19. 1	(F) Geo	9. 2.1708
Walker	W^m	AB	20. 4. 1	(B) Edwd	3. 3.1707
Walker	John	AB	17. 2. 2	(W) Kathrine	5. 3.1707
Ward	Jno	Ord	15. 6. 1	(M) Mary	2. 3.1707
Ward	Robt	Q^r G^r	22.19.10	(M) Rebecca	2. 3.1707
Warren	W^m	AB	15.17. 6	(M)Elizth	4. 3.1707
Watson	Robt	Chyr M^t	58. 0. 3	(F) Jno	1. 3.1707
Watson	Jno	AB	23.14. 2	Mr^y Thompsn	2. 3.1707
Wattson	W^m	AB	16.15.10	Mary Bourn	6. 3.1707
Weals	Saml	AB	15. 3. 4	(W)Elizabeth	6. 3.1707
Webb	Allen	Ord	26. 4.10	(F) James	9. 2.1708
Weekes	Will	Ord	23.17. 0	(W) Mary	1. 3.1707

Surname	First	Rank	Amount	NOK/Beneficry	D. Paid
Weekes	Jn°	AB	32.11. 0	(B) William	1. 3.1707
Welch	Robt	AB	17. 0. 4	(W) Elizth	4. 3.1707
Wellington	Jn°	AB	32. 7. 0	(W) Ann	1. 3.1707
Westbrook	Geo.	AB	15.13. 2	(W) Jane	4. 3.1707
Wheatley	Robt	AB	8.11. 3	(M) Mary	9. 3.1707
Wheeland	John	Ord	12.14. 4	Jos. Avery	9. 3.1707
Whethrgtn	Jn°	Capt Sv^t	6.16. 3	Cpt's (W) Mry	2. 3.1707
White	Tho	Ord	16.14. 1	(F) Jn°	2. 3.1707
White (2)	John	AB	12. 9. 6	(M) Mary Fox	5. 3.1707
Whitehead	Th°	Ord	24. 6. 2	Jno Layfield	1. 3.1707
Whitfield	Hend.	Mast^r	251.13. 9	(W) Rose	1. 3.1707
Whittaker	Thos	AB	15. 4. 6	Jane Sealy	19. 8.1708
Whittaker	Saml.	1st Capt	218. 0. 0	(W) Mary	2. 3.1707
Wilks	Chas.	AB	17. 2. 2	(W) Ursula	5. 3.1707
Willcocks	W^m	AB	19. 8. 0	(W) Elizth	19. 8.1709
Williams	W^m	Carp^r M^t	34.11. 2	(W) Elizabeth	1. 3.1707
Williams	John	AB	18. 7. 6	Jacob Askinsn	3. 3.1707
Williams	Hen.	AB	16.12. 8	(S) Joan	3. 3.1707
Williams	Jos.	AB	16.12. 8	(F) Hen^{ry}	4. 3.1707
Williams	Hen.	Ord	12.18. 8	(M) Anne	4. 3.1707
Williams	W^m	AB			
Williams	W^m	Capt Sv^t	6.16. 3	Benj Dwbrry	2. 3.1707
Williams	Jn°	AB	8. 5. 7	(F) Roger	9. 3.1707
Willis	Chas.	AB	16.12. 8	(W) Mary	4. 3.1707
Willson	Ralph	AB	21.15. 5	Mary Russell	2. 3.1707
Wingale	W^m	Ord	25.14. 8	(M) Joan	1. 3.1707
Winter	Jn°	AB			
Withers	R^d	AB			11. 9.1710
Withinghm	Jn°	AB	33. 8. 6	(W) Susan	1. 3.1707
Wood	Jn°	AB			
Wood	W^m	Q^r G^r			4. 3.1707
Wood	Jenkin	AB	16. 9. 6	Jna Reep	4. 3.1707
Woolcock	Thos	Bo^s M^t	24.16.11	(W) Mary	5. 3.1707
Woolfnton	E^d	AB	21.14. 1	Robt Rowles	8. 3.1707
Wootton	Amb^{se}	Mids	25. 9. 7	(F) Ambrose	5. 3.1707
Wotton	Hen.	AB	33. 5. 4	(W) Mary	1. 3.1707
Wright	Hen^r	AB	21.10. 6	(F) W^m	10. 2.1708
Wright	W^m	AB	15. 0.10	Saml Cloud	8. 3.1707
Wright	Cuthb^t	Ord	5.14. 5	Jn° Bonner	10. 2.1708
Yeardsley	Robt	AB	17. 1. 4	(F) Thos	9. 3.1707
Yeo	Arth.	AB	31. 9. 0	(W) Joan	1. 3.1707

APPENDIX I B

ASSOCIATION - ROYAL MARINES - OCTOBER 1707

Surname	First	Rank	Surname	First	Rank
Alstone	Sym^n	Mne	Johnson	Jno	Serj.
Beckley	Jno	Mne	Johnson	Jam.	Mne
Brooks	Pet^r	Mne	Loader	Rb^t	Mne
Burridge	Geo.	Mne	Marsh	Pet^r	Mne
Chandler	Hen.	Mne	McDonell	Arth.	Mne
Chandler	R^d	Mne	Napper	Jno	Mne
Cleater	W^m	Mne	Orland	Jas	Mne
Corps	Jno	Corp^l	Pinade	Jno	Mne
Cowles	Jno	Mne	Price	Jno	Mne
Fife	Rb^t	Mne	Pursett	Ed.	Mne
Gammitt	Tho.	Mne	Randolph	Corn^s	Mne
Gray	Nic^o	Drum^r	Sanders	R^d	Mne
Howard	Sa	Mne	Scott	Ed.	Mne

APPENDIX II A

EAGLE - NAVAL CREW - OCTOBER 1707

Surname	First	Rank	Amount	NOK/Beneficry	D. Paid
Alderton	R^d	AB	18.12.11	Robt Walker	14. 2.1708
Allen	Jo^s	AB	25.10. 1	(W) Hest^r	1. 4.1708
Anderson	Walt^r	AB	20. 6. 8	Jane Anderson	25. 3.1708
Answorth	Lewis	Ord	13. 6. 2	(S) Marg^t	30. 3.1708
Apsley	Ad^w	Mids	55. 0. 1	(S) Jane	13. 3.1707
Armerare	Paul	Ord	15. 7. 7	(F) Geo	30. 3.1708
Atkins	Saml	Ord	17.14. 6	(W) Sarah	27. 3.1708
Atkinson	Math.	AB	33.11. 8	(W) Deborah	13. 3.1707
Atkinson	Perci^l	AB	33. 6.11	Ann Jenkins	15. 3.1707
Attwood	Jno	Ord	26. 1. 8	(M) Joan	14. 2.1708
Bagnell	R^d	AB	17. 2. 2	Hanah Hollest^r	27. 3.1708
Baldwin	Jno	AB	26. 4. 9	(W) Hanah	30. 3.1708
Bale	Corn^s	AB	17. 2. 2	(W) Hanah	25. 3.1708
Baptisloe	Jno	Ord	13. 6. 2	Jos Whinead	8. 4.1708
Barber	W^m	Ord	17.18. 6	Leon^d Cullen	16. 3.1707
Barlow	W^m	AB	33. 6.11	(W) Elizth	15. 3.1707
Barnard	Tim^{ty}	Ord	19.11. 4	(S) Mary	23. 3.1707
Barter	Ben	AB	32.16. 3	(W) Sarah	13. 3.1707
Bartlett	W^m	Ord	29.12. 3	(W) Kth^{ne}	15. 3.1707
Bartlett	R^d	Ord	20. 6. 2	Saml North	16. 3.1707

Surname	First	Rank	Amount	NOK/Beneficry	D. Paid
Bass	Jn[o]	Ord	20. 4.10	(S) Mary	27. 3.1708
Baxter	Corn[s]	AB	17. 2. 2	Eliz[th] Cotton	30. 3.1708
Bayford	W[m]	Ord	19. 0. 7	(M) Mary Hancock	16. 3.1707
Beacham	R[t]	Ord	1.10. 0	(M) M. Bailey	14. 2.1708
Beale	Jn[o]	AB	2. 4. 1	(W) Ann	14. 2.1708
Beatie	W[m]	Schlmst[r]	11.16. 8	Edw[d] Sussex	30. 3.1708
Best	Ja[s]	AB	33.18.10	(W) Sarah	15. 3.1707
Bethele	Ben.	AB	32.18. 0	Ann	13. 3.1707
Bignall	Jn[o]	Ord	25.12. 4	(F) Emanuel	2. 6.1708
Bilton	Tho	AB	33.18. 0	(M) Experience	15. 3.1707
Bishop	Jn[o]	Gun[r] M[t]	46.14. 3	(W) Mary	13. 3.1707
Bishop	Tho	AB	33. 0. 6	(F) Thomas	13. 3.1707
Blackmore	Tho	Ord	26. 1. 8	(F) Charles	15. 3.1707
Boatswaine	Walt[r]	AB	25. 7.11	(W) Frances	14. 2.1708
Booker	W[m]	AB	33.12. 4	(M) Ann	13. 3.1707
Bosemen	Geo	AB	25.11.10	Eliz Lawson	18. 3.1707
Bowne	Jn[o]	Ord	25.12. 4	(W) Susan	13. 3.1707
Breman	Jn[o]	Ord	25.14. 2	(M) Mary	13. 3.1707
Bridgford	Edw[d]	Ord			
Bright	Jn[o]	AB	32.16. 2	(W) Eliz[th]	7. 6.1708
Brisben	Jn[o]	Ord	20. 4.10	Ann Collard	14. 2.1708
Broom	Ralph	3rd L[t] Sv[t]	18.19.11	(F) Patrick	20. 3.1707
Browne	Geo	AB	34.13. 2	Ann Finley	13. 3.1707
Browne	Jam.	Ord	24.19. 1	(M) Jane	15. 3.1707
Browne	Tho	AB	31. 9.11	Eliz[th] Brooks	15. 3.1707
Browne	R[d]	Q[r] M[r] M[t]	29. 7. 7	(W) Eliz[th]	23. 3.1707
Browne	Hen	AB	22.10. 0	(M) Ann	23. 3.1707
Browne (2)	Tho	AB	23. 2. 1	(W) Mary	25. 3.1708
Brwnrdge	Geo	Q[r] G[r]	35. 9. 1	(W) Mary	13. 3.1707
Buckinghm	Isa[c]	Ord	25.12. 4	R[d] Frinins	15. 3.1707
Buckland	R[t]	AB	17. 2. 2	(M) Anne	23. 3.1707
Burgis	Fra	Ord	26. 4. 2	(M) Eliz[th]	15. 3.1707
Burnham	Sam[l]	Ord	25.12. 4	Chas Demits	13. 3.1707
Cable	Tho	AB	32.18. 9	(F) Thomas	23. 3.1707
Canary	Tho	Mids	54. 4.11	Wm Risens	6. 7.1708
Canarys	W[m]	Chapl[n]	26. 7. 4	W[m] Rivers	11. 3.1707
Caperon	Ja[s]	Ord			
Carpenter	Jack	Mids	41.10. 4	(W) Marg[t]	23. 3.1707
Carpenter (2)	Jack	Cap[t] Sv[t]	19.18. 1	Cp[t]s (W) Mary	16. 3.1707
Carrington	Tho[s]	AB	23.16. 4	Cp[t]s (W) Mary	25. 3.1708
Carter	Ja[s]	AB	34.13. 2	Mary Roberts	7. 6.1708
Carter	Ste	AB	33. 5. 6	Dan[l] Robinson	13. 3.1707
Carter	Tho	Q[r] G[r]	26.14. 7	(M) Grace	23. 3.1707
Carthew	Tho	Ord	18.13. 5		
Cavell	R[d]	Ord	26. 7. 4	(F) Rich[d]	13. 3.1707
Chandler	Dan[l]	Ord	26. 4. 2	Geo Chandler	13. 3.1707

Surname	First	Rank	Amount	NOK/Beneficry	D. Paid
Channele	R^d	Arm^r	36. 3. 3	(W) Ann	11. 3.1707
Channell	Isaac	Capt Sv^t	19. 0. 7	Cpt^s (W) Mary	16. 3.1707
Chapman	Ja^s	Ord	13. 6. 2	Susanah Sice	30. 3.1708
Chappell	W^m	3rd L^t Sv^t	8.17. 4		
Charco	Jno	AB	34.10. 0	(W) Kath^{ne}	16. 3.1707
Checherin	Jno	Q^r G^r	24. 2. 5	Jos Deering	14. 2.1708
Chick	Jno	AB	32.16. 1	(W) Elizth	8. 4.1708
Chilcott	Jno	Ord	19. 5. 7	Chas Foard	30. 3.1708
Clarke	Tho	Capt Sv^t	18.10. 6	Cpt^s (W) Mary	16. 3.1707
Clarke (2)	Tho	Mids	41.10. 4	(W) Sarah	20. 3.1707
Clay	Robt	Q^r G^r	35. 8. 1	(B) W^m	13. 3.1707
Clist	Geo	Ord	19. 0. 7	(M) Susan	16. 4.1708
Coale	Nic^o	Ord	20. 2. 2	(F) Nic^o	30. 3.1708
Coats	Jno	Ord	17.10. 0	(B) Thomas	27. 3.1708
Cockrayne	Jno	3rd L^t	56.10.10	Wm Montgmry	5. 1.1708
Colebrand	Chas	AB	25. 4. 4	(W) Sarah	16. 3.1707
Conner	Phile	Ord	18.13.10	(W) Marg^t	16. 3.1707
Connolly	Jere	Purs^r			
Connor	Jno	Ord	24.14.10	(W) Dorothy	15. 3.1707
Cooke	W^m	AB	32. 7. 4	Sarah	13. 3.1707
Cooper	W^m	Ord	18. 7. 6	Isaac Ayliff	16. 3.1707
Corcking	Tobias	AB	26.11. 3	(W) Jane	16. 3.1707
Cotten	Tho	Capt Sv^t	10.19. 5	Cp^{t}s (W) Mary	16. 3.1707
Cotten (1)	W^m	Coop^r	16. 2. 1	(W) Susanna	16. 3.1707
Cotten (2)	W^m	Capt Sv^t	12. 2. 7	Cp^{t}s (W) Mary	16. 3.1707
Craford	Jam^s	3rd L^t	168.16. 0	(F) La?	20. 3.1708
Cribb	Tho	AB	33.13. 0	(W) Elizth	1. 4.1708
Crisp	R^d	AB	33. 8. 0	(F) Thomas	15. 3.1707
Culvert	Jno	AB	25.11.10	Wm Morley	27. 3.1708
Curtis	W^m	AB	32.18.10	Phillip Squire	14. 2.1708
Cuttance	Phil^p	Ord	16.17.11	Jno Seale	1. 4.1708
Davis	Jer^y	AB	18.12.11	Geo Selby	14. 2.1708
Davison	Ja^s	AB	17. 2. 2	Ste Fulford	30. 3.1708
Daw	W^m	AB	33.10. 6	(W) Elizth	15. 3.1707
Day	R^d	Ord	26. 4. 2	(F) Thomas	25. 3.1708
Descale	Tim^y	AB	17.11. 9	(W) Hanah	23. 3.1707
Dibdale	Jo^s	AB	34. 5. 8	(W) Barbara	27. 3.1707
Dickason	Jno	Q^r G^r	34.14.11	(W) Elizth	13. 3.1707
Dixon	Isaac	AB	33. 7. 4	Phill^p Squire	1. 4.1708
Dixon	Jno	Q^r G^r	26.14. 7	(W) Sarah	23. 3.1707
Draggit	Danl	AB	33.19.10	Ben Webster	13. 3.1707
Drane	W^m	Ord	25. 2.10	(M) Mary	15. 3.1707
Ducate	Jam^s	AB	32.14.10	Elias Armand	13. 3.1707
Dulgardner	Dv^d	Mids	54. 4.11	(W) Sarah	15. 3.1707
Dunn	Chas	Ord			
Eastcourt	Jno	Ord	26. 0. 6	(W) Mary	15. 3.1707

Surname	First	Rank	Amount	NOK/Beneficry	D. Paid
Eaton	Jno	Ord	26. 7. 4	(W) Sarah	15. 3.1707
Edwards	Jno	Ord	26. 3. 0	(M) Ann	1. 4.1708
Edwards	Jno	AB	17. 2. 2	Hen Cook	30. 3.1708
Edwards (1)	E^d	Ord	19. 2. 7	(B) Robert	23. 3.1707
Elcumb	Jno	Mids	42.12.11	(S) Mary Leach	15. 3.1707
Elliott	W^m	AB	22. 1. 9	Marg^t James	30. 3.1708
English	Tho	AB	33. 5. 6	(M) Kath^{ne}	13. 3.1707
English	R^d	AB	32. 7. 8	(M) Kath^{ne}	15. 3.1707
Farne	Thos	Ord	26. 2. 4	Sarah Groves	25. 3.1708
Fett	Martin	AB	32.14.10	Elias Armand	13. 3.1707
Fisher	Jno	Ord	18.16. 3	(F) Rd	16. 3.1707
Fisher	Lawr^{nc}	Chyr	148. 8. 9	(W) Jane	11. 3.1707
Foresight	W^m	AB	33.14. 4	Saml King	13. 3.1707
Frary	Jno	Ord			
Frazer	Jno	AB	33.18. 0	Alice Elder	13. 3.1707
Funter	Jno	Carp^r M^t	51. 6. 6	Frances Upton	14. 2.1708
Gardner	Jno	Q^r M^r M^t	40.13. 9	(W) Johanna	13. 3.1707
Gardner	Saml	AB	2. 5.10	(W) Clare	14. 2.1708
Getling	W^m	Ord	24.16. 0	(F) Jeremy	13. 3.1707
Gibson	Tho	AB	25.11.10	Elin^r Johnson	1. 4.1708
Goden	Jno	Capt Sv^t	17.15. 8	Cp^{t}s (W) Mary	16. 3.1707
Goding	Chris^r	Ord	17. 3. 9	(S) Jane	30. 3.1708
Gooden	Jno	Cook	25. 4.10	(W) Elizth	27. 3.1708
Gordon	Alex^r	2nd L^t	43. 4. 1	(B) Geo	30. 3.1708
Gould	Tho	AB	33.10. 6	(S) Ann	15. 3.1707
Grant	Jno	Carp^r Sv^t	13. 1.10	Carp^r (W) Elizth	16. 3.1707
Grigg	W^m	Ord	25. 5. 4	Jane Morrice	1. 4.1708
Grigg	Thos	Ord	13. 6. 2	(W) Elizth	13. 3.1707
Grindham	Jno	AB	32.17. 4	Robt Young	15. 3.1707
Hackswrth	Hen	AB	17. 2. 2	(W) Jane	30. 3.1708
Hale	Tho	AB	33.18. 0	(W) Elizth	15. 3.1707
Hale (2)	Thos	AB	25. 4. 6	Wm Wright	23. 3.1707
Hamond	Tho	AB	34. 5. 8	Sibil How	14. 2.1708
Hancock	Robt	Comd^r	418.14. 0	(W) Mary	16. 3.1707
Hancock	Robt	AB	2. 5.10	(M) Jane	14. 2.1708
Hand	Rich^d	Capt Sv^t	18. 6.10	Cpt^s (W) Mary	16. 3.1707
Hanson	Jno	AB	25. 3. 8	(W) Mary	1. 4.1708
Hardcastle	Cuthbt	Yeo Pdr	46.14. 3	(M) Anne	13. 3.1707
Harden	W^m	AB	33.11. 8	(W) June	13. 3.1707
Hare	Jno	Capt Sv^t	19.16. 7	Cp^{t}s (W) Mary	16. 3.1707
Hare	W^m	Capt Sv^t	14. 0. 8	Cp^{t}s (W) Mary	16. 3.1707
Harefinch	Tho	AB	33.13. 8	(W) Ann	15. 3.1707
Harley	W^m	AB	33.18. 0	(M) Elizth	13. 3.1707
Harrison	And^w	Mids	40. 9. 5	(W) Rachel	25. 3.1708
Hayman	Jas	Ord	17.19. 9	Martn Carsack	30. 3.1708
Heath	W^m	Q^r M^r M^t	35.18. 3	(W) Bridgett	13. 3.1707

Surname	First	Rank	Amount	NOK/Beneficry	D. Paid
Heley	Tho	AB	33.18. 0	(W) Lucretia	15. 3.1707
Henderson	Walt	AB	4. 6. 0	Jane Hendrson	25. 3.1708
Hewitt	Jno	3rd Lt Sv^t	19. 0. 7	(S) Mary	16. 3.1707
Hewitt	W^m	Trump^r	18. 6. 2	(W) Mary	14. 2.1708
Hide	Jno	Ord	18. 3. 9	Edwd Ebden	1. 4.1708
Hind	Harm^d	AB	24. 2.10	Wm Day	23. 3.1707
Hinkson	Jno	Ord	19. 1. 3	Saml Parcel	23. 3.1707
Holland	W^m	Capt Sv^t	19.16. 1	Cp^t's (W) Mary	16. 3.1707
Hooker	Tho	AB	33.18. 0	Jno Machin	22. 8.1709
Hopkins	Geo	AB	18.12.11	(W) Sarah	23. 3.1707
Hopps	Tho	Mids	55. 0. 1	W^m Ho?	25. 3.1708
Horlett	Isa^c	Ord	19.12. 5	Sylv^s Blackbrne	16. 3.1707
Horoe	W^m	AB	17. 2. 2	(W) Ann	20. 3.1707
Horrele	Thos	AB	26. 2. 2	(S) Johanah	16. 3.1707
Horwile	Jacob	AB	17. 1. 4	Edwd Foster	30. 3.1708
Hoskins	Fra	Capt Sv^t	19. 0. 7	Cp^t's (W) Mary	27. 3.1708
Howell	E^d	AB	33. 5. 6	(F) Edwd	13. 3.1707
Hudson	Thos	Ord	26. 4.10	R^d Price	16. 3.1707
Hule	Tho	AB	25.16. 7	(W) Anne	23. 3.1707
Humour	Thos	Ord	26. 3. 0	(F) Thomas	15. 3.1707
Hutchinson	Geo	Carp^r	44. 2.10	(W) Eliz^th	16. 3.1707
Hyatt	Rich^d	Mids	55. 0. 1	(W) Sarah	11. 3.1707
Hyde	Sylv^r	AB	33.14.10	(F)	1. 4.1708
Jacha	Bry^n	Ord	25.16. 2	Wm Stocker	8. 4.1708
Jackson	Walt^r	Mids	54. 4.11	(B) Wm	13. 3.1707
Jackson	W^m	AB	33.13. 0	Geo Grayden	15. 3.1707
James	Hen	Ord	25.19.10	Edwd Ebden	8. 3.1707
Jcnning	Ben	AB			
Jewell	Rich^d	Q^r M^r	45.19. 1	(W) Eliz^th	13. 3.1707
Johnson	W^m	AB	32.12. 6	Fra Acton	13. 3.1707
Jones	Tho	Ord	26. 7. 4	(F) Tho	13. 3.1707
Jones	Jno	AB	32.19.10	Sarah Bratt	8. 4.1708
Jones	W^m	Ord	17. 9. 4	(F) Jno Thomas	8. 4.1708
Jones	Jo^s	Ord	13. 6. 2	(B) Geo	30. 3.1708
Jones (1)	W^m	Ck Sv^t	18. 8. 2	Ck^s (W) Eliz^th	27. 3.1708
Jones (3)	Jno	Capt Sv^t	18.12. 6	Cpt^s (W) Mary	16. 3.1707
Joyner	Tho	Ord	26. 7. 1	(W) Jane	13. 3.1707
Kelly	E^d	Capt Sv^t	19. 0. 7	Cpt^s (W) Mary	16. 3.1707
Kent	W^m	Q^r M^r	46.14. 3	(W) Mary	15. 3.1707
Kidd	Jno	Ord	27. 7. 4	(F) John	15. 3.1707
Knight	Robt	AB	33.18. 0	(S) Joan	13. 3.1707
Knight	Jasp^r	Ord	12. 2. 7	(M) Jane	11. 3.1707
Lambert	W^m	Gun^r M^t	45.19. 1	(M) Mary	13. 3.1707
Lawnest	Dav^d	AB	25.11.10	Flora Christian	25. 3.1708
Lea	E^d	Ord	26. 7. 4	(F) Charles	15. 3.1707
Lebrock	Fra	Ord	26. 4. 2	Eliz^th Browne	27. 3.1708

Surname	First	Rank	Amount	NOK/Beneficry	D. Paid
Lenox	Dv^d	Ord	30. 5. 7	(W) Marg^t	14. 2.1708
Leo	Tho	Ord			
Lewis	Jno	Ord	18.16. 3	(W) Elizth	30. 3.1708
Lexton	Jno	AB	23. 6.10	(W) Mary	27. 3.1707
Longden	Ja^s	AB	17. 2. 2	(F) Justinian	8.10.1709
Longwrthy	Jno	Ord	18.16. 3	(M) Mary	30. 3.1708
Lovell	Jno	AB	18.12.11	(W) Elizth	30. 3.1708
Luffley	Jno	Ord	26. 8. 2	Mary Gittings	1. 4.1709
Lybourne	Rb^t	Ord			
Macklain	Geo	AB	39. 9. 7	(W) Mary	13. 3.1707
Mademan	R^d	Gun^r Sv^t	14. 5. 0	Gun^{r}s (W) Anne	30. 3.1708
Manning	Jno	Ord	26. 7. 4	Wm Simpson	15. 3.1707
Marcup	W^m	Q^r G^r	26.10. 4	Robt Staires	28. 3.1707
Marrow	Alex^r	Capt Sv^t	18.12. 6	Cpt^s (W) Mary	16. 3.1707
Marshall	Geo	Gun^r	47.12. 8	(W) Anne	30. 3.1708
Martin	Ben.	AB	33.14.10	Caleb Carrick	15. 3.1707
Mason	Pet^r	AB	33.18. 0	(W)	13. 3.1707
Mason	Ben.	AB	33.14.10	(B) Isaac	13. 3.1707
Mason	Chas	AB	33. 7. 6	(W) Judith	15. 3.1707
Mason	Saml	Ord	13. 6. 2	Mary Eldred	30. 3.1708
Mathews	Dav^d	Ord	19. 5.11	Wm Hinton	4. 4.1709
Matthews	W^m	AB	32. 0. 6	(W) Martha	13. 3.1707
Maturee	Elias	AB	32.15.10	Elias Armand	13. 3.1707
Maugh	R^d	Q^r G^r	26.14. 7	Jane Young	20. 3.1707
Maypowdr	Fra	Ord	10. 8. 8	(W) Hest^r	30. 3.1708
Messnghm	Fra	M^r M^t	63.18. 3	Susan Horton	25. 3.1707
Milburne	Geo	Chyr Mt	45. 0. 1	(M) Joyce	5. 3.1707
Mills	R^d	AB	25. 4.10	(B) W^m	15. 3.1707
Mntstphn	W^m	AB	33.13. 0	(F) John	13. 3.1707
Montooth	Geo	Q^r G^r	26.16. 0	(W) Susannah	16. 3.1707
Moor	Jos	Ord	26. 7. 4	(W) Hannah	13. 3.1707
More	Pat^k	Vol	16. 3. 9	(M) Barbara	16. 3.1707
Morris	Jno	Ord	13. 6. 2	(F) John	20. 3.1707
Morriss	Tho	AB	33. 7. 4	(M) Marg^t	13. 3.1707
Napman	R^t	Ord	19.14.11	Jno Collins	2. 6.1708
Nelson	Christ^n	Q^r G^r	32. 4. 7	(W) Elizth	11. 3.1707
Newman	W^m	Ord	24.12. 4	Wm Paine	13. 3.1707
Newton	Dav^d	AB	33.11. 2	Robt Bennet	15. 3.1707
Nicholes	Jno	Vol	19.12. 5	(F) Jno	16. 3.1707
Nicholes (2)	Jno	AB	17. 2. 2	(W) Elizth	30. 3.1708
Nicholson	Jno	VPO	17.15. 8	Jos Nicholson	14. 2.1708
Norman	Waltr	Carp^r Cr^w	35. 3. 1	Phill Squire	13. 3.1707
Noulton	E^d	AB	30.13. 0	(W) Elizth	15. 3.1707
Oar	Jno	Ord	25.18. 2	(W) Hest^r	13. 3.1707
Oswell	Jno	Capt Sv^t	18. 3. 9	Cpt^s (W) Mary	16. 3.1707
Overhale	Jo^s	Ord	26. 3. 0	(M) Elin^r	13. 3.1707

Surname	First	Rank	Amount	NOK/Beneficry	D. Paid
Overy	Jno	Ord	16.13. 5	(W) $Eliz^{th}$	27. 3.1708
Paine	Hen.	Pens	33.14.10	(W) Sarah	13. 3.1707
Palmer	Jno	AB	32.19.10	Ann Young	15. 3.1707
Palmer	Ja^s	$Cap^t Sv^t$			
Parrott	Robt	AB	33.14.10	$Rich^d$ Bowen	15. 3.1707
Pasco	Tho	AB	34.10. 0	(W) Mary	11. 3.1707
Pattman	Tho	Ord	25. 9. 2	Tho Bucknace	1. 4.1708
Pearson	Tho	Ord	26. 7. 4	(M) $Eliz^{th}$ West	16. 3.1707
Pele	Thos	$Carp^r Cr^w$	35. 2. 5	(W) Alice	15. 3.1707
Pennycoate	Jno	$Bo^s M^t$	46.14. 3	(W) Ann	11. 3.1707
Perkins	Sim^n	Ord	25. 9. 2	(F) Symon	15. 3.1707
Philles	Pet^r	AB	33. 6. 5	Jane Moltiver	16. 3.1707
Pinchard	Hen	Mids	38. 7. 4	(W) Mary	16. 3.1707
Pitts	Hugh	Ord	13. 6. 2	Geo Round	30. 3.1708
Ploughman	Tho	Ord	26. 1. 9	Edwd Miles	1. 4.1708
Pool	Jno	$Q^r G^r$	35. 8. 1	(W) Ann	13. 3.1707
Poole (2)	Jno	Ord	13. 6. 2	Robt Fuller	23. 9.1709
Porter	Geo	AB	25. 1.10	Sar^h Colebrone	16. 3.1707
Potts	Jno	Ord	19.10. 0	(W) June	27. 3.1708
Pratt	Coe	AB			
Price	Jno	AB	17. 2. 2	Elias Armand	30. 3.1708
Punch	Edwd	$Boat^s$	88.18. 3	(W) Mary	10. 3.1707
Punch (2)	E^d	$Bo^s Sv^t$	18. 3. 9	Bot^s (W) Mary	16. 3.1707
Purchance	E^d	Ord	17.14. 0	(F) Jos	30. 3.1708
Pursell	W^m	Ord			
Rabby	Jno	AB	33.18. 0	Jam La Roach	15. 3.1707
Radford	Rog^r	Ord	19.10. 8	$Alex^r$ Sampson	14. 2.1708
Randele	Jno	$Ck M^t$	31.12. 5	(W) Amy	15. 3.1707
Rayner	R^d	$Cap^t Sv^t$	19.18. 1	$Cp^t s$ (W) Mary	16. 3.1707
Reeves	Danl	AB	9.19. 4	Jno Bishop	18. 3.1707
Renne	Jno	AB	33.14.10	Elias Armand	13. 3.1707
Richer	W^m	AB	27. 7. 5	Jno Roker	15. 3.1707
Ridley (2)	Jno	AB	17. 2. 2	(W) Ansel	30. 3.1708
Roades	Chas	Ord	18. 3. 5	(M) Jillian	25. 3.1709
Robinson	Tho	$Carp^r Cr^w$	33.17. 5	Mary Goodwin	21. 4.1708
Robinson	Danl	AB	33.13. 8	Jno Woold	13. 3.1707
Rogers	Jno	$Stew^d$	26. 3. 8	Prize Vict Acc.	16. 3.1707
Rogers	$Oliv^r$	Ord	18. 4.11	(W) Mary	30. 3.1708
Rooke	Geo	Capt Clk	40. 3. 0	(F) Jno	23. 3.1707
Ross (2)	W^m	AB	33. 3. 0	Jno Woolridge	13. 3.1707
Roy	Jno	AB	33.14.10	Elias Armand	13. 3.1707
Ruman	Jno	AB	33. 6. 2	(W) June	13. 3.1707
Scater	Jno	$Cap^t Sv^t$	19.18. 1	$Cp^t s$ (W) Mary	16. 3.1707
Scott	Rand.	Ord	25.19.10	Phill Squire	13. 3.1707
Scott	R^t	Ord			
Seaten	Jno	AB	33.17. 6	(W) Susan	13. 3.1707

Surname	First	Rank	Amount	NOK/Beneficry	D. Paid
Sellacke	Ja^s	Ord	20. 2. 6	(W) Kath^ne	27. 3.1708
Sessions	Hen	AB	33. 3. 0	Wm Stretfield	30. 3.1708
Shannon	R^d	Capt Sv^t	17.15. 8	Cp^ts (W) Mary	16. 3.1707
Shiers	Math.	AB	30.16. 5	Phill^p Squire	29. 3.1709
Shillabeer	Jno	Ord	20.11. 3	(W) Grace	30. 3.1708
Shovell	**Jno**	**AB**	**22. 9. 4**	**(W) Judith**	**21. 4.1708**
Slade	Hen	AB	33.14.10	(S) Eliz^th	15. 3.1707
Smith	Ste	Q^r G^r	26.14. 7	(S) Eliz^th	16. 3.1707
Smith	Geo	Ord	17.19. 0	Mary Bennett	16. 3.1707
Smith	W^m	Mids	40. 9. 5	(S) Sarah	23. 3.1707
Smith	Ja^s	Chyr Sv^t	17. 1.11	(W) Jane	11. 3.1707
Smith (1)	Jno	Ord	25. 7. 6	(F) John	15. 3.1707
Soaper	Jo^s	Vol			
Spadua	Jno	Pens	24.16. 5	(W) Kath^ne	16. 3.1707
Spence	W^m	Ord			
Spragg	Christ^r	AB	33. 4.10	(W) Frances	13. 3.1707
St John	Paul	Vol			
Stinlly	Jno	AB	17. 2. 2	(M) Anne	15. 7.1708
Streach	Dav^d	Ord	26. 1. 8	R^d Wolstead	13. 3.1707
Symonds	Samp^n	AB	17. 2. 2	Eliz^th Player	22. 8.1709
Teat	Ja^s	AB	32.18. 0	Phillis Squire	13. 3.1707
Tidbury	Geo	Ord	24. 4. 4	(M) Mary	15. 3.1707
Tilly	Barn^d	AB	33.14.10	Dorothy	13. 3.1707
Tilly	Saml	Ord	26. 7. 4	(W) Alice	25. 3.1708
Tindale	R^d	Ord	18.16. 8	(W) Jane	16. 3.1707
Tippington	E^d	AB	25.11.10	(W) Eliz^th	23. 3.1707
Tre??	Tho	Cox^n	39.18. 7	(W) Lucy	1. 4.1708
Trigg	W^m	AB	34.13. 2	(W) Durance	13. 3.1707
Truscutt	Jno	Q^r M^r	46.14. 3	Ann Hardcast	13. 3.1707
Tucker	Paul	Mast^r	188. 7. 9	(W) Eliz^th	11. 3.1707
Turgis	Jno	AB	33.14.10	Jane Bodett	13. 3.1707
Turnball	W^m	Q^r M^r M^t	29.10. 2	(W) Marg^t	16. 3.1707
Turner	Tho	AB	33. 3.10	Ruth Wright	15. 3.1707
Urquart	W^m	Ord	26. 7. 4	Wm Christy	1. 4.1708
Vagers	Saml	Mr Sv^t	19. 8. 8	(W) Eliz^th	27. 3.1708
Valentine	Arch	Q^r M^r	34.12. 7	(W) Mary	13. 3.1707
Vaughn	Ja^s	Q^r G^r	35. 8. 1	(W) Mary	13. 3.1707
Veale	Tho	Ord	26. 7. 4	Edwd Ebden	1. 4.1708
Wallis	Danl	Ord	26. 7. 4	(F) Robt	13. 3.1707
Walton	Jno	Vol	17.17. 5	(F) John	20. 3.1707
Ward	R^t	Ord	13. 6. 2	(W) Eliz^th	14. 2.1708
Watts	W^m	Ord	17.12. 5	(W) Mary	25. 3.1709
Weatherhd	R^t	AB	25. 3. 1	(W) Susan	27. 3.1708
Webb	Jno	AB	33. 6. 3	(W) Ann	16. 3.1707
Webb	Thos	Ord	19.13. 1	(W) Agnes	30. 3.1708
Webber	Tho	Ord	17. 9. 3	Edwd Ebden	14. 2.1708

Surname	First	Rank	Amount	NOK/Beneficry	D. Paid
Welbeck	W^m	Ord	5.12. 5	(W) Elizth	25. 3.1708
Welch	W^m	Ord	25.10. 7	Edwd Ransford	16. 3.1707
Wells	Rog^r	Ord	19.10. 1	Sym^n How	30. 3.1708
West	Jno	Capt Sv^t	18. 3. 9	Cpt^s (W) Mary	16. 3.1707
Wetherby	W^m	Ord			15. 3.1707
White	Hen^y	AB	33.18. 2	(F) Robt	15. 3.1707
Whitmore	Clem^t	Q^r G^r	35. 8. 1	(W) Mary	13. 3.1707
Wilkins	Jno	AB	17. 2. 2	(W) Ann	23. 3.1707
Wilkinson	Cuthb^t	AB	34.10. 0	(W) Deborah	13. 3.1707
Wilkinson	Tho	Mids	39.18. 3	(B) Jno	23. 3.1707
Wilkinson	R^d	Purs^r Sv^t			
Willard	Geo	Ord	17.18. 7	Thos Braddon	30. 3.1708
Williams	Jno	AB	17. 2. 2	Sarah Brown	14. 2.1708
Williams(1)	Tho	AB	33.10. 6	(W) Ursula	15. 3.1707
Williams(2)	Tho	Ord	25.19.10	(M) Ursula	15. 3.1707
Willson	Hen	Ord	17. 7. 7	Elizth Turner	25. 3.1707
Wilson (2)	Geo	AB	33.18. 0	(A) Btrix Wilsn	25. 3.1708
Wishart	Gilb^t	AB	33.14.10	Elizth Finleson	13. 3.1707
Witherhed	Thos	Ord	17.15. 0	(W) Hanah	27. 3.1708
Wood	Jno	Ord			
Wooden	Hen	Ord	5.15. 1	Mary Bennett	30. 3.1708
Woodhead	R^d	AB	33.10.10	Marg^t Barton	1. 4.1708
Wooding	Jno	Capt Sv^t	18.12. 6	Cpt^s (W) Mary	16. 3.1707
Wordell	Jno	AB	17. 2. 2	Geo Storey	30. 3.1708
Worlett	Thos	Ord	18.10. 3	(M) Hanah	25. 3.1707
Wright	Jarvis	AB	34.10. 0	(W) Ruth	13. 3.1707
Wright	Ad^m	Ord	13. 6. 2	(W) Marg^t	25. 3.1708
Wright	Tho	AB	17. 2. 2	Ann Cook	30. 3.1708
Yellow	W^m	AB	33.10. 6	(W) Joyce	15. 3.1707
Yorke	R^t	Ord	17.10. 0	(F)	27. 3.1708

APPENDIX IIB

EAGLE - ROYAL MARINES - OCT 1707

Surname	First	Rank	Surname	First	Rank
Bartly	Edwd	Mne	Long	Ja^s	Mne
Bloxom	Thos	Mne	Shelks	Neil	Mne
Howard	Jno	Mne			

APPENDIX III A

ROMNEY - NAVAL CREW - OCTOBER 1707

Surname	First	Rank	Amount	NOK/Beneficry	Date
Abbot	Ben	AB	20.12. 3	(M) Sarah	9. 4.1708
Abrith	Lawr^c	AB	33. 2. 2	Jno Dickey	9. 4.1708
Albernet	Jno	Ord	23.18.10	Wm Martin	9. 4.1708
Albin	Tho	Ord	22.13. 9	(W) Ann	13. 4.1708
Alby	W^m	Ord	22. 9.10	(F) Henry	13. 4.1708
Allwerd	Hen	Gr M^t	22. 0. 8	(W) Mary	13. 4.1708
Ashon	Tho	Mids	33.13. 8	Mary Harris	13. 4.1708
Aspele	Tho	Ord			
Atkins	Jno	Ord			
Auden	Dom^n	AB	16. 3. 4	Elias Armnd	13. 4.1708
Axton	R^d	Ord	11.15. 4	Jno Richrds	14. 2.1708
Bailey	Jno	AB	33. 4. 7	(F) Thomas	13. 4.1708
Bailey	W^m	AB	8. 4. 9	(W) Honor	13. 4.1708
Barber	Jno	AB	30. 7. 2	Edwd Nu	9. 4.1708
Barnett	Jno	Q^r G^r	6.14. 2	Em Cooper	9. 6.1708
Barrow	W^m	AB	20.12. 3	(M) Sarah	9. 4.1708
Barry	Jno	AB	28. 2. 7	Joan Cockrum	14. 2.1708
Bayle	Jam^s	Ord	21.11. 0	(W) Elin^r	13. 4.1708
Bevan	Jno	Ord	22. 9.10	(B) Thos	14. 4.1708
Bigg	Jno	AB	24.14. 8	Wm Ousnam	14. 4.1708
Bird	Lew^s	Capt Sv^t	13. 3.10	Ben Dewbrry	13. 4.1708
Birkby	Tho	Chyr^n	103.12. 0	Oliver Birkby	13. 4.1708
Blake	Geo	Chyr^n M^t	73. 1. 8	Mry Wlbridge	9. 4.1708
Bond	Giles	Bo^s M^t	31. 1. 1	(W) Sarah	14. 4.1708
Botham	E^d	Ord	22. 9. 2	Wm Evans	13. 4.1708
Breadout	Chas.	Purs^r Sv^t	26. 7. 4	Elizth Hale	8. 1.1708
Browne (2)	Jno	AB	32.13. 0	(S) Elizth	9. 4.1708
Bryor	Tho	Capt Sv^t	17. 9. 4	Benj Dwbrry	13. 4.1708
Bryson	R^d	AB	7. 5. 4	Elizth Capter	14. 2.1708
Buck	Hen	Q^r G^r	18. 7.11	(W) Jane	13. 4.1708
Burcham	W^m	Ord	26. 3. 0	Jacob Bovis	9. 4.1708
Burton	Tho	Ord	22.19. 0	Mary Hanson	13. 4.1708
Carr	Jno	AB	15. 5.11	(W) Mary	13. 4.1708
Carter	Mich	Q^r M^r M^t	20. 0. 3	(W) Jane	13. 4.1708
Castle	Jos	Ord	23.14.10	Mat^w Jones	13. 4.1708
Caw	Jno	AB	28.12. 1	(W) Alice	13. 4.1708
Cawley	Fra	Mids	34. 7. 9	(B) W^m	13. 4.1708
Certain	W^m	Ord	21.13. 0	(W) Ann	13. 4.1708
Chappele	Marke	AB	20.14. 0	(W) Elizth	13. 4.1708
Charnock	W^m	Ord	23. 1. 8	Jno Foard	9. 4.1708
Cherry	Hugh	AB	28.15. 5	(W) Bridgett	13. 4.1708

Surname	First	Rank	Amount	NOK/Beneficry	Date
Clarke	Ben	AB	33.18. 0	(B) Jos	9. 4.1708
Clawson	Barth^w	AB			
Colpet	Pet^r	AB	14. 0. 1	(W) Elizth	14. 4.1708
Colwell	Ja^s	Sailmkr	8.11. 3	Geo Graydon	14. 2.1708
Cony	W^m	Comd^r	294. 0. 0	(W) Kathrine	13. 4.1708
Conyer	Jno	Ord	17.14. 4	(M) Elizth	13. 4.1708
Coper	Saml	AB	33.18. 0	Jam Register	13. 4.1708
Croscat	W^m	AB			
Crummell	E^d	AB	15. 0. 0	Ste Fulford	13. 4.1708
Culliford	Tho	Stew^d	32.17.11	Grace Rost	1. 4.1708
Cursitor	Jas	Ord	26. 3. 0	Christ^n Beaton	9. 4.1708
Dadd	Hen	Ord	10. 6. 3	Marg^t Aldrsn	13. 4.1708
Dant	E^d	Ord			
Dawson	W^m	AB	33.18. 0	Pet^r Parr	9. 4.1708
Day	R^d	Ord	24. 4. 4	Elizth Olive	14. 4.1708
Denson	Jno	Ord	26. 7. 4	(W) Elizth	13. 4.1708
Dentory	Mark	Cks Sv^t	4.19.11	Cooks (W)	6. 7.1708
Deplage	Luke	Ord	26. 7. 4	Mary France	9. 4.1708
Desiva	Eman^l	Ord			
Dickey	Jno	Mids	48. 6. 2	(W) Marg^t	9. 4.1708
Digging	Jo^s	AB	16. 0. 1	Jno Crafts	13. 4.1708
Drake	Hen	2nd L^t	39.16. 4	(F) Benjamin	15. 4.1708
Drew	R^d	AB	33.18. 0	Thos Bromhall	9. 4.1708
Drewry	Jno	Mids	30.16. 9	(F) John	13. 4.1708
Eastmen	Tho	AB	33.11. 2	(W) Elizth	9. 4.1708
Edwards	Jno	Ord			
Elliot	W^m	Q^r M^r	42.18.10	Elizth Allen	9. 4.1708
Elliott	W^m	Ord			
Endacout	Jno	Mids	48.11.10	(F) Thomas	9. 4.1708
Failsbury	W^m	Q^r M^r	42.18.10	(W) Mary	9. 4.1708
Faulk	Ben	AB	26. 3. 5	Jonas Helsin	13. 4.1708
Ferrara	Pas^{cl}	Ord			
Fido	Jno	2nd L^t Sv^t	13. 9. 3	2nd Lt^s (B)	13. 4.1708
Fisher	R^t	Ord	16.15. 7	(F) Robt	13. 4.1708
Fond	Hugh	Q^r G^r	34. 9. 1	(W) Jane	9. 4.1708
Ford	Tho	Ord	5. 4. 4	Jno Symonds	14. 4.1708
French	Ja^s	AB	7. 1. 5	(F) Jo^s	14. 4.1708
Frizzel	Alex^r	Ord			
Fry	W^m	Ord	19. 2. 5	Jno Brittle	9. 4.1708
Fry	Danl	AB	18.19. 5	(S) Elizth	21. 4.1708
Geally	Jno	AB	30.14. 2	(M) Sarah	9. 4.1708
Gill	Phile	Boat^s	73. 1. 8	Mary	13. 4.1708
Goat	Mich	Q^r M^r M^t	40. 7. 5	(W) Elizth	9. 4.1708
Goff	Jno	Capt Sv^t	9. 9. 5	Ben Dewbrry	13. 4.1708
Goody	Jno	Bo^s Yeo	37. 5. 6	Mary Jones	2. 6.1708
Gordon	Geo	Ord	24. 5. 8	Hector	9. 4.1708

Surname	First	Rank	Amount	NOK/Beneficry	Date
Grange	W^m	Capt Sv^t	17.14. 4	Benj Dwbrry	13. 4.1708
Grashell	Eman^l	Mast^r Sv^t	5. 7. 4	(M)	9. 4.1708
Gregson	Jno	AB	32. 6. 8	(W) Mary	13. 4.1708
Griffen	Tho	Ord	26. 1. 0	Frances Noble	9. 4.1708
Grigory	E^d	Ord	17. 5. 5	Edwd Withers	9. 4.1708
Gunn	Jam^s	Carp^r Cr^w	34. 4. 9	(F) James	14. 2.1708
Gwither	R^d	AB	32.10. 2	(F) Thom^s	9. 4.1708
Harbert	Robt	Ord	11.10. 1	John Ball	14. 2.1708
Harvey	Tho	2nd L^t	85.16. 3	(B) Robert	13. 4.1708
Heming	Robt	AB			
Hervey	R^d	Mids	18.14. 5	(B) Robt	13. 4.1708
Hockaday	Walt^r	M^r M^t	70. 5. 3	(W) Sarah	9. 4.1708
Holbore	Geo	Ord	24. 5. 1	Susan Paine	9. 4.1708
Holderness	W^m	AB	15. 2. 1	(W) Grace	13. 4.1708
Holstaff	Abr.	Ord	21.11. 4	Richd Langdn	9. 4.1708
Hood	Jno	Ord			13. 4.1708
Hoskins	Tho	AB	31.17. 3	(W) Tomalin	13. 4.1708
Hyab	Fra	Bo^s M^t	42.11. 7	(W) Mary	9. 4.1708
Izard	Tho	Ord	26. 4. 0	(F) Nich^o	9. 4.1708
Johnson	Jno	Cook	36. 3. 3	(W) Elizth	9. 4.1708
Jones	Hezk	Ord	15. 1. 1	Hugh Stevens	13. 3.1708
Jones	Danl	AB	17. 1. 6	Thos Mnday	14. 2.1708
Kelly	Jerre	Ord	23.11. 3	(W) Jane	9. 4.1708
Kelly	Ben	Capt Clk	32. 1. 6	(B) Jno	13. 4.1708
King	Tho	AB			
King	R^t	Ord	5. 7. 0	(F) Robt	1. 7.1708
Kingsbury	Jo^s	Ord	11.19.10	Abrm Ham	13. 4.1708
Lamb	Tho	Ord			
Larrimore	W^m	Mast^r	167. 5. 9	John Coxhead	9. 4.1708
Lassan	R^t	Ord	5. 4. 4	Wm Davison	8. 3.1708
Lawrence	Geo	AB	30.13. 7	G. Lawrence	9. 4.1708
Lester	Barn^d	VPO	26. 7. 4	Wm Headlam	9. 4.1708
Lindsay	Math	Ord	26. 7. 4	(F) Mathew	9. 4.1708
Lody	Allex	AB	16. 3. 4	Ant^y Brass	13. 4.1708
Loing	W^m	Ord	26. 7. 4	Christ^n Beaton	14. 2.1708
Lownds	Saml	Mids	33. 9. 9	(B) Jno	15. 3.1708
Loyd	Pet^r	AB	15.18. 8	Jno Holmes	21. 2.1708
Lyon	Jno	AB	13.13. 8	(B) Pat^k	13. 4.1708
Macklough	Mar^{tn}	Ord	22. 0. 9	(M) Mary	13. 4.1708
Marnes	Jos	AB	33.18. 0	Luke Haddock	9. 4.1708
Martin	Jo^s	Q^r G^r	34.18. 7	Elizth Allen	9. 4.1708
McDevale	Jno	AB			
McFerson	Danl	AB			
Merrifield	W^m	Capt Sv^t	12.16. 7	Benj Dwbrry	13. 4.1708
Michel	R^t	Q^r G^r	16.19. 1	(W) Mary	14. 4.1708
Miller	Tho	AB	34.13. 2	(W) Mary	

Surname	First	Rank	Amount	NOK/Beneficry	Date
Minard	Geo	Capt Sv^t	13.10. 7	Benj Dwbrry	13. 4.1708
Moore	Jno	Q^r G^r	36. 3. 3	(S) John	4.12.1708
More	Saml	G^r Sayl?	25. 7. 4	Elizth Croom	9. 4.1708
Morgan	Hw^d	AB			
Morris	Giles	Ord			
Morris	Jno	Ord			
Morriss	W^m	Ord	20. 1. 2	Thos Wood	13. 4.1708
Murray	Ben	Capt Sv^t	17.14. 4	Benj Dwbrry	13. 4.1708
Murrell	E^d	AB	32. 9. 0	(M) Mary	9. 4.1708
Mushaw	Jno	2nd L^t Sv^t	5.16. 9	2^d L^t (F) Benj	15. 4.1708
Nottingham	Saml	Ord	14.16.11	(B) Jno	13. 4.1708
Nutts	Bart	Cox^n	39.12. 3	(M) Mary	9. 4.1708
Oliphant	E^d	Chyr^n Sv^t	18. 8. 2	Oliver Birkby	13. 4.1708
Omem	Jno	AB	34.13. 2	Robt Burden	13. 4.1708
Osborne	R^d	Ord	26. 1. 0	Jno Cox	14. 4.1708
Overy	Pet^r	Ord	18.16. 3	Sus^n Granger	14. 4.1708
Parrish	E^d	Capt Sv^t	18. 7. 6	Benj Dwbrry	13. 3.1708
Pell	Stephn	Carp^r	7. 1.11	Geo Pell	1. 4.1709
Pembrook	Jno	Ord			
Pencene	Chitel	VPO	26. 7. 4	(M) Elizth	9. 4.1708
Petcod	W^m	AB	29. 9. 2	Chas Clark	13. 4.1708
Peterson	Er^k	AB	26.19. 5	Jonas Helsin	13. 4.1708
Philpott	Jno	AB	32.14. 8	(W) Mary	14. 4.1708
Pierce	Geo	M^r M^t	69. 0. 7	Elizth Foley	9. 4.1708
Pitcher	Jno	M^r M^t	54. 8.10	(W) Ann	14. 4.1708
Pitman	Hugh	AB	33.15. 6	Ann Hoskins	13. 4.1708
Plat	Geo	Ord	21.13. 6	Wm Blake	9. 4.1708
Plowden	Hen^{ry}	AB	28.18. 5	Mary	14. 2.1708
Plumb	Thos	AB	2. 8. 0.	(W) Rebecca	14. 2.1708
Pope	Dan	Ord	20.18. 0	(F) Danl	13. 4.1708
Pope	Geo	Ord	23.18.10	(F) Danl	13. 4.1708
Popham	Nic^o	AB	33.15. 6	Jno Levering	15. 4.1708
Price	Dav^d	Carp^r Cr^w	35. 5. 7	Geo Pell	9. 4.1708
Pritchett	Jno	Ord			
Putteford	W^m	Cable	22.11. 9	(B) Mrmaduke	13. 4.1708
Radford	Jno	Ord	21.19. 4	Dav^d Dorrall	9. 4.1708
Rainswall	Tho	Gun^r Sv^t	19. 0. 7	Gun^{rs} (W)	9. 4.1708
Ralph	Step	AB	16. 0. 7	(S) Elizth	13. 4.1708
Rapley	R^d	Ord	24.18. 0	Wm Townsend	9. 4.1708
Remonge	Jno	AB			
Rivero	Eman^l	Ord			
Roberston	R^d	AB	33.10. 6	Elizth Carter	21. 2.1708
Roberts	W^m	Ord	5.15. 1		9. 4.1708
Roberts	Jno	Corp^l	38. 5. 0	(W) Frances	9. 4.1708
Robinson	W^m	AB			
Rogers	Robt	Yeo Pwd^r	42.18.10	(W) Isabella	9. 4.1708

Surname	First	Rank	Amount	NOK/Beneficry	Date
Rouncevall	Thos	Gun^r	73.16. 0	(W) Martha	25. 3.1708
Rowlingson	Law^{rc}	AB			
Ruth	R^d	AB	29.12. 3	(W) Grace	9. 4.1708
Sarmays	Jno	Q^r G^r	35. 8. 1	Elizth Allen	9. 4.1708
Savage	Jno	AB	11.17. 2	(M) Elizth	13. 4.1708
Savel	R^d	Trump	23.14. 3	Sus^n Lillingtn	14. 4.1708
Scott	Jno	Chyr Mt	38.19. 7	Alex^r Creightn	14. 4.1708
Scriven	Hen	AB	20.12. 3	(F) Hen^{ry}	9. 4.1708
Self	Jno	Q^r M^r	40. 5. 0	(W) Ann	9. 4.1708
Sellaven	Cha	AB			
Selvey	Jno	AB	29.19. 6	(W) Elizth	13. 4.1708
Shephard	Jno	Ord	19. 9. 4	Pet^r Marke	13. 4.1708
Smith	Jno	AB	33.14. 0	Frances Smith	13. 4.1708
Smith	W^m	Ord	21.19. 7	(M) Susan	13. 4.1708
Smith	Hen	Ord	20. 3.10	Jno Pilcher	13. 4.1708
Smith	W^m	VPO			
Sorvter	Jno	AB	33. 8. 0	(W) Sarah	9. 4.1708
Spicer	Saml	Purs^r	73.16.10	Elizth Hales	8. 1.1708
Stabb	Barn^d	Capt Sv^t	9.13. 9	(F) Saml	14. 2.1708
Standford	W^m	Ord			
Stevens	W^m	Ord			
Supple	Abr	Capt Sv^t	18. 7. 6	Benj Dwbrry	13. 3.1708
Swaine	Jno	Mids	24.18. 7	Sarah Allison	13. 4.1708
Swanson	Tho	AB	26.11. 2	Jonas Helsin	13. 4.1708
Swinwright	Jno	AB	31.15. 7	(W) Elin^r	13. 4.1708
Thaxton	Tho	Ord	24. 9. 2	(M) Elizth	13. 4.1708
Thomas	Jno	AB	24.11. 2	(W) Mary	13. 4.1708
Thomlinson	Jno	Tchr Mths	24.18. 7	(W) Jane	14. 4.1708
True	Am	Ord	5. 4. 4	Ste Roy	14. 4.1708
Verrier	E^d	Mids	32. 0. 5	(B) W^m	13. 4.1708
Waller	Jno	Ord	23.15. 8	(M) Mary	9. 4.1708
Warren	Jno	Ord	17. 9. 0	Wm Backshll	14. 4.1708
Warwick	Jno	Ord	25.12. 7	(B) Thomas	9. 4.1708
Way	Alex	AB	33.18. 0	Marg^t Newman	14. 4.1708
Weatherly	Tre^r	AB	32.18. 0	(W) Ann	9. 4.1708
Weymon	Jo^s	AB			
Weymouth	Jno	AB	33.18. 0	(W) Mary	9. 4.1708
Whitear	Oliv^r	Carp^r Cr^w	24. 5. 1	(F) Richard	3. 7.1708
Wiggen	R^d	Capt Sv^t	17. 7. 0	Benj Dwbrry	13. 4.1708
Wilkins	W^m	AB	6. 14. 1	Danl Fox	14. 4.1708
Wilson	Ben	M^r M^t	48.13. 0	(S) Sarah	9. 4.1708
Woodard	Geo	Ord	15. 2.11	(W) Alice	13. 4.1708
Woolgar	W^m	Carp^r M^t	49.14. 7	(W) Elizth	9. 4.1708
Wright	And^w	Ord	24. 8. 8	(B) Alex^r	9. 4.1708
Wright	Jno	AB	16. 6. 9	(F) W^m	13. 4.1708
Young	E^d	Ord	17. 7.10	Jno Woodgate	13. 4.1708

APPENDIX III B

ROMNEY - ROYAL MARINES - OCT 1707
Major Desideer's Company in Brigadier Holt's Regiment

Surname	First	Rank	Surname	First	Rank
Bunn	Ben.	Mne	Hill	Tho.	Mne
Clayton	Jno	Mne	Nicholls	Rd	Mne
Clogsdell	Chas	Mne	South	Jno	Mne
Decoy	Lews	Mne	Thomason	Tho.	Mne
Denham	Jno	Corpl	Thompson	Robt	Mne
Gilbert	Ph	Mne	Withings	Rd	Mne

APPENDIX IV

FIREBRAND - NAVAL CREW - OCTOBER 1707

Surname	First	Rank	Amount	NOK/Beneficry	Date	
Anderson	Rich^d	Capt S^t	6. 1.10	Capt (W) Hester	9. 2.1708	D
Baker	Kerby	Gun^r M^t	9. 8. 0	(F) Jno	9. 2.1708	D
Banister	Jno	AB	29.12. 1	Mary Steward	9. 2.1708	D
Barrillo	Fr^a	Capt S^t	4. 7. 6			S
Bradford	Cha^a	Chyr	112.18. 4			S
Bradford	Pet^r	AB	17. 3. 6		9. 2.1708	D
Brickstock	Th^o	Ord	15.16. 0	Hen Lyn	9. 2.1708	D
Browne	R^{bt}	Gun^r M^t	24.19. 7			S
Chappell	Geo	Carp^r	8. 4. 8		20.02.1707	S
Colebourne	Rich^d	AB	54.13. 2	Aaron Lamb	9. 2.1708	D
Deane (1)	Jno	Q^r M^r	39. 2. 9	(W) Mary	9. 2.1708	D
Drayton	W^m	AB	33.14. 2	(W) Mary	9. 3.1707	D
Dukman	W^m	AB	33.10. 0	(W) Charity	30. 1.1707	D
Edwards	Th^o	AB	21.13.10	R^d Cuse	1. 7.1708	D
Evans	Th^o	AB	31. 7. 5	(S) Marg^t	25. 3.1708	D
Gardiner	Jno	Ord	15.14.10	Wm Quash	9. 2.1708	D
Goreings	Jno	AB	32.11.11	(M) Susan	9. 2.1708	D
Griffith	Griff	AB	30. 1. 6	(B) Jno	1. 7.1708	D
Harling	Hnry	Boat^s	57.13. 4	Sarah	10. 7.1708	S
Harminow	M^{ke}	Bo^s M^t	39. 2. 9		9. 3.1708	S
Harrison	Th^o	M^r M^t	41.19. 2	Sarah	31.12.1707	D
Harte	Fr^a	Ord	10.11. 9			S
Hingston	W^m	Capt Sv^t	18. 6. 2			S

Surname	First	Rank	Amount	NOK/Beneficry	Date	
Johnson	James	AB	32. 0. 0	Mary Stew^d	17. 2.1708	**D**
Lewis	W^m	AB	8. 4. 8			**S**
Loader	Ge^o	AB	17. 4. 3	Johanah	9. 3.1709	**D**
Marshall	Ben	Mids	30.17. 8			**S**
Morris	Nich^{el}	Gunner	66. 6. 2	(W) Elizabeth	9. 3.1708	**D**
Morris	Jno	Gun^r Sv^t	5.13. 1	(M) Elizabeth	9. 3.1708	**D**
Morris	Jno	Ord	18. 1. 9	(M) Elizth	9. 3.1707	**D**
Pearson	Th^o	Capt Sv^t	18.19. 3			**S**
Percy	Fr^a	Com^{dr}	254. 0. 0			**S**
Percy	Robt	AB	22. 6. 8	Liz Forster	9. 1.1708	**D**
Probyn	W^m	L^t	41. 0. 0			**S**
Reed	Ant	AB	7.14. 1	(W) Ann	20. 3.1709	**D**
Robinson	W^m	AB				**S**
Small	W^m	Ord	23.09. 5	(W) Jane	9. 3.1707	**D**
Statt	W^m	Cox	36. 9. 8	(W Sarah	8. 3.1708	**D**
Vicount	Th^o	Q^r M^r M^t	37.13. 5		16. 1.1708	**S**
Watkins	Wl^{tr}	AB	9. 7. 2	Ann Hook	16. 3.1707	**D**
Watson	Rch^d	AB	20.12.11	Tho Cotterill	31. 8.1709	**D**
Watson	W^m	AB	21. 2. 9			**S**
Whitehead	Rich^d	AB	19. 6. 5		4. 2.1708	**D**
Willford	Ed^{wd}	Mids	32. 5. 3			**S**
Willson	W^m	Ord	14. 0. 4	Jam Wilde	9. 2.1708	**D**
Wilson	James	AB	15. 7. 2	R^d Hunter	12. 2.1708	**D**
Wilson	Th^o	AB	11.16. 3	R^d Coleburn	9. 2.1708	**D**
Wood	E^m	Lt^s Sv^t	6. 8. 6			**S**

NB. Abbreviation in the extreme right hand column of the *Firebrand* list above indicates:

D = Drowned/Lost

S = Survivor

Bibliography

Andrews H.(Ed) *The Quest for Longitude.* (Harvard Symposium 1993)

Anon. *The Life and Glorious Actions of Sir Cloudisley Shovell.* (London 1707) BM No10815 c5

Archibald E.H. *The Wooden Fighting Ship.* (London 1968)

Backscheider P.R. *Daniel Defoe; His Life.* John Hopkins University Press (London and Baltimore 1989)

Black's Guide to the Duchy of Cornwall. (Edinburgh 1885)

Du Boulay J. *Wrecks of the Isles of Scilly.* Mariner's Mirror Vols 45 & 46 (NRS)

Boyer, *History of the Reign of Queen Anne.* Vol VI (London 1703-14)

Bradford E. *The Story of the Mary Rose.* (London 1982)

Brown D. *Secret Memoirs of the Life of the Honourable Sir Cloudsley Shovell, Kt. Admiral of Great Britain.* (London 1708) BM Vol 221 Ref 615 a b

Brun V. *Guerres Maritime de la France.* (Paris 1861)

Burchett J. *The Complete History of Transactions at Sea.* (London 1720)

Campbell R. *The Lives of the Admirals.* Vols III & IV (London 1812)

Carriss C.V. *A Ghost of Old Hastings.* Sussex County Magazine Vol 21

Charnock J. *Biographia Navalis.* Vol II & III (London 1795)

Coffin L.W. *Holwell and Villages Past and Present* (Bridport 1990)

Colledge J.J. *Ships of the Royal Navy.* Vol I (Newton Abbot 1969)

Cooke J.H. *The Shipwreck of Sir Clowdisley Shovell.* Society of Antiquaries (Gloucester 1883)

Corbett J. *England in the Mediterranean.* Vol II (London 1904)

Cousins H. *Hastings of Bygone Days and the Present.* (Hastings 1911)

Crokkat, Rev. G.A. *A Consolatory Letter to Lady Shovell.* (London 1708) BM Vol 46 Ref. 4406. bb 33

Daily Courant (Newspaper 1707)

Defoe D. *A Tour through the Whole Island of Britain.* (London 1927) First published 1724

Defoe D. *The Storm.* (London 1704)

De Jonge J.C. *Geschiedenis Van Het Nederlansche Zeewezen.* (1835-62)

Dictionary of National Biography. (London 1897)

Dorrien-Smith C. *Shipwrecks of the Isles of Scilly.* (1953)

Dunbar J. *The Lost Land.* (London 1958)

Dyer F.E. *The Life of Sir John Narborough.* (London 1931)

Earle P. *The Wreck of the Almirante.* (London 1979)

Fowles J. *Shipwreck.* (1974)

Franzen A. *The Warship Vasa.* (Stockholm 1974)

Gill, Crispin. *The Isles of Scilly.* (Newton Abbot 1975)

Greenville Collins. *Great Britain's Coasting Pilot.* (London 1753)

Hastings and St.Leonards Pictorial Advertiser and Visitors List.(1914)

HMC Report, *12th Report of the Historical Manuscripts Commission*

HMC Report, *Dartmouth Manuscripts.*

HMC Report, *Finch Manuscripts.*

HMC Report, *House of Lord's Manuscripts.*

Howse D. *Britain's Board of Longitude: The Finances 1714-1828*. Mariner's Mirror, Vol 84 (NRS 1998)

Iago, Rev. W. *Bishop Trelawney*. Journal of the Royal Institute of Cornwall, Vol VII (1882)

Isles of Scilly Burial Records.

Jeffries and McDonald, *The Wreck Hunters.* (London 1966)

Journal of James Yonge. (London 1963)

Kelly S. *An Eighteenth Century Seaman.* (London 1925)

Laird-Clowes W. *The Royal Navy, A History.* Vol VI (London 1897)

Lane W.H. & Son, *Sales Catalogue, 23rd November, 1973*

Lane W.H. & Son, *Sales Catalogue, 24th September, 1974*

Lane W.H. & Son, *Sales Catalogue, 26th September, 1975*

Lane W.H. & Son, *Sales Catalogue, 24th November, 1977*

Lane W.H. & Son, *Sales Catalogue, 30th November, 1979*

Lane W.H. & Son, *Sales Catalogue, 1st June, 1983*

Larn R. *Cornish Shipwrecks, The Isles of Scilly.* (Newton Abbot 1971)

Laughton J.K. *Physical Geography.* (London 1870)

Lecky H.S. *The King's Ships.* (London 1913)

Lilly C.L. *Survey and Census of the Isles of Scilly.* (1715)

Locker E.H. *Memoirs of Celebrated Naval Commanders.* (London 1832)

London Gazette. (Newspaper 1707)

London Letter. (Newspaper 1710)

Mace M. *A Diver's Report on the Association.* (Penzance 1974)

Marcus G. *Sir Clowdisley Shovell's Last Passage.* Journal of the Royal United Services Institute, Vol C II (1957)

Marsham-Townsend R. *The Death of Sir Clowdisley Shovell.* Notes and Queries 6th Series Vol X (1884)

Marsham-Townsend R. *The Death of Sir John Narborough.* Notes and Queries 7th Series Vol VI (1888)

Marsham-Townsend R. *The Parentage of Sir Clowdisley Shovell.* Notes and Queries 8th Series Vol VII (1895)

May W.E. *Compasses in 1707.* Journal of the Institute of Navigation, Vol VI (1953)

May W.E. *A History of Marine Navigation.* (London 1973)

May W.E. *The Last Voyage of Sir Clowdisley Shovell.* Journal of the Institute of Navigation, Vol XIII

McBride P. & Cowan R. *Cannon Survey - Tearing Ledge Site.* (1975-6)

McDonald K. *The Treasure Divers.* (London 1974)

McDonald K. *The Wreck Hunters.* (London 1966)

McKee A. *History Under the Sea.* (London 1968)

Morris R. *Island Treasure.* (London 1969)

Morris R. Salvors *Report on the Undersea Wreck of HMS Eagle.* (Penzance 1970) (NB. Title in error - the subject is an unidentified wreck on the Crim Rock- not the Eagle)

Mudd D. *The Cruel Cornish Sea.* (Bodmin 1981)

Mumford C. *Portrait of the Isles of Scilly.* (London 1967)

Murray, General Sir G.J. *The Letters of John Churchill - First Duke of Marlborough, 1702-12.*

Naval Air Command Sub-Aqua Club, MOD(N) Expedition Report - July 1970.
Naval Air Command Sub-Aqua Club, MOD(N) Expedition Report - Survey and Sketch Plan of the Tearing Ledge Site - July 1971.
Naval Chronology
Naval Gazetteer, Biographer and Chronologist. (London 1827)
Noall C. *Cornish Lights and Shipwrecks.* (Truro 1968)
Norfolk Fair Magazine. (April 1968)
North I.W. *A Week in the Isles of Scilly.* (Penzance 1850)
NRS Series. *Journals and Narratives of the 3rd Dutch War.* (NRS 1946)
NRS Series. *Letters and Papers of Sir George Byng.* (NRS 1930)
NRS Series. *Tangier Papers of Samuel Pepys.* (NRS 1935)
Owen J.H. *War at Sea under Queen Anne, 1702-8.* (Cambridge 1938)
Page W. (Ed) *The Victoria History of the Counties of England - Cornwall.* (1906)
Pattison S.R. *Sir Cloudsley Shovell.* Journal of Royal Institute of Cornwall, Vol I (1864-5)
Pearson C. *Early Tours in Devon and Cornwall.* (Newton Abbot 1967)
Pickwell J.G. *Improbable Legends Surrounding the Shipwreck of Sir Clowdisley Shovell.* Mariner's Mirror, Vol LIX p221-3 (NRS 1973)
Pinder A. *A Kent Life.* (1978)
Pryme, A. De La, *Diary of Abraham De La Pryme.* (1697)
Quiller-Couch T. *Sir Cloudesley Shovell.* Journal of the Royal Institute of Cornwall, Vol II (1866-7)
Rennel J. *Observations on a Current to the West of Scilly.* (London 1873)
Robinson J.A. *A Narrative of the Victory at La Hogue in 1692.* (London 1744)
Ronciere C. De La, *Histoire de la Marine Francaise.* (Paris 1899)
Royal Cornwall Gazette. (Newspaper 1847)
Rule M. *The Mary Rose.* (London 1982)
Smith F.F. *A History of Rochester*
Sobell D. *Longitude. (London 1995)*
Sotheby and Co. *Sale Catalogue -14th July 1969.*
Strike F. *Cornish Shipwrecks.* (Porthleven 1965)
Styles S. *Admiral of England.* (London 1978) (Fiction)
Sussex Archaeological Collections.
Sutherland W. *Shipbuilding Unveil'd.* (1717)
Taylor E.G.R. *Reward for Longitude.* Mariner's Mirror, Vol XLV (NRS 1959)
The Post Boy. (Newspaper 1707)
Toynbee A. *A Study of History.* Vol IV (London 1951)
Trevelyan G.M. *England Under Queen Anne - Ramillies and the Union with Scotland.* (London 1932)
Westminster Abbey Official Guide. (London 1977)
Whiston W. & Ditton H. *A New Method for Discovering the Longitude both at Sea and Land, Humbly Proposed to the Consideration of the Publick.* (London 1714)
Whitfield H.J. *Scilly and Its Legends.* (1852)
Williams M. *Deep Sea Treasure.* (London 1981)
Williams M. *Sunken Treasure.* (London 1980)
Woodley Rev. G. *The Present State of the Isles of Scilly.* (London 1833)

Acknowledgments

Without the assistance of those personally involved in the relocation and subsequent salvage of Shovell's ships, this publication would have been impossible. The authors therefore wish to extend their grateful thanks and public appreciation to the following, who have made available information, photographs, or other material, or participated in a major role in the underwater search and recovery phase between 1967 and 1972. To Lieut. Roy Graham RN(Retd) of St. Mary's; Lieut. Cdr. Jack Gayton RN(Retd), of Veryan, Cornwall; Wardmaster Lieut. Terry Montgomery RN(Retd) now believed to be living in Australia; Cdr. Alan Baldwin RN(Retd) Bay of Islands, New Zealand; Lieut. Andrew Lindsey RN(Retd); Lieut. Minchin RN(Retd), and the late Lieut. Cdr. Ted Barter RN(Retd). Particularly to Terry Hiron and Jim Heslin of Scillonian Diving Services Ltd; Mark Horobin of Porthhallow, Cornwall; Frank Gibson, Geoffrey and Pam Coldwell and Noel Jenkins, all of St. Mary's, Isles of Scilly; also to Trevor Newman of Plymouth, who traced and supplied a copy of the Court Martial of Captain Piercy of the *Firebrand.* Also the late Roland Morris of Penzance, Terry Roe and Barry Fairest, of St. Mary's.

To Ernest Perry, of Bexhill-on-Sea; Paul Armiger, of St. Mawes; Rex Cowan, of Hampstead, London; Mrs R.G. Purle, Reference Assistant, County Library, Rochester; Mr and Mrs Fox-Pit, Mrs Cowdrey, Knowlton Court Estate Office, Deal, Kent; Paul Presswell; Showell Styles; Naval History and Reference Section Librarians and Staff, Plymouth Central Library; Steven Ottery, Curator of the Isles of Scilly Museum.

Also to Christine North and staff, County Records Office, Truro; J.N. Allen and staff, Hastings Area Library; C. Wilkins-Jones, Local Studies Librarian, Norwich; Norwich City Museum and Art Gallery; D.J. Lyon, London; Mrs. Holness, Brian Turner and Roger Marshall, Deal Camera Club and the late Commander W.E. May RN; Ivan Corbett of Tormark Press, St. Day for advice and comments and many others who have not been named individually, but are acknowledged either in the text or reference sources. Special acknowledgment is also given to Bridget Larn, for assistance with research; also Mary Richards, of Gorran Haven, Cornwall and Carolyne McBride for their keyboarding, reading and correction of the manuscript.

Peter McBride   1999   Richard Larn

Index